D1029607

NICHOLAS OF CUSA AND
MEDIEVAL POLITICAL THOUGHT

HARVARD POLITICAL STUDIES

Published under the direction
of the Department of Government
in Harvard University

NICHOLAS OF CUSA

Detail from the memorial in the church
of St. Peter in Chains, Rome.

NICHOLAS OF CUSA AND MEDIEVAL POLITICAL THOUGHT

. . . .

PAUL E. SIGMUND

HARVARD UNIVERSITY PRESS

CAMBRIDGE, MASSACHUSETTS · 1963

Distributed in Great Britain by
Oxford University Press, London

Publication of this book
has been aided by a grant from the Ford Foundation

Library of Congress Catalog Card Number: 63-20772

Printed in the United States of America

TO JOSEF KOCH

PREFACE

.   .   .

T H E   A U T H O R was first attracted to the study of the political thought of Nicholas of Cusa because the standard histories of political thought singled him out as one of the first theorists to make consent the basis of the legitimacy of law and government. In the course of the critical examination of Cusanus' thought, my first impression of his political theory as a revolutionary break with the past has been substantially modified, but this has not led to any lessening of the intrinsic interest of his thought. Cusanus is an original thinker, not as a radical innovator, but as the creator in both philosophy and politics of a new synthesis and recombination of traditional elements. He is, as one of his German commentators put it, "an unconscious revolutionary . . . the last of the scholastics and at the same time, the herald of a new age."

In the last thirty-five years, there has been lively interest in Cusanus in Germany, France, and Italy, and I am grateful for the opportunity to put before an English-speaking audience the results of the research done by European scholars, insofar as it has aided in an understanding of Cusanus as a political theorist. Those who, through their writings and through personal discussion, have contributed to this study are too numerous to list, but many are mentioned in the footnotes. Special thanks are due to Professor H. S. Offler of the University of Durham, England, for originally suggesting that there was a need for a full-length study of Nicholas of Cusa's political thought, to the late Professor Bruno Decker of the University of Mainz for lending me the first two books of the Heidelberg edition of *De Concordantia Catholica,* now out of print, and particularly to Professor Josef Koch of the University of

Cologne, without the benefit of whose knowledge and understanding of Nicholas of Cusa's thought this study would never have been possible. On this side of the Atlantic, Reverend Daniel A. Power, S.J., of Georgetown University first aroused my interest in medieval political theory, and I owe a special debt of gratitude to Professor Carl J. Friedrich of Harvard University for his advice, assistance, and encouragement, especially when the linguistic and research difficulties seemed insurmountable. My thanks also go to the Catherwood Foundation for the grant which enabled me to do the basic research in Europe in 1955-56, and to the Department of Government in Harvard University for including this book in the Harvard Political Studies.

PAUL E. SIGMUND

Princeton, New Jersey
June, 1963

CONTENTS

.　　　.　　　.

NICHOLAS OF CUSA AND
MEDIEVAL POLITICAL THOUGHT

ABBREVIATIONS

WORKS OF NICHOLAS OF CUSA

DAP *De Auctoritate Presidendi in Concilio Generali*

DCC *De Concordantia Catholica*

DDI *De Docta Ignorantia*

PERIODICALS AND OTHER PUBLICATIONS

Archives d'histoire *Archives d'histoire doctrinale et littéraire du moyen âge* (Paris)

HJ *Historisches Jahrbuch* (Munich)

HZ *Historische Zeitschrift* (Munich)

Mitteilungen *Mitteilungen und Forschungsbeiträge der Cusanus-Gesellschaft* (Mainz)

Quellen *Quellen und Forschungen aus italienischen Archiven und Biblioteken* (Tübingen)

RTA *Deutsche Reichstagsakten*

SBH *Sitzungsberichte der Heidelberger Akademie der Wissenschaften,* Philosophisch-historische Klasse (Heidelberg)

INTRODUCTION

SITUATED on a bend in the river Moselle, about midway between Trier and Koblenz, is the town of Bernkastel-Kues. Today it is known principally as the producer of a particularly fine brand of Moselle wine (*Bernkasteler Doktor*) and as the goal of tourist excursions from the Rhineland cities situated within a radius of ninety miles. Tourists find the town worth visiting because much of it has remained exactly as it was four or five centuries ago. Among the tourist sights to be seen in Kues, across the river from Bernkastel, are the hospice, library, and chapel of Nicholas of Cusa, which celebrated their five hundredth anniversary in December 1958. Perhaps the most impressive of the various rooms in the collection of buildings on the banks of the Moselle is the library, where a single pillar in the center of the room unites the Gothic arches which form the roof. Surrounding the pillar, on the reading stand at its base and in shelves around the room, are the writings and personal library of Nicholas of Cusa.[1] The single pillar supporting the many arches seems to symbolize the central concern of the author whose writings are contained in this room—the problem of

---

1 The library at Kues has been catalogued in J. Marx, *Verzeichnis der Handschriften-Sammlung des Hospitals zu Cues* (Trier, 1905). It contains over three hundred manuscripts and two hundred first editions. Not all of its present contents were in the possession of Cusanus at his death, but internal evidence, including extensive marginal annotations and, in some cases, actual dates, enable us to relate many of the manuscripts to Cusanus' intellectual development. Thirty-eight manuscripts in the British Museum and several in the Bibliothèque Royale in Brussels have been identified as originally from the library at Kues. A list of the books in Cusanus' possession at the time of his death, recently discovered in Vicenza, Italy, gives further information on the subject. See Giovanni Mantese, "Ein notarielles Inventar von Büchern und Wertgegenständen aus dem Nachlass des Nikolaus von Kues," *Mitteilungen*, 2:85-116 (1962).

unity in diversity, the one and the many, the reconciling of differences in one harmonious whole.

Nicholas of Cusa's vision, best expressed in political terms in *De Concordantia Catholica* but also given metaphysical expression in his work *De Docta Ignorantia*, has not ceased to be of interest since its delineation over half a millenium ago. The religious reformers of the sixteenth century looked back to him as a forerunner of the Reformation. Early scientific investigators such as Kepler and Copernicus referred to his cosmological conceptions. The thinkers of the Enlightenment interpreted one of his works as a medieval anticipation of their doctrines. In Germany in the nineteenth century, the Romantic movement revived interest in his work, and nationalist sentiment impelled German scholars to investigate his thought. In the 1920's scholarly interest was aroused by the work of Ernst Cassirer, who characterized Cusanus as "the first great modern thinker"[2] at the same time that Ernst Hoffmann established a Cusanus Commission at Heidelberg to study and edit his works. The study of Cusanus continues today at the Institut für Cusanusforschung of the University of Mainz. A Cusanus Society (*Cusanus-Gesellschaft*) has also recently been established, which publishes an annual collection of articles on various aspects of Cusanus' life and thought and supervises work at the library of Kues.

The interest in Cusanus has led to a great increase in knowledge of his life and works, but so far this has not been utilized in studying his political thought. Most histories of political theory adjudge the political writings of Nicholas of Cusa as the most important between Marsilius and Machiavelli, but there have been no attempts in Eng-

---

2 Ernst Cassirer, *Individuum und Kosmos in der Philosophie der Renaissance* (Leipzig, 1927), p. 10.

lish and few efforts in other languages to give an over-all evaluation of his thinking on politics.

In the nineteenth century Otto von Gierke, the great German pioneer in the study of medieval political thought, was drawn to Cusanus' political writings as an early attempt to give institutional expression to the moral restraints which medieval constitutionalism never succeeded in effectively enforcing on either lay or spiritual leaders.[3] Gierke and those who followed him were also interested in Cusanus' use of consent as the basis for his theory of political obligation. It was the theory of consent that Figgis praised in his study of the conciliarists, and more recent works on the history of political ideas, such as those of George Sabine or the massive six-volume history of medieval political thought by the Carlyle brothers, also concentrate on this aspect of his thought.[4]

Because of their interest in Cusanus' theories of consent and representation, the summary accounts of his theory by the historians of political thought often give an inaccurate version of his thought by overemphasizing the "democratic" aspects. For instance, the single lengthy translated excerpt from the *Concordantia Catholica,* the section on Nicholas of Cusa in Coker's *Readings in Political Philosophy,* includes only the various statements of the theory of consent and Nicholas' proposal for the incorporation of a system of representative councils in the medieval empire.[5] Sabine's history of political theory notes that there are

[3] Otto von Gierke, *Das deutsche Genossenschaftsrecht,* III (Berlin, 1881), 602.

[4] John Neville Figgis, *Studies of Political Thought from Gerson to Grotius* (New York, 1960), p. 70; George Sabine, *A History of Political Theory,* 3rd ed. (New York, 1961), pp. 318-324; R. W. and A. J. Carlyle, *A History of Medieval Political Theory in the West* (Edinburgh and London, 1950), VI, 136-137 and 169-171.

[5] Francis W. Coker, *Readings in Political Philosophy* (New York, 1938), pp. 257-276.

other elements in his thought but repeatedly misstates the content of *De Concordantia Catholica* (see especially the supposed contradictions listed on page 324 of Sabine's work) and ignores the rest of Cusanus' writings. Of the shorter accounts in English, only E. F. Jacob's lecture in the Hearnshaw series on social and political thinkers and this writer's recent article, written while the present work was in progress, discuss other aspects of his political theory, and both of these are necessarily incomplete.[6]

A brief biography by Henry Bett (London, 1932) and three translations of his philosophic writings exhaust the books in English concerned exclusively with Nicholas of Cusa;[7] there is nothing on his political writings, although a recent revival of interest in the conciliar movement has produced a number of studies of his predecessors.[8] The best single work on the political theory of Cusanus is a German study which is confined to his principal political work, *Die "Concordantia Catholica" des Nikolaus von Cusa* by Andreas Posch (Paderborn, 1930). More recent but less satisfactory efforts by German scholars to evaluate and analyze his political thought include E. Bohnenstädt, *Kirche und Reich im Schrijtum des Nikolaus von Cues*, in the

6 E. F. Jacob, "Nicholas of Cusa," in F. J. C. Hearnshaw, ed., *Social and Political Ideas of Some Great Thinkers of the Renaissance and Reformation* (London, 1925), pp. 32-60; Paul E. Sigmund, "Cusanus' *Concordantia*: a Re-interpretation," *Political Studies*, 10:180-197 (1962). There is also a brief but reliable account of the *Concordantia* in Hubert Jedin, *A History of the Council of Trent*, trans. Ernest Graf, I (London, 1957), 22-24.

7 Nicolas Cusanus, *Of Learned Ignorance*, trans. Germain Heron, O.P. (London, 1954); Nicholas of Cusa, *The Vision of God*, trans. E. Gurney Salter (New York, 1928); *Unity and Reform; Selected Writings of Nicholas de Cusa*, trans. with an introduction by John Patrick Dolan (Notre Dame, Ind., 1962).

8 E.g., Alan Gewirth, *Marsilius of Padua*, 2 vols. (New York, 1951, 1956); Walter Ullmann, *The Origins of the Great Schism* (London, 1948); E. F. Jacob, *Essays in the Conciliar Epoch* (Manchester, 1953); Brian Tierney, *Foundations of Conciliar Theory* (Cambridge, 1955); and John B. Morrall, *Gerson and the Great Schism* (Manchester, 1960).

INTRODUCTION

proceedings of the Heidelberg Academy of Sciences *(SBH* 1938-39, no. 1, Heidelberg, 1939); Rudolf Schultz, *Die Staatsphilosophie des Nikolaus von Kues* (Meisenheim am Glan, 1948), and Gerd Heinz-Mohr, *Unitas Christiana* (Trier, 1958). In French, Edmond Vansteenberghe, *Le cardinal Nicolas de Cues* (Lille, 1920), is an excellent, if somewhat dated, biography which is also an analysis of Cusanus' thought. Unlike most of the other writers, Vansteenberghe does not restrict himself to the *Concordantia* in writing about Cusanus' political ideas, but makes full use of the letters and speeches which were accessible to him at the time. (Many more are now available.) The only other major study in French is that of Maurice de Gandillac, *La Philosophie de Nicolas de Cues* (Paris, 1941), a difficult work with little relevance to political theory. In Italian, Paolo Rotta has produced several works, the most recent being *Nicolò Cusano* (Milan, 1942), but he has not concerned himself particularly with political theory. The specialized study of Posch and the political sections of Vansteenberghe's biography are of value, but as this review of the literature indicates, there has thus far been no satisfactory attempt to treat the whole of Cusanus' political theory, or relate it to his metaphysical outlook and to the medieval traditions upon which he drew.

Such a study must begin with Cusanus' major political work, *De Concordantia Catholica* *(DCC)*. It is printed in the 1514 Paris edition of his works and in that published at Basel in 1565, the latter recognized until recently as the standard scholarly edition. In 1928 Gerhard Kallen issued a facsimile reprint of the *Concordantia* from the 1514 edition, and the entire 1514 *Opera* of Cusanus were reprinted in Frankfurt in 1961. However, the definitive critical version of the *Concordantia* is now that edited by Gerhard Kallen and issued as volume XIV of the new edition of Cusanus' works published by the Heidelberg Academy of Sciences (*Akademie der Wissenschaften*). Volume XIV has appeared in three sections, corresponding to the three books of the original work. Books I and II were originally published in Leipzig, in 1939 and 1941 respectively. The publication of Book III was delayed by World War II, but it appeared in Hamburg in 1959, and it is expected that the first two books with corrections by Professor Kallen will be reissued in the near future.

Another work of interest for an understanding of Cusanus' political thought, *De Auctoritate Presidendi in Concilio Generali (DAP)* has also been edited by Gerhard Kallen in the proceedings of the Heidelberg Academy of Sciences.[9] In addition, the Heidelberg Academy has published collections of Cusanus' letters and sermons, as well as a series of specialized studies on various aspects of his life and works. Cusanus' speeches to the *Reichstag* after his abandonment of conciliarism appear in volumes XIV-XVII of the series of *Deutsche Reichstagsakten (RTA)*, initiated by the Academy of Sciences (*Akademie der Wissenschaften*) of Bavaria. A part of a manuscript in the library of the city of Trier has also recently been identified as an anti-conciliar dialogue written by Cusanus at some point after 1439.

The most important of Cusanus' philosophical works in terms of its influence on his political theory is his well-known *De Docta Ignorantia (DDI)*. It appears as volume I of the Heidelberg edition, edited by Raymond Klibansky and Ernst Hoffmann (Leipzig, 1932). Other works which are useful for an understanding of his ecclesiology include his treatise on religious understanding, *De Pace Fidei*, which is volume VII of the Heidelberg edition, edited by

---

9 *Sitzungsberichte der Heidelberger Akademie der Wissenschaften*, Philosophisch-historische Klasse (SBH), 1935-36, no. 3 (Heidelberg, 1935).

Raymond Klibansky and Hildebrand Bascour, O.P. (Hamburg, 1959), and a project for a general reform of the church, written late in his life.[10]

On the basis of the improved texts in the Heidelberg edition of Cusanus' works, and the published results of research done in recent years, it is now possible to make a critical evaluation of the political thought of the last and greatest of the conciliar thinkers. In this book, several methods have been used to analyze Nicholas of Cusa's political theory. It has been considered in relation to the theories which preceded and influenced it, so as to gain an understanding of the various terms and concepts used in Cusanus' political writing and to determine what, if anything, is novel or original in his work. These include not only earlier works of conciliar theory but also others not specifically concerned with politics, since in the medieval period the relationship of theology, philosophy, law, and political thought was a close and intimate one and no one demonstrates this better than Cusanus, who drew on what might be regarded as unrelated cosmological, theological, and philosophical ideas in order to fashion his political theory. Much of the writing of both Cusanus and his predecessors is concerned with the government of the church, an area which is not often considered by political theorists today. However, theories of church government form an important and often neglected part of the history of Western political thought.[11] There is in Cusanus' theory, as often in medieval thought, a transfer of categories and modes of argument from one sphere to another—from ecclesiology to political theory. A crisis in the church constitution was the occasion for the develop-

10 The reform project is printed in Stephan Ehses, "Der Reformentwurf des Kardinals Nikolaus Cusanus," *HJ*, 32:281-297 (1911).

11 Two studies which recognize this relationship are Ernest Barker, *The Dominican Order and Convocation* (Oxford, 1913), and Ernst Kantorowicz, *The King's Two Bodies* (Princeton, 1957).

ment of Cusanus' political thought, but he discusses issues broader than church government, including such general political topics as the nature of authority, consent, and representation.

In this book two major traditions with different origins and political implications have been singled out for particular attention because of their influence on Cusanus' political theory. His thinking on politics is interpreted as an attempt to combine the hierarchical theories of Christian Neo-Platonism concerning the origin and structure of authority with the more equalitarian corporatist theories of consent and representation derived from Roman and canon law. While the first view might tend towards unitary government and the second might lead to a type of pluralism, in fact Cusanus' political thought, like that of most of the Middle Ages, was characterized by dualism—a parallelism of function and office in the spiritual and temporal orders.

Utilizing these categories of hierarchy, consent, and parallelism, the study of Cusanus' thought in terms of antecedent influences thus leads to a second method, the analysis of his political ideas in order to determine the various senses in which key concepts are used, and to relate them to one another—an effort which is particularly necessary in the case of theory as complex, and at times obscure, as that of Cusanus. His belief in the fundamental unity and harmony of all things, even those which are in apparent opposition to one another, means that his theory will often contain tensions and ambiguities which must be identified and analyzed in any study of his philosophy.

A third method utilized is a detailed examination of the historical circumstances surrounding the composition of Cusanus' political theory. There are historians of political theory who defend the study of texts apart from their historical context,[12] but this would be foolish in a writer as involved in contemporary political and legal controversy as Cusanus. Like most of the great works of political theory, Cusanus' writing on the subject was a generalized response to specific political problems, a critical analysis of the claims of existing governmental institutions in the fifteenth century at a time when they were in conflict. To understand the meaning of the terms used, and the full implications of the theory as a whole, it is necessary to know the context from which they emerged. Moreover, the study of the historical details of Cusanus' life is also helpful in determining the sources which influenced his thought.

This reference to the historical and biographical background is especially useful in the case of Cusanus because one of the most tantalizing questions suggested by his life and works is the relation of his conciliarist writings to his transfer of allegiance to the papacy only four years after these writings were published. One of the reasons that this change has appeared so difficult to understand is lack of acquaintance with the original theories. The day has not yet arrived when "the average professor of political theory . . . will be able to dip into his well-underlined copy of Cusa's *De Concordantia Catholica* with the same facility as that with which . . . he had turned to the *Politics* of Aristotle,"[13] but perhaps this study will contribute to an understanding of the reasons for a change which has often been attributed to sheer opportunism. When examined in context and particularly when adequate attention is given to the hierarchical elements in his thought, Cusanus' political theory emerges as more traditional in content than it appears in the summaries and excerpts presently available,

12 This is the method of Leo Strauss. See, for example, Leo Strauss and Joseph Cropsey, eds., *History of Political Philosophy* (Chicago, 1963).
13 Ewart Lewis, *Medieval Political Ideas* (New York, 1954), I, vii.

and his shift of allegiance to the side of the papacy becomes more consistent with his fundamental political principles.

To study his political ideas after the change of allegiance we must draw on his letters, speeches, and philosophical works, since he never wrote a systematic work on politics after his espousal of the papacy. As this work will show, he never felt that this was necessary, since underlying his apparent reversal of attitudes there was a fundamental consistency between his early and later thought. This belief in the possibility of a concordance of apparently opposed conceptions lies at the root of his political thought as it does of his philosophy as a whole. The two poles of authority and freedom, order and liberty, structure and spontaneity, which in more recent political theory have been considered as fundamentally opposed, appear in Cusanus' political thought as united in *concordantia catholica*—universal harmony—combining the principal themes of classical and medieval thought in a final synthesis before the breakdown of the medieval order.

CHAPTER I

. . .

THE HISTORICAL
AND INSTITUTIONAL
BACKGROUND

THE THEORIES of the conciliar movement, of which the *Concordantia Catholica* is the last and most nearly complete expression, were at once a reflection of, and a reaction against, current church practice. The historians of the church in this period note that during the so-called Babylonian captivity, which preceded the conciliar movement, the church, far from being disunited, was becoming increasingly centralized in the papacy.[1] The claims for the plenitude of power in the church which had been made by the great thirteenth century popes and canonists were given concrete expression through increasing papal expansion of ecclesiastical taxation and an ever-widening list of cases in which the pope might appoint candidates to lower church offices.[2] The system of canon law which had been developed by the Decretists and Decretalists in the twelfth and thirteenth centuries was now in full flower, and it codified and justified the expansion of papal powers of appoint-

[1] J. Haller, *Papstum und Kirchenreform* (Berlin, 1903), esp. pp. 96-103 and 125-151, gives a good account of the development of papal centralization in the fourteenth century, as does Paul Hinschius, *Das Kirchenrecht der Katholiken und Protestanten in Deutschland*, vol. III (Berlin, 1881). More recent accounts include Geoffrey Barraclough, *Papal Provisions* (Oxford, 1935); H. E. Feine, *Kirchliche Rechtsgeschichte* (Weimar, 1950), I, 261ff; and Ludwig Buisson, *Potestas und Caritas* (Cologne, 1958).

[2] Clement IV claimed the right to dispose of all ecclesiastical benefices in a decretal of August 27, 1265. However, the actual centralization of appointments through such devices as reservations, expectancies, etc., took place principally in the fourteenth century.

ment, taxation, and legal jurisdiction. Although church tradition and practice called for the election of bishops and metropolitans by their chapters and councils, a lengthening list of exceptions was made providing for direct appointment from Rome. Thus the pope as *judex ordinarius* of all Christians could intervene in cases of disputed elections, could appoint successors to sees when their incumbents died at Rome (later extended to cases of transfer or new appointment by the papacy), and could reserve appointments for the remuneration of papal servants and the members of the *curia* in Rome. From 1316 the annate, a fixed part of the first year's income, was paid from every benefice appointed by the pope. Beginning in the thirteenth century, bishops or their representatives were also bound to make periodic visits, *ad limina,* to Rome and to pay a special tax. Archbishops were bound to swear their obedience and to pay fees for the reception of the *pallium,* or shawl from the pope, which signified papal confirmation of their election or appointment.

The thirteenth century popes had also made repeated claims to authority over the temporal power, culminating in the bull *Unam sanctam* issued by Boniface VIII in 1302. During the first part of the fourteenth century, the controversy was continued in the conflict of the papacy with the emperor, Lewis the Bavarian. War raged between empire and papacy intermittently from the date of Lewis' election in 1314 until his death in 1349. His successor, Charles IV, following his coronation in Rome in 1355, issued the "Golden Bull," repudiating the claims of the papacy to approve imperial elections and restricting the choice of the emperor to the seven prince electors, four secular and three ecclesiastical. This effectively marked the end of a controversy which had dominated political thought ever since the reign of Pope Gregory VII three centuries before. Future discussions were to center around the nature of the constitution of the church itself, and in particular the position of the papacy within the church.

This controversy arose out of attempts to settle the Western Schism, which broke out immediately after the return of the popes from Avignon in 1378. Since Pope Nicholas II in 1059 had determined that the popes should be elected by the cardinals, they had taken an increasingly important part in the government of the church.[3] After the return from Avignon, the cardinals elected Urban VI in Rome. Subsequently a number of them claimed that the election had been carried out under intimidation from the Roman mob, and five months later at Fondi they elected Clement VII.[4] With Clement's election as "the Avignon pope" the Great Schism began.

Less than two years later came the first proposal for settlement of the dispute by means of a general council. In 1380 Henry of Langenstein, Vice-Chancellor of the University of Paris, published the *Epistola Pacis,* which drew on theories already put forward earlier in the century by John of Paris, Gulielmus Durandus the Younger, Marsilius of Padua, and William of Occam, and proposed the solution of the controversy by means of a general council. A year later he published his *Epistola Concilii Pacis,* which called for the use of the council not only to end the schism but also for the purposes of church reform. At the same time Conrad of Gelnhausen, a professor at the same university, composed the *Epistola Concordiae* for the guid-

3 Previously they had been appointed by the emperor, or elected by the "clerus et populus Romanus." Nicholas' reform diminished the dependence of the pope on the emperor and on the vagaries of Roman politics. Nevertheless, the large families of Rome continued to exercise a very important influence.

4 For an account of the circumstances surrounding the disputed election of 1378, see Ullmann, *Origins.*

ance of the French king, a work which came to a similar conclusion.[5]

For forty years Christendom remained divided between the two allegiances, one in Rome and the other in Avignon. In the search for a solution to the division, the University of Paris continued to be the principal center of activity. Its chancellor, Pierre d'Ailly, and his successor, Jean Gerson, were active in the furtherance of the conciliar idea, and the French king periodically intervened in an attempt first to force adherence to the Avignon pope, and later to call for his resignation. It was not, however, until the Council of Pisa in 1409 that the *via concilii* was actually utilized as a method for ending the schism. Although cardinals of both obediences attended the council, they succeeded only in electing a third claimant to the papal chair after deposing the other two claimants (not, it should be noted, on the grounds of any general superiority of the council to the pope, but because both were declared to be heretics and schismatics).[6]

Two years later the empire, which had also been in dispute, passed to Sigismund of Luxemburg, a vigorous ruler, who from this time until his death in 1438 attempted to carry out his responsibilities as protector of the Christian religion. When the pope who had been elected at Pisa was in military difficulties with the King of Naples, he appealed to Sigismund for assistance. Sigismund's reply was to demand the convocation of a general council. Reluctantly the Pisan pope agreed to the site chosen by the emperor—

5 The relationship of the works of Gelnhausen and Langenstein is treated by K. Hirsch, *Die Ausbildung der konziliaren Theorie im XIV. Jahrhundert* (Vienna, 1903), pp. 78ff.

6 The most nearly complete treatment of the period of the Great Schism is in Noel Valois, *La France et le grand Schisme de l'Occident*, 4 vols. (Paris, 1886-1902). There is also a good discussion in Carl Joseph Hefele, *Conziliengeschichte*, trans. and rev. H. Leclercq, *Histoire des Conciles*, vol. VI, part 2 (Paris, 1915).

Constance—and on November 16, 1414, the council held its first session.[7]

The Council of Constance lasted three years and five months. At its height, there were in attendance 29 cardinals, 3 patriarchs, 33 archbishops, 150 bishops, and 100 doctors of theology. The participation of the last-named category in the voting was an innovation introduced at the Council of Pisa and retained at Constance. It testified to the desire of the non-Italian delegates to outvote the supporters of the Pisan pope, who constituted almost half of the bishops present. A vote was also given to the representatives of the universities, and to the envoys of the princes, who numbered 23, at least some of whom were laymen. An additional electoral device intended to assure the dominance of the non-Italian faction was the division of the council into "nations," with final decisions being taken by a vote in which each of the four (and later five) nations in the council voted as a unit, regardless of the number of representatives which it had at the council.

The first step which the council took to end the schism was to force the resignation of the Pisan pope. Although he pledged to abdicate in March of 1415, he soon changed his mind and fled in disguise, annulling all his previous promises. As a result, the council at the fifth session of 1415 (April 6) passed the famous decree *Sacrosancta*, declaring, "This holy Synod of Constance, being a General Council . . . declares that it is lawfully convoked in the Holy Spirit, that it forms a General Council, that it represents the Catholic Church militant, and has its power imme-

---

[7] Ludwig Pastor's *History of the Popes*, vol. I (London, 1891), begins with the Council of Constance. He relies, as does Hefele-Leclercq, *Histoire*, vol. VII (Paris, 1916), on the collection of documents by Hermann von der Hardt, *Rerum Concilii Oecumenici Constantiensis*, 7 vols. (Frankfurt-Berlin, 1697-1742). This collection has now been superseded by Heinrich Finke, *Acta Concilii Constanciensis*, 4 vols. (Münster, 1896-1928).

diately from Christ, and that all men, no matter what their status or dignity, including the pope, are obliged to obey it in matters concerning faith, the ending of the present schism, and the general reform of the Church of God in head and members."[8]

Within a few months the Pisan pope had surrendered himself to the council and the emperor, and on May 29 he was formally deposed. That same summer the Roman pope, Gregory XII, authorized his representatives to convoke the council (thus asserting the validity of his power to call a council), and he submitted his abdication. There remained only the last representative of the Avignon popes, and two years of fruitless negotiation in Aragon between the emperor's envoys and Benedict XIII ended with his formal deposition by the council in July 1417. After an extended controversy over how a new pope was to be elected, an expanded electoral college composed of the twenty-three cardinals and six delegates from each of the five nations represented at the council elected Martin V as universally acknowledged pope on November 11, 1417.

The council was not only concerned with ending the schism and asserting its own supremacy, but it also viewed itself as the divinely appointed instrument of reform. The emperor and the German nation had been in favor of carrying out the work of reform before electing the pope, but the opposition of the cardinals led to a compromise in accordance with which the two works were carried out simultaneously. A month before the election of Martin,

---

8 *DAP,* ed. Kallen, p. 104: "Haec sancta Synodus Constantiensis generale Concilium faciens . . . declarat, quod ipsa in spiritu sancto legitime congregata, Concilium generale faciens, et ecclesiam catholicam militantem repraesentans, potestatem a Christo immediate habet, cui quilibet cuiuscumque status vel dignitatis, etiamsi papalis existat, obedire tenetur in his quae pertinent ad fidem et exstirpationem dicti schismatis et generalem reformationem ecclesiae Dei in capite et in membris."

the council had adopted five reform decrees, which once again asserted its prerogatives as highest ruling body in the church. The most famous of these, the decree *Frequens*, called for another general council within five years of the termination of the one at Constance, followed by a third after an additional seven years, and then regular councils at ten-year intervals. It also forbade the pope to dissolve or transfer the council except by its own consent. Following Martin's election, a set of seven decrees for universal reform were adopted, as well as a series of individual concordats between the pope and the various nations. The decrees abolished the papal rights to revenues from vacant sees, and restricted (but did not abolish) papal rights to tax by tithes and annates and to appoint to vacant benefices.[9] Having made these partial efforts at reform, and with the schism terminated, the council adjourned with the intention of reassembling in five years.

The Council of Constance appeared to be a decisive demonstration of the validity of the conciliar theory of church government. It had succeeded in ending the schism, and in making at least partial reforms. While the significance of the decree *Frequens* may be somewhat exaggerated by Dr. Figgis when he calls it "the most revolutionary official document in the history of the world,"[10] the council appeared to have established itself as a permanent part of the machinery of church government, and as the highest legislative body in Christendom.

Important for subsequent thought on the subject was

9 See for example the English concordat, given in Hefele-Leclercq, *Histoire*, vol. VII, part 1, pp. 560-565, which forbids giving more than one benefice to the same person "unless he is of noble birth or outstanding learning." The German concordat (pp. 536-549) restricts papal appointments to (1) benefices vacated in Rome, or belonging to a papal officer, (2) those made vacant by papal deposition or transfer, and (3) cases of disputed elections. Thus ample grounds still remained for papal intervention.
10 Figgis, *Gerson to Grotius*, p. 41.

the active role taken by the Emperor Sigismund in support of the goals of the council. Particularly in the negotiations with the rival popes, it was the emperor's legates whose action was decisive, and in the efforts to reform the church the imperial party was much more anxious to press forward than were the cardinals. The very fact that the council was held in Constance, in the imperial domain proper, is an indication of the active role of the emperor.

The changes in voting procedure are also important, since they mark a break with the tradition of the past, according to which the councils were a meeting of all bishops to declare what was the belief of the churches. At Constance a very different body met, in which doctors of theology and representatives of the laity participated in the voting, which was carried out by nations—another break with past procedure.[11]

The new pope approved the decrees of Constance with a vague formula which was later to be used to demonstrate that he had never formally adhered to the doctrine of conciliar supremacy. He indicated his approval of all that had been done, "in materiis fidei, conciliariter." The qualifying phrase *conciliariter* ("as a council") could be used to maintain that he was not approving the decrees *Sacrosancta* and *Frequens,* which had been passed before his election, and, in the case of *Sacrosancta,* before the convocation of the council by the Roman pope.[12]

In addition to the ending of the schism and the reform of the church, the council had also interested itself in the problem of the Hussite heresy. Constance will be forever associated with the burning of John Hus in violation of

11 The division into "nations" had also been utilized at the Council of Vienne (1311).
12 For the elaboration of this view, see Hefele-Leclercq, *Histoire,* vol. VII, part 1, p. 592.

the safe-conduct granted by the emperor (July 6, 1415). The condemnation of Hus and of Jerome of Prague led the Czech populace and nobility under King Wenceslaus to defy the council and to defend the Hussite doctrine. The emperor was the legal heir of Wenceslaus, but when the latter died in 1419 the Hussites revolted rather than submit to Sigismund. The combination of aroused Czech nationalism and superb Hussite generalship prevented the emperor and the pope from asserting their claims over Bohemia, and despite a temporary agreement in 1436 the Bohemian question remained a burning one (in more than one sense) throughout the rest of the century.

The Council of Siena, held in 1423-24 in accordance with the decrees of Constance, adopted several decrees against the Hussites, and became involved in a controversy over the validity of the papal transfer of the council from Pavia, its original site. The pope had never shown any enthusiasm for the council, and it finally dissolved itself after resolving to meet again at Basel in seven years.

In February 1431, Martin V appointed Cardinal Cesarini as his legate to preside over a new council at Basel, and a month later the pope died. His successor, Eugene IV, had been made a cardinal by the Roman pope during the schism, and had not participated in the Council of Constance until that pope had abdicated. Thus he had never been a proponent of the doctrine of conciliar supremacy. He had, however, signed an agreement before his election that he would give the College of Cardinals a considerable share in church government, including securing their consent for any transfer in the site of the general council, for a declaration of war, and for the conclusion of treaties. He also had promised the cardinals one half of the papal revenues. This attempt to augment the power of the cardinals meant that, in addition to the question of the relationship of pope and council, the role of the College of Cardinals was another constitutional issue in the church.

Cardinal Cesarini organized a crusade against the Hussites in the summer of 1431, which ended in a disastrous defeat for the forces of the papacy. It was clear that another method than force had to be used, and this appeared to lend a new urgency to the demand for the opening of the Council of Basel. On September 9, Cesarini arrived at Basel, and on October 30 a sparsely attended council invited the Hussites to come to Basel and state their case.

Despite the efforts of Cesarini to carry out his responsibilities as papal legate, the council and pope faced each other as adversaries from the outset. The atmosphere of mutual suspicion was aggravated by geographical separation, with the pope at Rome and the council and papal legate at Basel. When the pope heard of the invitation to the Hussites, he used this as a reason to issue a bull (December 18, 1431) dissolving the council.[13] When it arrived, Cesarini resigned as papal legate and chairman of the council, although he continued to participate in his capacity as cardinal. The council's reaction to the bull of dissolution was to reaffirm the decree of Constance which declared that the pope was subordinate to the general council and that it could not be dissolved or transferred without its own consent. It was at this point that a certain doctor of canon law and churchman from Koblenz arrived in Basel to defend the right of Ulrich von Manderscheid to the archbishopric of Trier. The constitution of the church was in question, the empire in need of reform, and the Bohemian revolt still in progress. Nicholas of Cusa was to become involved in all three questions, both by his writings as a theorist and by his actions as an ecclesiastical diplomat.

13 Other reasons included the existence of heresy around Basel, the war between Austria and Burgundy, and the difficulties of getting to Basel in wintertime. The dissolution also included provision for another council in Bologna in 1433.

CHAPTER II

·   ·   ·

BIOGRAPHICAL
BACKGROUND

NICHOLAS OF CUSA was born in 1401 at Kues, on the banks of the Moselle River, between Trier and Koblenz. His father was a boatman, according to the records, with the surname Kryfts (or Krebs), a name which is still common in the present town of Bernkastel-Kues. The family seems to have been moderately well-to-do, and had financial relations with the local nobility in the Moselle Valley. Although there are numerous legends and stories which have been utilized in writing popular novels about him in the twentieth century, we know very little about Cusanus' early life. The existence of a scholarship named after him (the *Bursa Cusana*), and a special visit later in his life, seem to indicate that he studied at the school of Deventer in central Holland, which was directed by the Brothers of the Common Life. This order, which was typical of the revival of popular piety in the fourteenth and fifteenth centuries, had been founded by Gerard de Groote a half century before, and its best-known member, Thomas a Kempis, was ordained at Zwolle near Deventer at the time that Nicholas may have been studying with the Brothers. The Brothers' education emphasized the classical authors Virgil and Cicero, and they tried by practical methods to develop the inner piety and sense of union with God which was the object of the *devotio moderna*, developed at Deventer under De Groote's influence. It may have been also from the Brothers that Nicholas first developed his interest in Christian mysticism and his aversion to scholastic modes of thought.[1]

In 1416, when he was fifteen years old, he registered at the University of Heidelberg, and the record indicates that he was a cleric of the diocese of Trier, although this only meant that he had received the tonsure from the bishop and had adopted the clerical dress. He stayed in Heidelberg only a year and a half, and the strong nominalist tendency of the university does not seem to have left any impression on his thought.[2]

In 1417 Nicholas transferred to the University of Padua, which in the fifteenth century was one of the great universities of Europe.[3] Originally established in 1222 by the departure of a group of masters and students from Bologna, Padua had become part of the territory of the wealthy city-state of Venice in 1404, and by the time of the arrival

[1] A manuscript in the Strasbourg University and National Library (no. 84) contains a version of Gerson's *Theologia Mystica* which Cusanus may have acquired while studying with the Brothers of the Common Life. It is discussed in E. Vansteenberghe, "Quelques lectures de jeunesse de Nicolas de Cues," *Archives d'histoire,* 3:275-284 (1928). Vansteenberghe's faulty attempt to assess the date of the manuscript is corrected in Rudolf Haubst, "Die Thomas- und Proklos-Exzerpte des 'Nicolaus Treverensis' in Codicillus Strassburg 84," *Mitteilungen,* 1:17-51 (1961). On the "devotio moderna," see A. Hyma, *The Christian Renaissance* (Grand Rapids, 1924), and Jacob, *Essays,* chap. vii. Concerning the political situation in the Moselle Valley in the first part of the fifteenth century, and the relations of Nicholas' family to the local nobility, see Erich Meuthen, "Obedienz und Absolutionslisten aus dem Trierer Bistumsstreit (1430-1435)," *Quellen,* 40:43-64 (1960), and "Nikolaus von Kues und der Laie in der Kirche," *HJ,* 81:101-122 (1962).

[2] Hastings Rashdall, *The Universities of Europe in the Middle Ages* (Oxford, 1936), I, 181 (on the meaning of the term *clericatus*) and II, 253 (on the relative strength of realism and nominalism at Heidelberg).

[3] "What Paris had been in the thirteenth century, what Oxford and Paris together had been in the fourteenth, Padua became in the fifteenth; the center in which ideas from all Europe were combined into an organized and cumulative body of knowledge." J. H. Randall, Jr., "The Development of the Scientific Method in the School of Padua," in *Roots of Scientific Thought,* ed. Philip Wiener and Aaron Noland (New York, 1957), pp. 144-145.

of Cusanus it was, in Renan's phrase, "the Latin quarter of Venice."[4]

From the thirteenth century Padua had been known as the center of medical studies and of civil and canon law. By the fifteenth century it surpassed even its famous parent university in legal training. Nicholas elected to take his degree in canon law. From 1417 to 1423 he attended lectures, in the morning devoted to the *Decretum* of Gratian and the Decretals of Gregory IX, and in the afternoon to the *Liber Sextus,* the *Clementinae,* and the *Extravagantes* collections of the later popes.[5] In 1423 he was awarded the degree of *doctor decretorum,* which qualified him as a canon lawyer.

While there is no clear evidence that Cusanus attended lectures outside his own faculty, it is possible that he may have been influenced by some of the famous teachers in other schools of Padua. At a time when knowledge of Greek was not widespread in Italy, it was being taught in Venice, and Vittorino da Feltre, who was professor of rhetoric at Padua from 1420 to 1422, knew the language. Thus it may have been at this time that Nicholas first began his studies of Greek. Italy was already well into the Renaissance when Nicholas was at Padua. Four years before his arrival the city had celebrated the supposed rediscovery of the bones of Livy with the rites formerly reserved for relics of the saints. Nicholas was affected by the prevailing atmosphere,

4 Ernest Renan, *Averroes et L'Averroisme* (Paris, 1869), p. 326.

5 Rashdall, *Universities,* I, 205-207. The professors in arts and canon law at Padua in 1424 are listed in Lynn Thorndike, *University Records and Life in the Middle Ages* (New York, 1944), p. 302. From a note in a manuscript in Cusanus' library at Kues (a treatise on canon law procedures dated April 1423, listed as no. 220, 4 in Marx, *Verzeichnis,* p. 218), we know that one of Cusanus' teachers in canon law was Prosdocimus de Comitibus; cf. Alois Krchňák, "Die kanonistischen Aufzeichnungen des Nikolaus von Kues in Cod. Cus. 220 als Mitschrift einer Vorlesung seines Paduaner Lehrers Prosdocimus de Comitibus," *Mitteilungen,* 2:67-84 (1962).

and when he returned to Germany he played an important part in the rediscovery of classical manuscripts there. Padua also provided the stimulus to his later interests in mathematics and astronomy. In the company of Paolo Toscanelli, the Florentine scholar who was to be his lifelong friend, he probably listened to lectures by the famed mathematician and astronomer, Prosdocimo de' Beldomandi. In 1422 Prosdocimo was appointed professor of astrology at Padua, and it is possible that his teaching was the source of Cusanus' interest in the influence of the stars on human behavior—an interest which is in evidence even in his political writings.[6]

Attendance at Padua was decisive for the rise of the young churchman from Germany. It gave him a thorough grounding in canon law, which was the avenue to ecclesiastical preferment and the framework within which he wrote his most famous political work, *De Concordantia Catholica.* He also had an opportunity to observe the governmental institutions of the Italian city-states, especially Venice. In addition, Padua gave him personal contacts with the present and future elite of Christendom, among them Giuliano Cesarini, later papal legate at the Council of Basel, whom Cusanus describes as his teacher *(preceptor)* in the dedication to his work, *De Docta Ignorantia.* (Cesarini was not a professor but probably did some teaching as a doctoral candidate.)

After Nicholas received his doctoral degree, he visited Rome for the Jubilee. Many years later in the introduction to his work, *De Mente,* he described this first visit, and

---

6 The first chair of Greek at Padua was established only in 1463. On the teaching of Greek, see William Harrison Woodward, *Vittorino da Feltre* (Cambridge, 1897), and Deno John Geanakoplos, *Greek Scholars in Venice* (Cambridge, Mass., 1962), chap. i. On Prosdocimo de' Beldomandi, see Lynn Thorndike, *History of Magic and Experimental Science,* IV (New York, 1934), 70, 79, 152, and literature cited there.

in a sermon in 1457 he alluded to hearing the famous preacher Bernardino da Siena. It is possible that during this visit he established the contacts with the Italian humanists which were continued in succeeding years. From Rome he returned to the Rhineland, where as a student in orders, although not a priest, he received the income from a church post in the archdiocese of Trier which enabled him to study philosophy and theology at the University of Cologne, registering there on April 8, 1425. A fruitful year was spent in Cologne, which, under the influence of the dean of the faculty of arts, Heimericus de Campo, was a center for the study of the works of Albert the Great and Raymond Lull. Heimericus' works, most of them unpublished, and at least one dating from Cusanus' period in Cologne, are preserved in the library at Kues, and it has been demonstrated that in 1428 Cusanus copied a work of Raymond Lull from an original manuscript which Heimericus secured for him from Paris.[7]

In an *Apologia* written later in his life, Heimericus

7 Nicholas of Cusa's church offices from 1425 until the time of his death are studied on the basis of the Vatican archives in Erich Meuthen, "Die Pfründen des Cusanus," *Mitteilungen* 2:15-66 (1962). Meuthen demonstrates that Nicholas became a priest only much later in his life—between 1436 and 1440. Rudolf Haubst in his article "Zum Fortleben Alberts des Grossen bei Heymerich von Kamp und Nikolaus von Kues," *Studia Albertina*, Supplement IV, *Beiträge zur Geschichte der Philosophie und Theologie des Mittelalters* (Münster, 1952), pp. 420-447, analyzes *Codex Cusanus* no. 106 from the library of Kues containing the works of Heimericus, including a conciliar treatise composed in 1433-34 listing several hundred arguments for the superiority of the council. The existence of an "Albertist" school in Paris where Heimericus studied is discussed in G. Meersseman, *Geschichte des Albertismus*, I (Paris, 1933), 16-23. The further development of the study of Albertus Magnus under Heimericus after his arrival in Cologne in 1423 is treated in Meersseman, *Geschichte*, II (Rome, 1935), 23ff, who cites his publication of a *Tractatus* in 1428 devoted to proving the superiority of Albertus Magnus to St. Thomas Aquinas in the solution of eighteen philosophical problems. On Heimericus as intermediary for the text and study of Lull by Cusanus see Eusebio Colomer, *Nikolaus von Kues und Raimund Llull* (Berlin, 1961), pp. 8-46.

describes three philosophical schools as current in Paris when he studied there—the followers of Albertus Magnus, the Thomists, and the adherents of the *via moderna* of William of Occam. Heimericus followed the Albertists, and Cusanus' library indicates that the Cologne dean found a willing pupil in the young canon lawyer from Kues. While no medieval philosopher after the thirteenth century was uninfluenced by Aristotle, it was the Neo-Platonized Aristotelianism of Albertus Magnus and the mathematical metaphysics of Raymond Lull with which Cusanus came into contact in Cologne—and this was consciously distinguished both from nominalism and from the Thomistic version of Aristotelianism. As the contents of his library and writings indicate, Cusanus' studies at Cologne left a lasting imprint on his philosophical outlook, placing him in the tradition of Christian Neo-Platonism.

Nicholas practised law at this time and gained a familiarity with German legal procedures which he later demonstrated in the *Concordantia*. In 1424 or 1426 he appeared as one of sixty-two theologians and canon lawyers who submitted advisory opinions to Cardinal Giordano Orsini, the papal legate in Germany, on the legal aspects of a tax exemption for a church in Bacharach. In the margin of the manuscript, now in the Munich library, there is a sketch of Cusanus (not drawn from life) and the description "juvenis magnus." It is doubtful that he was Orsini's secretary at this time, as most of his biographers assert. In 1427 the Vatican archives describe him as the secretary of the Archbishop of Trier, acting as the Archbishop's representative in Rome.[8]

8   See Meuthen, "Die Pfründen," p. 22, and "Nikolaus von Kues und der Laie," p. 109. Alois Schmidt, "Nikolaus von Kues Sekretär des Kardinals Giordano Orsini?" in *Aus Mittelalter und Neuzeit*, ed. Josef Engel and Hans Martin Klinkenberg (Bonn, 1957), pp. 137-143, discusses Cusanus' supposed

BIOGRAPHICAL BACKGROUND

Beginning in that year, the name *Nicolaus Treverensis* appears in the correspondence of Poggio Bracciolini, the noted Italian humanist who for a decade had been attempting to recover lost manuscripts of the classical authors from the monasteries of northern Europe. In May 1427 Poggio writes from Rome that he has discussed with Nicholas a report that the manuscript of Cicero's *De Re Publica* had been found in Cologne, as well as Cusanus' own testimony that he had seen a history of Roman wars in Germany by Pliny which did not correspond to any known work by the author. He describes Nicholas as "learned and not boastful or deceitful" *(doctus et . . . minime verbosus aut fallax)*, but a week later he writes that Nicholas is angry and disappointed to have come to Rome and not received anything from the pope, apparently an indication that Cusanus had already begun his lifelong avocation of collecting ecclesiastical benefices. Despite his initial disappointment, he did not do badly. He already possessed the benefice given him by the Archbishop of Trier on January 31, 1425, to support him in his studies at Cologne. The papal registers indicate that in August and September 1427 he was also reserved a benefice in Trier, as well as the posts of dean of the church of Our Lady in Oberwesel (which he subsequently gave up) and dean of the church of St. Florin in Koblenz. In November he was still in Rome, making financial arrangements for payment of annates on his benefices.[9]

After he returned to Germany, Nicholas continued to

---

position with Orsini. The text of the opinion is printed as appendix 6 in Erich Koenig, *Kardinal Giordano Orsini* (Freiburg, 1906), p. 112. The sketch of Cusanus is reproduced in Ernst Hoffmann, "Nikolaus von Cues und die deutsche Philosophie," *Neue Heidelberger Jahrbücher*, 1940, facing p. 58.

9 The citations from Vatican archives are noted by Ludwig Pralle, *Die Wiederentdeckung des Tacitus* (Fulda, 1953), p. 81, and discussed in Meuthen, "Die Pfründen," pp. 16-25.

correspond with Poggio about works which he was trying to obtain. In February 1429 Poggio writes that Nicholas has reported that he has manuscripts of several speeches of Cicero, twenty works of Cyprian, and twenty of the comedies of Plautus. Nicholas also confessed to Poggio that the supposed manuscript of Cicero's *De Re Publica* had turned out to be Macrobius' *Commentary on the Dream of Scipio*—a work known throughout the Middle Ages. Poggio wrote excitedly of the discovery of the Plautus comedies and eagerly awaited Nicholas' arrival in Rome. When Cusanus came in December 1429, he brought with him a total of sixteen comedies of Plautus, twelve of them hitherto unknown, in an eleventh century manuscript which is still preserved in the Vatican library.[10]

Nicholas had already begun to gather the manuscripts which were to form one of the most useful collections surviving from the Middle Ages. In his library at Kues a manuscript of the works of William of Auvergne, a thirteenth century bishop of Paris, contains the note in Cusanus' handwriting that he acquired it along with the sermons of Raymond Lull and the *Sentences* of Peter Lombard on July 8, 1428. The discovery of the Plautus manuscript made the young cleric from the diocese of Trier well known among the Italian humanists, and when he came to the Council of Basel in February 1432 to plead in a case involving a disputed election to the archbishopric of Trier, he was in contact with the noted bibliophile, Francesco Pizzolpasso, the Bishop of Pavia and later Archbishop of Milan. A letter written by Francesco to Nicholas from

---

10 Poggio's correspondence has been printed in *Poggii Epistulae*, ed. T. de Tonellis, 3 vols. (Florence, 1832-1861). The relevant letters appear in vol. III, pp. 207ff. Substantial excerpts are reproduced in Alois Meister, "Die humanistischen Anfänge des Nikolaus von Cues," *Annalen des historischen Vereins für den Niederrhein*, XLII (1896), 5-9, and in Pralle, *Wiederentdeckung*, pp. 33-36.

Basel after he had returned to Koblenz discusses various manuscripts which he was having copied, including a volume of Greek proverbs. Pizzolpasso, addressing Nicholas as "most learned" *(doctissimo)*, sent his letters with his nephew, who was making a pilgrimage to the shrine of the Three Kings in Cologne and wished to see Nicholas "whose fame had attracted him" *(illectus est fama)*. Around the same time, Ambrogio Traversari wrote from Florence to Cesarini, papal legate at Basel, referring to reports of "a large manuscript of exceeding age" of the works of Cicero which Nicholas had shown to one of the council participants, and other volumes which he promised to bring to Basel.[11]

From the surviving correspondence of the Italian humanists, Nicholas appears as an enterprising researcher and manuscript collector, probably not very thorough in his methods or profound in his knowledge of the classics, who used his access to the German manuscript sources to develop contacts with Italian churchmen and to secure various ecclesiastical appointments. When he arrived at the Council of Basel, he was hardly past his thirtieth year, but he was well known in Italy, had visited Rome often, and had personal friendships among propapal churchmen. If, given the tradition of the Council of Constance and the physical separation of Basel and Rome, the council is seen as doomed from the start to develop into a power struggle with the

11 The letters have been published in R. Sabbadini, "Niccolò da Cusa e i conciliari di Basilea alla scoperta dei codici," *Rendiconti della Reale Accademia dei Lincei*, 5th series, XX (1911), 9-19, and Sabbadini has also published excerpts in *Le Scoperte dei codici latini e greci ne secoli XIV e XV*, II (Florence, 1914), 18-20. Nicholas' source seems to have been the cathedral library at Cologne (not Fulda, as Pralle, *Wiederentdeckung*, attempts to prove). At Cologne he had particularly good contacts since his later client, Ulrich von Manderscheid, was dean of the cathedral chapter. The manuscript of William of Auvergne is listed as no. 94 in the catalogue of the library at Kues (Marx, *Verzeichnis*, pp. 94-95).

papacy, Nicholas from the beginning had a foot in each camp, and it is not surprising that his conciliar theory should be a moderate one.

Cusanus' interest in the classical manuscripts which he was collecting was, at least at first, largely a means to another end. From his library and his writings, he seems to have had a genuine interest in church history and, as a professional canon lawyer, he was already collecting works that would be useful to him in this career. However, it would be inaccurate to describe him as a humanist in the sense of an enthusiast for classical culture. His primary interest was in the history and law of the church, and it was as a canon lawyer that he first appeared at the council which was the occasion for the writing of his first major work.[12]

The records of the council indicate that he was formally incorporated on February 29, 1432, as one of three representatives of Ulrich von Manderscheid. The Archbishop of Trier had died in 1430, and the chapter had elected Jacob von Sirck as his successor. Ulrich, however, with the support of the local nobility, contested the election. When Sirck appealed the case to Rome as a disputed election, the pope replied by conferring the archbishopric on still another candidate, Raban, the Bishop of Speyer. In the meantime, however, Ulrich succeeded in putting sufficient pressure on the chapter that it changed its position and cast its unanimous vote for him. The dispute, then, was between Ulrich, as the elected candidate of the cathedral chapter, and Raban, the papal appointee. Nicholas was the chief

12 Nicholas' abilities as a canon lawyer were recognized as early as 1428 when he was offered a professorship at the new University of Louvain, possibly indicating that he taught canon law at Cologne. The invitation was refused, both at that time and when it was tendered a second time in 1435. Cf. Vansteenberghe, "Quelques lectures," p. 277, quoting the records of the city of Louvain.

of a six-man delegation which came to the council to plead the cause of van Manderscheid. Manderscheid had the support of the nobility in the Trier area and such clergy as they controlled. Raban had the city of Trier and most of the clergy behind him.

Abandoning the division into nations used at Constance, the council had divided into four committees, or deputations, to deal with its business: on faith, on matters of common interest, on reform, and on peace. Each deputation contained an equal number of each of the four nations present—French, German, Italian, and Spanish. Nicholas' case was referred to the deputation *pro Communibus* and the deputation *pro Pace* in March 1432, and when the former group decided to postpone decision on the matter he left the council for three months. In June he returned and was active in trying to get the deputation to make a decision. The council, however, was very reluctant to decide the case, which divided the nobility and bourgeoisie of the diocese of Trier. It was repeatedly discussed in the deputation, but the full council did not take up the case until 1434.[13]

On his arrival at Basel, Nicholas had been made a member of the deputation *de Fide*, and since the Manderscheid case was delayed he began to take an active part in the more general concerns of the council. The reply of the conciliar party to the papal bull of dissolution of December 1431 was to reaffirm repeatedly the Constance doctrine that the council was superior to the pope and could not be dissolved or transferred without its own consent. (Eugene had tried to do both, since his earlier bull had called for

---

[13] The documentation on the case of Ulrich von Manderscheid appears in Johannes Haller, *Concilium Basiliense,* vols. II-III (Basel, 1897, 1900); the von Manderscheid delegation is listed in III, 70. Cusanus' role in the von Manderscheid case is re-examined in a forthcoming book by Erich Meuthen.

the transfer of the council to Bologna.) In August 1432 the Archbishop of Taranto came with the pope's latest offer. Eugene agreed to allow the council to continue its negotiations with the Bohemians and its work of reform, but he maintained that by divine intention the church was under a monarchical form of government, that the council could only be valid with the pope's approval, that it could not depose the pope except for heresy, and that the pope could dispense with conciliar decrees, including those of the Council of Constance.

The council answered that it alone was infallible and the pope was merely a minister of the church as a whole, even though he was its head. At the same time, the council decided to give the vote to the lower clergy in attendance, a move which completely altered the balance of power in the meeting, making a parish priest or a master of arts the equivalent of a bishop or cardinal when it came to voting in the deputations and plenary sessions. This decision had an important effect on the later history of the council, when many of the higher clergy went over to the papal side.[14]

Nicholas had returned to Koblenz after his appearance in Basel in June, but he reappeared in Basel in October, returned to Koblenz for Christmas, and was back in Basel in early 1433.[15] The negotiations between Pope Eugene and the council dragged on at a very slow pace, principally because of the difficulties of communications between Basel and Rome, and no real progress was made towards a solu-

14 At the end of 1433 there were about 500 members incorporated in the council, of whom about 100 were of episcopal rank. Cf. Joseph Gill, *The Council of Florence* (Cambridge, Mass., 1959), p. 50, n. 4.

15 Vansteenberghe, *Le cardinal Nicolas de Cues* (Lille, 1920), p. 54, n. 2, and p. 213, n. 7. The house which Nicholas occupied during his periods of residence in Koblenz was in continuous use until it was destroyed in World War II. Its history is given in Meuthen, "Die Pfründen," p. 25, n. 56a, and a picture appears facing p. 64 of *Mitteilungen*, vol. II.

tion. In the meantime the delegates from Bohemia arrived, and Nicholas of Cusa was one of those named by the council on February 11, 1433, to meet with them.[16] It was he who finally proposed a compromise, according to which the Bohemians were to be allowed communion under both forms, provided they abandoned their demands that mortal sin be punished by the civil power and that church property be confiscated. While the proposal was not accepted by the Hussite representatives who left the council in April, it became the basis of a subsequent settlement in 1436. The negotiations also led Nicholas to write an opinion on the Bohemian question, printed as two *Letters to the Bohemians*.[17]

The *de Fide* deputation of which Nicholas was a member continued to concern itself with the still unsolved question of relations with the papacy, in particular with the status of the papal bull of December 1431 dissolving the

---

16 Haller, *Concilium Basiliense*, II, 348ff.

17 The letters to the Bohemians appear as *Epistolae* II and III in the Basel edition of Cusanus' *Opera*, pp. 829-846 (soon to be republished in vol. X of the Heidelberg edition). The infrequent mention of the council, and the great emphasis on unity with the *sedes Romana*, have led Vansteenberghe, *Nicolas*, p. 216, n. 1, to question whether the text of the letters was later modified in a propapal direction. However, an early copy of the original text of the two letters, which are in reality a single work entitled *De Usu Communionis*, is located in the Trier Municipal Library and has not been altered. As subsequent analysis of *De Concordantia Catholica* will show, the emphasis on the necessity of unity with the *sedes Romana* and the *cathedra Petri* (p. 835) does not necessarily imply an anticonciliar position, since these terms are not always identical with the papacy in Cusanus' thought. (Cf. *DCC*, Book I, chap. 14, pp. 77-79, and analysis below.) The lengthy discussion (p. 836) of the place of the primacy (*primatus*) in the church "to avoid schism" coincides with Cusanus' views in the *Concordantia*. In the letters, he does not take a position on whether infallibility inheres in the papacy or the church as a whole, restricting himself to attributing it to the union of the *sedes* and the *ecclesia*. A more subtle analysis is developed in *De Concordantia*. That the two works are closely related is proved by the reference in the *Concordantia* (Book II, chap. 26, p. 254) to "a certain little work against the error of the Bohemians."

council. The pope was under pressure from the secular rulers, especially Emperor Sigismund (whom he had crowned in Rome in May 1433), to arrive at some compromise. On August 1, therefore, he formally annulled the dissolution and recognized the council's decrees, except for those which prejudiced the rights of the Holy See. However, just such a decree had been passed at Basel one month earlier, when the council declared that all church offices must be filled by election, and that the pope could not appoint to or reserve sees except in the diocese of Rome and where canon law specifically provided for papal appointment. It is true that the council did allow the pope the possibility of exceptions to the rule, but these could only be *ex magna rationali et evidenti causa,* and he was required to give his reasons in writing.[18] When the pope received news of this decree, he refused to accept it. At the same time, in Basel, a subcommittee of the deputation, including in its membership Nicholas of Cusa, examined the papal bull of submission and pronounced it insufficient. The council then decided to suspend the pope, an action which it had threatened repeatedly in the past but had not yet taken.

In October 1433 the emperor returned from Italy and began to take an active part in the council. Meanwhile, the pope was under heavy pressure from his enemies in Italy, and on December 15, 1433, he issued a bull granting all that the council had demanded. Eugene admitted that his dissolution was null and void and that the council had been canonical from its inception. He accepted all the requirements of the council, although in a letter written at the same time he said that he would never approve the

---

18 For the decree, see J. D. Mansi, ed., *Sacrorum Conciliorum Nova et Amplissima Collectio,* vol. XXIX (Venice, 1788), cols. 56-64. The papal bull of August 1 appears in col. 57 and that of December in col. 78.

decrees asserting the superiority of the council to the pope.[19] It was during this period that Nicholas submitted his major work of political theory, *De Concordantia Catholica*, to the council. A reference in the first book of the work indicates that the opening section was written elsewhere than in Basel, probably in Koblenz during Cusanus' frequent stays there in 1432, and possibly also in Cologne, since he seems to have had access to a large library there and speaks proudly of having gathered his authorities "not from any abbreviated collection but drawing from original materials."[20] The second book refers to "this council" and cites a decree of the council adopted in August 1432, so that it must have been written after that date. It also refers to Nicholas' writings against the Bohemians which were composed in early 1433, but there is no mention of papal concessions made in August of that year.[21] Much of it must have been written in Basel, and in its composition Nicholas probably used the other members of the Manderscheid delegation to do research for him. The third book repeatedly mentions the presence in Basel of the emperor, who arrived in October 1433, and there is no reference to the papal submission which took place in December. The

19 Letter to Doge of Venice, 1433, quoted by Gill, *Council of Florence,* p. 344, n. 1. When Eugene, after initial resistance, agreed that the Council at Basel had been and continued to be legitimate for the purposes of "reform of the church in head and members," it appeared to everyone but Eugene himself that he was conceding the superiority of the council to the pope. Subsequent developments made it clear that this was only a tactical move. Cf. N. Valois, *Le Pape et le Concile,* 1418-1450 (Paris, 1909), I, 304-306.

20 *DCC,* preface, p. 3 (Heidelberg edition). In 1426 the humanists in Italy heard about a library in Cologne which contained over 800 manuscripts. Pralle, *Wiederentdeckung,* pp. 67-68, doubts that there was such a library, but Nicholas often refers to Cologne as the source of his materials (e.g., *DCC,* Book III, chap. 3, p. 340, chap. 25, p. 422). The reference to the Council of Basel as *"ibi congregatis"* in *DCC,* Book I, chap. 12, p. 73, indicates that this section was written elsewhere.

21 *DCC,* Book II, chap. 17, p. 189, chap. 20, p. 226, chap. 26, p. 254.

internal evidence, therefore, seems to indicate that the first two books were written in Koblenz and Basel in 1432 and early 1433, while the third book was composed in Basel late in 1433, the entire work being submitted to the council at the end of 1433 or the beginning of 1434.[22]

A study of the manuscript sources has revealed that the work went through several versions before reaching its present form. Originally it was "A Pamphlet on Harmony in the Church," written to demonstrate the superiority of the council to the pope. This first version corresponds to Book I and Book II, chapters 1-7, 16-21, and 26-30, of the *Concordantia Catholica* as we know it today. A subsequent version involved the insertion in the middle of the second book of several chapters on consent as the prerequisite for legitimate law and government, a conception which was probably related to Cusanus' legal argument in favor of Ulrich von Manderscheid as the elected candidate for the archbishopric of Trier over the papal appointee, Raban. Then it appears that the impending arrival of the emperor at the Council of Basel led Nicholas to extend his concerns to the reform of the empire on the same basis—the establishment of councils to give consent to law and government. Finally, he added a preface to the third book and new final chapters to the second and third books.

De Concordantia Catholica, as it was retitled in its final form, sets the problem of the respective jurisdictions of pope and council in the framework of a broader consideration of the nature and government and society and relates

22 *DCC,* Book III, chap. 3, p. 339, chap. 19, p. 397, chap. 24, p. 418, chap. 41, p. 473. On the manuscript evidence see G. Kallen, "Der Reichsgedanke in der Reformschrift 'De Concordantia Catholica' des Nikolaus von Cues," *Neue Heidelberger Jahrbücher,* 1940, p. 66, and "Die handschriftliche Überlieferung der Concordantia catholica des Nikolaus von Kues," *SBH* 1963, no. 2 (Heidelberg, 1963).

it to Cusanus' view of the structure of the universe. This is what makes the *Concordantia* much more than a polemical tract in defense of the Council of Basel. Whether considered from the point of view of sheer length, of subtlety of thought, or range of acquaintance with the principal medieval writers, it ranges far beyond all the other works written in the conciliar period. It is the last great work of political theory before Machiavelli. In it nearly all the great schools of medieval philosophical and legal thinking are combined in a magnificent and soaring harmony drawn from the diversity of medieval thought.

Because of the wealth of resource material in Cusanus' library and the ample citations which accompany his works, as well as the comparative abundance of historical evidence regarding his intellectual formation, it is not difficult to trace the principal influences upon the theory of Nicholas of Cusa. In philosophy he was particularly influenced by medieval Neo-Platonist philosophers and theologians. By profession he was a canon lawyer, and the occasion for writing the *Concordantia* was the determination of the fundamental law of the church. From medieval Neo-Platonism and canon law, symbolized respectively by his studies at Cologne and Padua, Nicholas constructed a theory which was at once an original synthesis and a summing up of a century and a half of conciliar theory. Perhaps "he who predicates originality of any single passage of conciliar theory is a bold man,"[23] but the political philosophy of Nicholas of Cusa illustrates the variety, complexity, and subtlety possible in a reworking of the common elements of medieval thought. At the risk of some oversimplification, and because an appreciation of the magnitude of Nicholas' accomplishment is only possible by

[23] Jacob, *Essays*, p. 53.

an understanding of the sources on which he drew, the analysis of his political thought will begin with a review of the two major traditions out of which it was formed— the philosophy (and theology) of Christian Neo-Platonism, and the legal theories of Roman and canon law.

CHAPTER III

. . .

CHRISTIAN
NEO-PLATONISM

THE PHILOSOPHICAL
ANTECEDENTS

W HITEHEAD'S statement that the history of Western philosophy is a series of footnotes to Plato applies with particular validity to the Middle Ages, although most of Plato's works were unknown to medieval writers. Two of Plato's dialogues were translated in the twelfth century, and most of the *Timaeus* was known through the Latin translation and commentary by Chalcidius, but the principal medieval contact with Platonic thought came through other writers, such as Cicero, the church fathers, and certain of the Neo-Platonic philosophers of the early Christian era.[1] Only in the fifteenth century did Western Europe recover the corpus of Platonic writings and develop a different Platonism from that of the Middle Ages. Nicholas of Cusa spent the last part of his life in Italy at a time when it was experiencing the impact of the revived interest in the original Plato, but his major works of political theory and of metaphysics are influenced by medieval rather than Renaissance Platonism.[2] It is true that he visited Constan-

[1] Chalcidius' commentary has been printed in an edition by Johann Wrobel (Leipzig, 1876). The Warburg Institute of London has published a new edition by J. H. Waszink, as Vol. IV of its series, *Plato Latinus* (London, 1962).

[2] Cusanus' library contains Petrus Candidus Decembrius' translation of the *Republic*, but it was not completed until 1439, well after the composition of the *Concordantia* (Marx, *Verzeichnis*, no. 178, p. 166).

tinople after his break with the Council of Basel and he seems to have had a rudimentary knowledge of the Greek language,[3] but the principal sources of his thought were the common founts of medieval Platonism—Plato's Neo-Platonic commentators and the writings of the fathers of the church. While he may have read some of these writers during his years of study of canon law at Padua, he probably studied them most intensively during and after his stay at Cologne. The authors represented in his library at Kues attest to his lifelong interest in the writers influenced by Neo-Platonism. Utilizing the writers whom he is known to have read, it is possible to reconstruct the tradition of Christian Neo-Platonism as it affected his thought.

The influence of these writers upon the metaphysical and theological works which Nicholas wrote later in his life is already acknowledged. Less widely recognized is their effect upon his political works, most of which were written while he was still a young man. Those who have studied his conciliar writings have tended to treat them in relation to their legal aspects as a part of the conciliarist attempt to constitutionalize the church. Yet there is another important element with radically different implications in Cusanus' political thought which he drew from the Neo-Platonic tradition—the belief in the principle of hierarchy as the basis for a divinely intended order in the universe, in society, in the church and the empire, and in man himself. However much it might be at odds with theories drawn from other sources, the principle of hierarchy was one of the central organizing conceptions of Cusanus' political theory, as it was of medieval society. As a Christian, Cusanus would be led to believe in a purposive order in the universe as a conclusion from the doctrines of Creation and

3 Cf. M. Honecker, *Nikolaus von Cues und die griechische Sprache*, in *SBH* 1937-38, no. 2 (Heidelberg, 1938).

Divine Providence. Moreover, the ultimate source of political authority for the Christian is God, for "there is no power but of God; the powers that be are ordained of God" (Rom. 13:1). However, Cusanus' conception of the order which would best carry out the divine will in the world—a series of analogical hierarchical structures in man, in society, and in the universe—was derived from Neo-Platonic philosophy and its Christian intermediaries rather than directly from Christian revelation.

This hierarchical world view had originally been anticipated in the writings of Plato but had received a more systematic formulation from Plotinus early in the Christian era (A.D. 205-270). On the basis of certain passages in Plato, especially in the *Parmenides* (the nonpredicability of the One), in the *Timaeus* (the description of the activity of the creative Demiurge), and in the *Republic* (Plato's assertion —no. 509—that the Good is "beyond Being"), a Neo-Platonic theology had been developed which described the One as the source of all Being, yet Itself infinitely removed from them. By a process of overflowing or emanation, the One creates first *nous* or mind, then *psyche* or soul, and in turn this creative triad produces successively lower grades of being, sensation, plant nature, and so on. As the process is described in Macrobius' *Commentary on the Dream of Scipio* (Cusanus did not know Plotinus, but we know from Poggio's correspondence that he read Macrobius' *Commentary* in 1428):

> Since from the Supreme God, Mind arises, and from Mind, Soul and since this in turn creates all subsequent things and fills them all with Life, and since this single radiance illumines all and is reflected in each, as a single face might be reflected in many mirrors placed in a series; and since all things follow in continuous succession degenerating in sequence to the bottom of the series, the attentive observer

will discover a connection of parts, from the Supreme God down to the last dregs of things, mutually linked together without a break.[4]

Writing a generation after Plotinus, Eusebius of Caesarea believed that Plato as interpreted by Plotinus had already anticipated the Christian doctrine of the Trinity in his belief in the One, Mind, and Soul. An example of the fusion of Christian and Platonic triadic thinking occurs in Augustine's doctrine of the "traces of the Trinity," *vestigia Trinitatis,* a theory which Cusanus as well as other medieval Platonists adopted. The Triune God, reasoned Augustine, has imprinted His creation with a series of threefold divisions, making the universe a symbolic representation of His nature. Anyone observing the natural divisions of the created world (e.g., the three faculties of memory, intellect, and will in man) would be led, in Augustine's view, to an appreciation of the reality of the Trinity.[5]

In the *Confessions* Augustine acknowledges the debt which he owes to "the Platonists" (probably Porphyry and Plotinus in Latin translation) for leading him to Christianity. Passages in the *City of God* make it clear that he shared with them the belief in an ordered and hierarchical universe. As he states it in the twenty-second chapter of Book XI, "From things earthly to things heavenly, from

4 Macrobius, *Commentarium in Somnium Scipionis,* I, 14, 15, quoted in Arthur O. Lovejoy, *The Great Chain of Being* (Cambridge, Mass., 1936), p. 63. The complete text of the *Commentary* has been translated with an introduction and notes by William Henry Stahl (New York, 1952). Thomas Whittaker has also done a critical study on *Macrobius* (Cambridge, 1923). On the tracing of a copy of Macrobius to Nicholas' library at Kues, see Raymond Klibansky, *The Continuity of the Platonic Tradition during the Middle Ages* (London, 1939), p. 31.

5 Augustine, *De Trinitate,* Book XV, chaps. xxi-xxiii, English translation by M. Dods, in *The Works of Aurelius Augustine,* VII (London, 1873), 424-29.

the visible to the invisible, there are some things better than others; and for this purpose are they unequal in order that they might all exist."[6] Similarly in the thirteenth chapter of Book XIX, Augustine defines peaces as "the tranquillity of order." In Augustine's view, peace is the result of "an ordered harmony of obedience and rule" in the parts of the human organism, in man's relationship to God and to his fellow man, in the family, and in the earthly and heavenly cities. "Order is the distribution which allots to things equal and unequal, each its own place."[7]

St. Augustine's assumption was that each equal and unequal thing had its own place—that he lived in an ordered universe. In the earthly city, therefore, there should be a proper order of obedience and rule with the implication that there were some who should rule and others who should be ruled, on the basis of objective qualifications of equality and inequality. While he never defined the structure of this ideal order as it applied to society and government, and the ambiguity of his political theory in this respect continues to provide material for scholarly controversy, Augustine's definition of peace could be interpreted to imply that there was one proper order of obedience and rule in the political community, the establishment of which would bring peace and order. The medieval philosophers and theologians followed Augustine in his quest for order and in his belief in a rational universe distinguished by differences of levels of existence and value.

6 Augustine, *The City of God* (trans. M. Dods), Book XI, chap. 22 (Modern Library edition, New York, 1950, p. 365). On St. Augustine and Neo-Platonism, see M. F. Sciacca, *Saint Augustin et le Neoplatonisme* (Louvain, 1956), and M. P. Garvey, *St. Augustine, Christian or Neo-Platonist?* (Milwaukee, 1939). On Augustine's relation to Cusanus, see F. Edward Cranz, "St. Augustine and Nicholas of Cusa in the Tradition of Western Christian Thought," *Speculum*, 28:297-315 (April 1953).

7 Augustine, *The City of God*, Book XIX, chap. 13, p. 690.

NICHOLAS OF CUSA

The Neo-Platonic cosmology and theology were available directly to Cusanus and the later Middle Ages in the writings of Proclus (418-485). His *Elements of Theology, Commentary on Plato's Parmenides,* and other works were translated by William of Moerbeke between 1260 and 1286. An Arabic summary of his doctrines, the *Liber de Causis,* attributed to Aristotle until St. Thomas noted its resemblance to Proclus' ideas, also influenced the scholastics, in particular Albertus Magnus. In his later writings Nicholas of Cusa refers frequently to Proclus. Copies of his works with heavy marginal notations appear in the library at Kues.[8]

Although Proclus was aware that the discussion of the One and the Many in Plato's *Parmenides* could be interpreted simply as an exercise in logic, his commentary gave a theological interpretation to the conclusion of its first hypothesis, that nothing can be predicated about the One. When the original dialogue was translated in its entirety by George of Trapezunt at the instigation of Nicholas of Cusa in 1450-51, it became apparent that the *Parmenides* also had a nontheological purpose, but Cusanus continued

---

8 Copies of Proclus' *Platonic Theology* and *Commentary on the Parmenides* are listed as no. 185 and no. 186 in the library at Kues (Marx, *Verzeichnis,* pp. 172-173). The Latin and English texts of Proclus' *Commentary on the Parmenides* as well as Cusanus' marginal notes have been published by Raymond Klibansky and Charlotte Labowsky as vol. III of the *Plato Latinus* series of the Warburg Institute under the title, *Parmenides nec non Procli Commentarium in Parmenidem* (London, 1953). On the influence of Proclus' *Commentary on the Parmenides* on the Middle Ages and especially on Cusanus, see the following writings of Raymond Klibansky: *Ein Proklos-Fund und seine Bedeutung, SBH,* 1928-29, no. 5 (Heidelberg, 1929); *Continuity of Platonic Tradition;* "Plato's Parmenides in the Middle Ages and the Renaissance," *Medieval and Renaissance Studies,* 1:281-335 (1943). Klibansky is mistaken when he describes quotations from Proclus in the Strasbourg manuscript discussed in Chapter II, note 1, as dating from the period of Cusanus' youth. For this question, as well as an assessment of the influence of Proclus on Cusanus, see Haubst, "Die Thomas- und Proklos-Exzerpte."

to regard the dialogue as a treatise in theology rather than in logic.[9]

In Proclus' handbook of his teachings, *The Elements of Theology*, the triadic divisions of the Platonic tradition are related to a fundamental property of Being—the fact that, for one thing to cause another, there must be a middle term, so that the hierarchy of creation operates in three steps: cause, intermediary, and effect. Similarly creation is described in three stages, the One, the Procession, and the Reversion, and within each grade of being there is a threefold subdivision.

Yet the One is absolutely removed, above the secondary principles of Being, Life, and Intelligence (prop. 115). He is the Good and the First Cause of all things (prop. 5, 12, and 13).[10] This paradoxical juxtaposition of divine transcendance and triadic emanation was developed out of hints in Plato, and passed on to the medieval thinkers. Yet, although some of Proclus' works were translated in the thirteenth century, his ideas would never have been accepted so readily had it not been for the mediation of "the unknown eccentric who within a generation of Proclus' death conceived the idea of dressing his philosophy in Christian draperies and passing it off as the work of a convert of St. Paul."[11]

Dionysius the Areopagite, often referred to as Pseudo-Dionysius, was a Syrian Christian disciple of Proclus, who wrote around A.D. 500. In what seems to have been a deliberate deception, he was successful in persuading his medieval readers that he was the "Dionysius, the Areopa-

---

[9] Cf. Klibansky, "Plato's Parmenides," pp. 9-24. The *Commentary on the Parmenides* is summarized in Thomas Whittaker, *The Neo-Platonists* (Cambridge, 1928), pp. 248-264.

[10] Proclus, *The Elements of Theology*, trans. E. R. Dodds (Oxford, 1933), *passim*.

[11] E. R. Dodds, introduction to Proclus, *Elements*, p. xxvi.

gite," mentioned in the Acts of the Apostles as a convert of St. Paul after his sermon on the altar of the Unknown God in Athens (Acts 17:34). Because of his supposed mention in the New Testament, his writings received a nearly scriptural veneration in the Middle Ages. Commentaries were written on his works by John Scotus Eriugena in the ninth century (who did a translation into Latin), by Robert Grosseteste in the twelfth century (also with translation), and by Albertus Magnus and Thomas Aquinas in the thirteenth century. St. Thomas mentions Dionysius one hundred and forty-three times, and Dante places him beside Aquinas in paradise. Down to the Renaissance Dionysius was one of the most important intellectual influences on Western thought.[12]

Yet from the time of Nicholas of Cusa, increased knowledge of the history of the church gave rise to doubts about the authenticity of the work of the supposed disciple of St. Paul. Cusanus himself, although very much influenced by Dionysius, wrote in the margin of one of his manuscripts asking why the church fathers before Gregory the Great failed to mention him.[13]

Dionysius' writings include *The Mystical Theology,* the *Divine Names,* the *Celestial Hierarchy* and the *Ecclesiastical Hierarchy,* and ten letters. Together they constitute the principal medium of transmission of Neo-Platonic theological and hierarchical ideas to the Middle Ages.

12 The most convenient summary of the vast German and French scholarship concerning Dionysius is contained in Thomas L. Campbell, *Dionysius, the Pseudo-Areopagite, the Ecclesiastical Hierarchy* (Washington, 1955). The best edition of his works has been published in two volumes by the abbey of Solesmes as *Dionysiaca* (Bruges, 1937). In it the original Greek and the various Latin translations of Dionysius' works appear on parallel lines along with a French version.

13 Henry Bett, *Nicholas of Cusa* (London, 1932), p. 19, n. 2, quoting from no. 44 in the library at Kues. Several translations and commentaries on Dionysius are listed in the library at Kues, some from late in Cusanus' life (Marx, *Verzeichnis,* numbers 43, 44, 45, 96, pp. 38-42, 97-98).

The *Divine Names* outlines a method of attaining a knowledge of God which was to become the basis of medieval scholastic theology—the affirmative way or way of analogy. The affirmative way consists in predicating of God to an infinite degree the qualities found in a limited fashion in His creatures. Thus, if any of His creatures are beautiful, good or just, He can be said to be Infinite Beauty, Goodness, Justice. The method resembles the process of arriving at the Idea of the Good in Book VI of Plato's *Republic* by means of progressive dialectical stages of abstraction.

In both the *Divine Names* and the *Mystical Theology* Dionysius also describes "the negative way" of theology, derived from Proclus' interpretation of Plato's *Parmenides*. In this method, the theologian or mystic begins with limited created things in all their imperfection and progresses by exclusion until he arrives at a conception of God as "super-essential darkness"—as the One above Being, about whom nothing can be asserted. When Dionysius attempts to describe God in the *Divine Names,* he prefaces his descriptions with the warning that this is impossible, since "the One, the Unknown, the Being above Being, the Good in Itself can neither be described nor understood."[14] The *Mystical Theology* speaks of the negative way as one by which "we may know that not-knowing [*ignorantiam,* in the medieval Latin translations] . . . and see that darkness above Being which is hidden in Light among existing things." The last chapter of the work consists of a single sentence listing what God is not: "He is not soul or mind . . . nor is He one nor is He unity, nor is He Godhead nor Goodness . . . nor can any affirmation or negation apply to Him. . . He transcends all affirmation by being the perfect and unique cause of all things, and all negation

14 *Divine Names,* chap. i (*Dionysiaca,* I, 36).

by the plenitude of His simple and absolute nature."[15] Cusanus' conception of "learned ignorance" is a development of these ideas in Dionysius, which he knew directly and through later medieval mystics and philosophers familiar with Dionysius' works.[16]

Although the idea was not a new one, Dionysius seems to have been the first to use the term "hierarchy." In the *Celestial Hierarchy,* he defines it as "a holy order, science, and action, as far as possible reflecting the likeness of God." In the *Ecclesiastical Hierarchy,* it is defined as "an orderly arrangement *(logos)* of sacred things."[17] In the two works, the Neo-Platonic triads of being become Christianized and personified—in the *Celestial Hierarchy* as the angelic choirs next to the throne of God, and in the *Ecclesiastical Hierarchy* as officers of the church. Dionysius' scheme for the order among the angels became the definitive classification of the heavenly hosts, and the model of the angelic hierarchy was later used by medieval political theorists to give theological support to the political structure of feudal monarchy.[18] The hierarchies of Dionysius are incorporated into the political thought of Cusanus and form the model for the political and ecclesiastical structures which he proposes.

The heavenly hierarchy is divided into a first rank comprising the Seraphim, Cherubim, and Thrones; an intermediate rank consisting of Dominations, Powers, and Virtues; and a lowest rank of Principalities, Archangels, and

15 *Mystical Theology,* chaps. ii and v *(Dionysiaca,* I, 582-583, 597-602).

16 He also may have seen the term in one of St. Augustine's letters. See discussion in Chapter XII.

17 *Celestial Hierarchy,* chap. iii *(Dionysiaca,* II, 785); *Ecclesiastical Hierarchy,* chap. i *(Dionysiaca,* II, 1086).

18 For examples of the "angelic analogy" in medieval political theory, cf. Wilhelm Berges, *Die Fürstenspiegel des hohen und späten Mittelalters* (Leipzig, 1938), pp. 32-34, 52-59.

Angels. The first group perfects all below, the second illuminates, and the third purifies. Each level draws the lower levels up to God. The first rank is in direct contact with Him. "The second rank is elevated similarly by the first, the third by the second, and our (earthly) hierarchy by the third according to a well-ordered cosmic system in divine harmony and following the analogy of the good order of the whole."[19]

Beneath the celestial hierarchy and directly modeled on it are the ecclesiastical hierarchy and the hierarchy of the law. While Dionysius does not go into great detail about the legal hierarchy, he indicates that the first "representation of the heavenly archetypes" was in the Law of the Old Testament, which has given way to the "fulfillment and sacred end of the legal hierarchy in the ecclesiastical hierarchy."[20]

The *Ecclesiastical Hierarchy* is arranged in the same triadic fashion. It is divided into sacraments, priesthood, and people, and while the sacramental order is not broken down into a triple subdivision, the sacerdotal order is divided into three ranks, following those of the celestial hierarchy. The highest sacerdotal rank, those who consecrate and perfect, "possessing the priestly power in its fullness," are the bishops *(hierarchai)*. Below them are those who illumine, the priests *(hiereis)*, and the lowest rank is composed of those who purify, the ministers or deacons *(leitourgoi)*. The sacerdotal order administers (mediates) the sacraments to the laity, who are in turn divided into the monks *(monachoi)*, who are consecrated, the faithful *(hieros laos)*, who have been illuminated, and the cate-

---

[19] *Celestial Hierarchy*, chap. x *(Dionysiaca*, II, 919). The division into nine orders of angels is also found before Dionysius in Cyril of Jerusalem. See R. Roques, *L'Univers Dionysien* (Paris, 1954), p. 175, n. 5.
[20] *Ecclesiastical Hierarchy*, chap. v *(Dionysiaca*, II, 1322).

chumens (described but not given a special name), who are being purified.[21]

There is an important difference, which Dionysius does not bring out, between the ecclesiastical and the celestial hierarchy. The ecclesiastical hierarchy is not necessarily based on intrinsic qualities. To justify its rule the church used a different principle from that of superiority in sanctity or wisdom. The bishop might be a very saintly person, but what made him a bishop was the fact that he had received orders from a church official with the power to consecrate bishops or priests. The transmission of the power of orders could be traced back ultimately to the original consecration of the apostles by Christ. Augustine's recognition that not everyone who was a member of the church on earth or even in a high place in the ecclesiastical hierarchy was thereby a citizen of the *civitas Dei* was another way of emphasizing the difference between the view of hierarchy as based on intrinsic qualitative differences, and the view of hierarchy as based on the transmission of orders.

In addition, in the ecclesiastical hierarchy there are only two triads, or six ranks, instead of the nine choirs of angels which Dionysius ascribed to the celestial hierarchy. Moreover, he does not adhere strictly to the Neo-Platonic principle that each order transmits to the order immediately beneath it the power which it has received from the order above. Thus the bishops consecrate the deacons, and the priests perfect the monks. However, some departure from a perfect hierarchical scheme was necessary in order to conform to the ecclesiastical practice of the day.

In the *Divine Names*, Peter is referred to as "the chief, and eldest and highest of the apostles," and in the *Ecclesi-*

---

21 *Ecclesiastical Hierarchy*, chaps. v and vi (*Dionysiaca*, II, 1322-1351 and 1377-1387).

astical Hierarchy he is described as "the head of the disciples" who took the lead in the election of Matthias to replace Judas among the twelve, but there is no attempt to give a special place to the bishop who is Peter's successor.[22] One would expect that the hierarchy should be given unity at its summit, but the *Ecclesiastical Hierarchy* appears to set forth an ecclesiology in which each bishop is supreme in his own church, under the divine High Priest, who is Christ. A similar conception was to be the basis of later episcopalist tendencies in the conciliar movement.

The hierarchical outlook as applied to the church by Dionysius does not, therefore, imply necessarily that the structure of authority in the church be rigorously centralized under one visible authority. It does connote a clear distinction between the laity and the clergy, and between priests and bishops—a distinction which is based on a supernatural power of orders which comes from Christ through his apostles and their successors. Only those who possess this power can perform the sacraments, and only those who possess it in its fullness can pass this power on to their successors.

In the eighth and ninth centuries the French kings possessed Greek manuscripts of Dionysius' works sent by the pope and by the Byzantine emperor. A faulty translation completed between 832 and 835 by Hilduin, the Abbot of St. Denis, the famous monastery near Paris supposed to have been founded by Dionysius (St. Denis in Latin is *Sanctus Dionysius*), was superseded by that of John Scotus Eriugena, who published translations and commentaries of the works of Dionysius around 858.[23] Between 862 and

---

[22] *Divine Names,* chap. iii (*Dionysiaca,* I, 136); *Ecclesiastical Hierarchy,* chap. v (*Dionysiaca,* II, 1363).

[23] Cf. P. G. Thery, *Hilduin, Traducteur de Denys,* vol. I of *Études Dionysiennes* (Paris, 1932).

866, Eriugena also wrote a long philosophical work, *On the Division of Nature,* which was a development of some of the ideas which he had found in Dionysius.

Eriugena transmitted and developed Dionysius' distinction between negative and affirmative theology, and pronounced himself in favor of the negative way as the most effective way to reach God.[24] The anticipation in Eriugena's negative theology of Cusanus' conception of the coincidence of opposites is demonstrable in passages in which Eriugena speaks of God as "the opposition of oppositions, the contrary of contraries," in whom are "all similitude and dissimilitude, all contraries and oppositions."[25] He is at once infinitely removed, and the cause of all created things.

In emphasizing the intimate relationship between God and the world, the negative theology was always in danger of pantheism, and Eriugena comes close to this doctrine in his writings. When the question is posed in the *Division of Nature,* "Can you deny that Creator and creature are one?" the reply is negative.[26] Because of this answer, Eriugena's works were condemned by the pope in 1225 as the inspiration for heretical doctrines in southern France. Despite the ban, however, Eriugena continued to be read, and Cusanus specifically recommends his works for study.[27]

To Dionysius and Eriugena as mediators of Neo-Pla-

24 Migne, *Patrologia Latina,* vol. CXXII (Paris, 1853), "De Divisione Naturae," col. 684D.
25 *Ibid.,* cols. 517B, 510D.
26 *Ibid.,* col. 528B.
27 Nicolai de Cusa, *Apologia Doctae Ignorantiae,* ed. Raymond Klibansky (Leipzig, 1932), vol. II of *Opera Omnia,* p. 21. Cusanus calls him "Joannes Scotigena" and later, in a bit of affectation of his knowledge of Greek, gives his Latin work a Greek title, "Peri Physeos" (p. 30). The library at Kues formerly had a copy of *De Divisione Naturae* with marginal notes by Cusanus. Cf. introduction by Raymond Klibansky to Nicolai de Cusa, *De Pace Fidei,* vol. VII of *Opera Omnia* (Hamburg, 1959), p. xxxv. The description of the hierarchies in the opening book of Cusanus' *Concordantia* uses a vocabulary similar to that of Eriugena.

tonism to Cusanus, one must add a fifth century contemporary, Boethius, one of the principal philosophical
sources of scholastic logic and of the Platonism of the
twelfth century school of Chartres. Like Dionysius, he was
placed in Paradise by Dante, who considered him a Christian martyr. His *Consolation of Philosophy,* written while
in prison, was one of the most frequently copied works of
the Middle Ages. The ninth meter of the third book of
the *Consolation,* a poem to the creator of heaven and earth,
is a short summary of Plato's *Timaeus,* based on the Neo-
Platonic view of the creation of the universe in accordance
with exemplars in the divine mind. The work is not
specifically Christian in inspiration, but Boethius wrote
several theological works which were a defense of the
doctrines of Catholicism.

Boethius' *Commentary on the Isagoge* and the *Consolation of Philosophy* are in the library at Kues, but the
influence of Boethius on Cusanus was principally an
indirect one through the theologians of the twelfth century
school of Chartres.[28] Some of Cusanus' most important
philosophic conceptions, including the explanation of the
relation of God to the world through the dualism *complicatio-explicatio,* were derived from the commentaries of
the school of Chartres upon Boethius' *De Trinitate.*

Besides the influence of their writings on Cusanus, the
theologians of the school of Chartres also directly affected
another important figure in the history of political thought,
John of Salisbury. Pupil of some of the leading teachers at
Chartres, and later bishop of that city, John wrote the
Policraticus, the most important work of political theory
between the writings of Augustine and Aquinas.

The *Policraticus* is the work of a cultured churchman

---

28 Marx, *Verzeichnis,* no. 190, 191, pp. 177-78.

and litterateur with a broad acquaintance with the classics as they were known in the twelfth century. Its relevance for the tradition which we are tracing lies in the extended use by John of Salisbury of the organic analogy to describe the relations which exist among the various parts of society. Under the guise of a lost work of Plutarch sent to the Emperor Trajan, the entire fifth book, as well as most of the sixth book of the work, is devoted to an analysis of the *res publica* in terms of a comparison with the various parts of the human organism. The prince is the head of the commonwealth, the priests are the soul, the senate is the heart, the judges and governors are the eyes, ears, and tongue, the soldiers are the hands, and those in charge of finance are the stomach and intestines. Lowest of all are the peasants, who support, sustain, and move the whole commonwealth. At a later point, John adds other groups to the peasants: wool workers, mechanics, and metal workers. The commonwealth has so many different groups among its feet, he says, that it could be described as a centipede.[29]

The organic analogy is not identical with the hierarchical approach and may even be used in support of a juristic corporation theory, as discussed in the next chapter. However, when the analogy serves to emphasize the interrelation and subordination of the members to the "body politic," and when the various functions in society are regarded as higher and lower in dignity, as is clearly the case in the *Policraticus,* the conclusions of the organic approach to the social order are similar to those drawn from hierarchical

29 *Joannis Saresberiensis Episcopi Carnotensis Policratici Libri VIII,* ed. C. C. J. Webb, 2 vols. (Oxford, 1919). The organic analogy is summarized in Book V, chap. ii, and the elaboration of the role of the *pedes* is developed in Book VI, chap. xx. Substantial portions of the Policraticus have been translated in John Dickinson, *The Statesman's Book of John of Salisbury* (Cambridge, Mass., 1927). On the extent to which medieval thought can properly be called organic, see Lewis, *Medieval Political Ideas,* II, 195-224.

modes of thought. The Neo-Platonic philosophers saw the social order as hierarchical because this was the structure of reality, emanating by degrees from God, while the organic theorist sees it as hierarchical because it is a counterpart or projection of the nature of man, but both theories come to the same conclusion about the proper structure of society. Plato's *Republic,* which John of Salisbury only knew from references in Chalcidius, was based on a similar analogy between the individual and the city-state, which was the individual "writ large."[30] Christian thought, beginning with St. Paul, also frequently used the analogy between the church and Christ's body to demonstrate the differentiation of function in the church and the interdependence of the faithful in their common subordination to Christ as its head.[31] Hence when Cusanus in the *Concordantia* develops extensive parallels between the individual and the Christian commonwealth, he is drawing not only on John of Salisbury but on earlier Christian and Platonic antecedents, for it was characteristic of the Platonic tradition to see man, society, and the universe as ordered in an analogical fashion, and the organic analogy was one example of this type of thinking.

Another twelfth century writer, Hugh of St. Victor, in his major work, *De Sacramentis,* argues in a similar analogical manner. The church is defined as the *universitas* of all Christians. It is composed of clergy and laity, who are respectively its soul and body. As the eyes, ears, feet,

[30] John refers to the *Republic* in Book VI, chap. xxv, summarizing a reference made in Chalcidius' *Commentary on the Timaeus* (Webb, *Policraticus,* II, 73).

[31] Cf. Rom. 12:4-6; I Cor. 12:27; Eph. 4:16. For references to the mystical body in the writings of Tertullian, Clement of Alexandria, Augustine, and Gregory the Great, see Henri de Lubac, *Corpus Mysticum* (Paris, 1949), pp. 14-16. The later history of the doctrine with special reference to its significance for political theory is treated in Ernst Kantorowicz, *The King's Two Bodies* (Princeton, 1957).

and so forth, are all parts of one body, but carry out different functions, so in the church there are various grades and orders derived from and related to the one source of all being.[32] The Augustinian abbey of St. Victor rivalled Chartres in its theological works, and Hugh also wrote commentaries on Dionysius' *Mystical Theology* and *Celestial Hierarchy*. The writings of the Victorines served to propagate the doctrines of Dionysius and to integrate his mystical system into the developing scholastic movement, so that the condemnation of Eriugena in the early thirteenth century did not affect Dionysius, his mentor. The negative way, the description of God as "divine darkness," the injunction to purge the mind of all other attachments until it attains a state of union with God, remained a powerful element of Catholic mysticism in such writers as Bonaventure and Albertus Magnus in the thirteenth, Eckhart in the fourteenth, and Gerson in the fifteenth century. Except for Gerson, whose *Mystical Theology* appears in the Strasbourg manuscript dating from Cusanus' youth, all are strongly represented in the library at Kues.[33]

Despite the intellectual revolution caused by the translation of Aristotle into Latin, the hierarchical cosmology continued to dominate scholastic thought in the thirteenth century. The Neo-Platonic cosmos, a universe of ascending degrees of being rising to God, was not in contradiction to Aristotelian ideas. God now was described as pure Act and

32 Hugh of St. Victor, *De Sacramentis,* in A. Migne, *Patrologia Latina,* vol. CLXXVI (Paris, 1879), col. 418. Cusanus refers to Hugh of St. Victor in *De concordantia Catholica* as "our German" (Book II, chap. xxix, p. 267) and "our most excellent Saxon" (Book III, chap. xxxix, p. 456). The library at Kues contains his commentaries on the *Mystical Theology* and the *Celestial Hierarchy* (Marx, *Verzeichnis,* no. 45, 4 and 6, pp. 40-41).

33 Marx, *Verzeichnis, passim.* The Strasbourg manuscript also contains Bonaventure's *Itinerarium Mentis in Deum,* dating from the period of Cusanus' studies in Cologne. The possible direct influence of Bonaventure on Cusanus' *Docta Ignorantia* is noted below in Chapter X, note 2.

the Unmoved Mover, but Albertus Magnus in his commentary on the Neo-Platonic work, *Liber de Causis,* still viewed creation as an emanation or flowing-out (*fluxus*) from the First Principle through a series of subordinate intelligences, each lesser cause working in dependence on the cause above it and acting on the one below. In addition to the *Liber de Causis,* which he mistakenly attributed to Aristotle, Albert also wrote commentaries on Dionysius' *Divine Names* and *Celestial Hierarchy.* Through his teacher at Cologne, Heimericus de Campo, Nicholas of Cusa became acquainted with Albert's works, and through Albert he acquired a knowledge of the substance of Dionysius' teachings, which he knew directly only at a later date.[34]

Albert's great pupil, St. Thomas Aquinas, also wrote a commentary on Dionysius, early in his life. Aquinas' *Summa Contra Gentiles,* the *Summa Theologica,* and his other works are filled with references, paraphrases, and quotations from Dionysius' works. From Dionysius and St. Augustine, as well as Proclus, Chalcidius, and Macrobius, St. Thomas drew the Platonic elements which figure prominently in the Thomistic synthesis.[35]

The influence of St. Thomas on Cusanus was very slight, but it should be noted that the hierarchies and parallelisms of the Neo-Platonic view of the universe survived in the Thomistic synthesis.[36] Question 108 of the First Part of

34 On the direct or indirect influences of Albert on Cusanus, see below, Chapter X, notes 4 and 9.

35 The Platonic elements in Aquinas have been discussed by Arthur Little (*The Platonic Heritage of Thomism,* Dublin, 1950) and more exhaustively by R. J. Henle (*St. Thomas and Plato,* The Hague, 1956), who examines and traces the origin of every citation of Plato in St. Thomas' writings. J. Durantel, *Saint Thomas et le Pseudo-Denis* (Paris, 1919), is a similar study of the influence of Dionysius on Aquinas.

36 Cusanus quoted Aquinas only rarely in his political works—once in a letter to the Bohemians (p. 856 of the Basel edition of his works), and once in his letter to the Carthusians—*Briefwechsel des Nikolaus von Kues,* part 1, ed. Josef Koch, in *SBH* 1942-43, no. 2 (Heidelberg, 1944), p. 42.

the *Summa Theologica* discusses the hierarchies and orders among the angels and the other orders modeled on them. Aquinas argues that each of the levels of the angelic hierarchy is subdivided into three orders, "the summit, the middle, and the base; and so in every hierarchy, Dionysius placed three orders" (art. 2). Similarly, in every city there is a threefold order. "Some are supreme, as the nobles, others are the last, as the common people, while others hold a place between these, as the middle class *(populus honorabilis)*." The structure of the church follows the same model. "The ecclesiastical hierarchy is derived from and represents the heavenly hierarchy. By Divine Law, inferior things are led to God by the superior" (art. 4). However, in the *Summa Contra Gentiles,* Aquinas does not adhere strictly to the analogy with the angelic choirs since he divides the church hierarchy into pope, bishops, priests, and faithful, and he also departs from Dionysius in arguing that papal monarchy is the best form of government because the church is one, as God is one.[37]

There is little of the negative theology in St. Thomas' approach to God. He recognizes that "it is impossible for

There is also a passing reference to *De Regimine Principum* in the *Concordantia* (Book III, chap. xii, p. 376). The great number of manuscripts of the writings of Albertus Magnus in the library at Kues (Marx, *Verzeichnis,* numbers 95, 96, 124, 130, 192-4, 204, 207, and 209, at pp. 96-98, 120, 126, 178-81, 189, 194, and 200-201) contrasts with the meager representation of the writings of Aquinas (Marx, *Verzeichnis,* numbers 68-74, at pp. 76-78), consisting of a complete text of the *Summa Theologica* bought after Cusanus' death, an excerpt from the same work bought by Nicholas after 1448, and the *Summa contra Gentiles,* purchased between 1429 and 1448. Marginal notes by Cusanus in a Belgian manuscript, indicating his preference for Albertus Magnus over Aquinas, are discussed by E. van de Vyver in "Annotations de Nicolas de Cues dans plusieurs manuscrits de la bibliothèque royale de Bruxelles," *Nicolò Cusano, Relazioni presentate al Convegno Interuniversitario di Bressanone* (Florence, 1962), pp. 47-62.

37 Aquinas, *Summa contra Gentiles,* Book IV, chap. lxxvi (trans. English Dominicans, London, 1929).

any created intellect to comprehend God" in the sense of knowing Him perfectly *(Summa Theologica,* I, q. 12, a. 7), but he insists that affirmative propositions can be formed about God *(S.T.,* I, q. 13, a. 12). The tendency of Thomistic thought is to exalt the powers of the human reason to attain to a knowledge of God, and when in the same article Aquinas quotes Dionysius' statement that negative statements about God are true in a way that affirmations cannot be, he treats this as an objection and is careful to answer it in such a way as to undermine the whole force of the statement.

After the revival of Aristotle, three writers can be singled out as belonging to the philosophical and theological tradition of Christian Neo-Platonism (which now included some Aristotelian elements as well) as it influenced Cusanus: Raymond Lull, Meister Eckhart, and Jean Gerson.

Raymond Lull (1235-1315) was a Spanish (Majorcan) member of the third order of St. Francis, who wrote a great number of works of theology, philosophy, poetry, mathematics, and morals. His ambitious plan to include in one method, the *ars generalis,* all branches of human knowledge was based on the belief that by a mathematical and geometrical system one could attain certainty. Any religious or moral truth, he felt, even the mystery of the Trinity, could be demonstrated mathematically.

There are more manuscripts of Raymond Lull at Kues than of any other author, a total of sixty-eight works, or one fourth of all the titles produced by this prolific author. Among Lull's works which influenced Cusanus were a proposal on squaring the circle, a problem about which both authors wrote; the *Liber De Gentili,* a disputation between a Jew, a Christian, and a Moslem, which formed a model for Cusanus' attempt in his work, *De Pace Fidei,* to reconcile all religions and nations to the essential truths of Christianity; and a proposal for a method of election of the Holy Roman Emperor which inspired a similar proposal by Cusanus in the *Concordantia*. From a note in one of the manuscripts (no. 83 at Kues), it is certain that Cusanus had copied some of Lull's spiritual writings as early as 1428, and he quotes Lull directly in a sermon in 1431. It also seems clear that he was introduced to Lull's writings by his teacher at Cologne, Heimericus de Campo.[38]

Indeed, it appears that many of the most important metaphysical conceptions of Cusanus, such as the approach to God through mathematics and geometric symbols, the triadic structure of the universe (this may also have come from Augustine), and the conception of Christ's incarnation as the link of the finite universe with the infinite, have their roots in the writings of Lull, or those of Heimericus de Campo which were influenced by the study of Lull.

The title of Cusanus' major political work, *De Concordantia Catholica*, may also have been suggested by his reading of Lull. The excerpts which Cusanus copied in 1428 include a short section from Lull's *De Concordantia et Contrarietate*, and the same manuscripts include other discussions of Lull's triad: *differentia, concordantia,* and *contrarietas*.[39] More persuasive evidence of Lull's influence is the discussion in the first chapter of the *Concordantia* of the concordance of one and three in the Holy Trinity, a favorite theme of Lull's and Cusanus' definition of *concordantia*, which is very similar to that of Raymond Lull

---

38 Colomer, *Nikolaus und Llull*, pp. 39-46, 47, 68-69. For the foregoing, see the introduction by Ludwig Mohler (trans.) to Nikolaus von Kues, *Über den Frieden im Glauben* (Leipzig, 1943), pp. 42ff; J. E. Hofmann, *Die Quellen der Cusanischen Mathematik I: Ramon Lulls Kreisquadratur*, *SBH* 1941-42, no. 4 (Heidelberg, 1942); and Martin Honecker, "Ramon Lulls Wahlvorschlag," *HJ*, 57:563-574 (1937).

39 Colomer, *Nikolaus und Llull*, prints the text of Cusanus' excerpts on pp. 125-186. See especially pp. 140 and 149.

in the *Ars Generalis,* several copies of which are in the library at Kues.[40]

In contrast to his early reading of Lull, Cusanus seems to have come much later to the work of the great German mystic, Meister Eckhart (1260-1327?). In Eckhart the negative theology of Christian Neo-Platonism becomes far more important than the affirmative way of reaching God. Developing the thinking of Dionysius and Eriugena, Eckhart describes God as "a being above being and a superessential negation."[41] The soul reaches God not through any ladder of creation but by direct intuition. "There is in the soul something which is above the soul, Divine, simple, a pure nothing; rather nameless than named, rather unknown than known."[42] This divine spark *(scintilla animae)* is the essence of the soul, the means of communication with the divine.

The writings of Eriugena, from whom Eckhart drew much of his thought, had already been condemned by the church for failing to distinguish between God and His creation. Eckhart himself was in difficulty with the ecclesiastical authorities at the end of his life, and a number of the more extravagant statements drawn from his writings were condemned after his death.

It is not certain that Cusanus read all of Eckhart's major work, *Opus Tripartitum,* but the prologue of the first part is in his library along with other biblical commentaries and sermons.[43] Nicholas mentions seeing Eckhart's defense

40 Cf. *DCC,* Book I, chap. 1 (pp. 33-34), and compare Cusanus' definition of *concordantia* as *id ratione cuius ecclesia catholica in uno et pluribus concordat* with that of Lull in *Ars Generalis* (Part III, Strasbourg, 1617, p. 222): *id ratione cuius bonitas etc. in una et pluribus concordant.*

41 J. Ancelet-Hustache, *Master Eckhart* (New York, 1957), p. 55, quoting a sermon, *Renovamini spiritu mentis vestrae.* Eckhart's works in German and Latin are being published by the *Deutsche Forschungsgemeinschaft* (Stuttgart-Berlin, 1936-   ).

42 Quoted in W. R. Inge, *Christian Mysticism* (New York, 1956), p. 157.

43 Marx, *Verzeichnis,* no. 21, pp. 15-17.

against the charges of heresy before 1439, and a manuscript of Eckhart's works in Kues, dated 1444 (no. 15), is heavily annotated. Eckhart seems to have influenced Cusanus in the composition of his major philosophical work, *De Docta Ignorantia*, in 1439, in 1449 he defended Eckhart from the charge of pantheism, and after 1453 his sermons show clear dependence on Eckhart's writings.[44]

Eckhart drew on the negative theology of Christian Neo-Platonism to undermine the Plotinian conception of a hierarchical universe proceeding by emanation from God to the lowest orders of creation. For Eckhart, there was no question of an overflowing or emanation; God was present everywhere and identified with everything. The soul could commune directly with Him, and was not required to rise through the various levels of creation. God was a super-essential Nothingness, who could not be described except by negations, yet He was present in the individual soul. Paradoxically, the negative theology by removing God from creation brought Him closer to it. A similar turning of Neo-Platonism against itself took place in Nicholas of Cusa's thought when he composed his *On Learned Ignorance*.

The theories of Jean Charlier de Gerson with regard to church organization will be treated in the next chapter. Here it should be noted that in the Strasbourg manuscript discussed earlier we have evidence of the early influence of Gerson's mystical thought upon Cusanus. His *Mystical Theology* takes the speculations of Dionysius as its starting

44 *Vier Predigten im Geiste Eckharts*, ed. Josef Koch (Cusanus-Texte), *SBH* 1936-37, no. 2 (Heidelberg, 1937), esp. pp. 36-40. Eckhart is defended in the *Apologia Doctae Ignorantiae*, pp. 24-26. On the question of earlier influences, see Herbert Wackerzapp, "Der Einfluss Meister Eckharts auf die ersten philosophischen Schriften des Nikolaus von Kues," *Beiträge zur Geschichte der Philosophie und Theologie des Mittelalters*, vol. XXXIX, no. 3 (Münster, 1962).

point and explains the *via negativa* as an approach to union with God, concluding (consideration 34), "the greatest philosophers at the end of their researches concluded that they only knew one thing, that they knew nothing."[45] In combining an active life in church politics with a concern with mystical problems, as well as in the profound influence of Dionysius upon his thought, Gerson comes closest to anticipating the theories of Nicholas of Cusa.

Augustine had sought a principle of order which could bring harmony and peace to the universe, to society, and to man. Platonism, as developed by Plotinus and transmitted by Pseudo-Dionysius, provided that principle for the Middle Ages in the theory of the hierarchical structure of all creation. Each part of the hierarchy received its existence and value from that above, and all beings were ordered in grades of value from God down to the lowest ranking element of inanimate existence. In this "great chain of being," each part of the hierarchy reflected the whole, "as a single face might be reflected in many mirrors placed in a series." The structure of the universe, the structure of society, and the structure of the human person were ordered in a parallel fashion, as participants in a harmonious and purposive universe created by a rational God.

The political thought of Cusanus draws on this tradition of hierarchy and parallelism. Politics is part of a larger order which is at once natural, moral, mathematical, cosmological, and theological. The world is a graduated whole, a value hierarchy perceptible to human intelligence, whose order imposes a moral obligation on those who perceive it. The parts of the universe correspond to one another in structure, so that the Triune God produces a triadic

45 Vansteenberghe, "Quelques Lectures," p. 280. On the influence of Dionysius on Gerson, see André Combes, *Jean Gerson, Commentateur Dionysien* (Paris, 1940).

universe. The members of this structure are characterized by an organic interdependence, each carrying out the function for which it is naturally fitted and all contributing to the good of the whole and being radically subordinated to the head. Each rank is assisted by those above it, and, as the triads of the hierarchical order are ascended, each level of being participates more fully in reality until the ultimate Reality is reached which absorptively contains all subordinate ranks and has created them. Augustine's objectives of peace and order are attained when everyone conforms to the hierarchy of being inbuilt in a value-laden universe and orients his life to God, who is the source and fulfillment of the entire structure and at the same time infinitely removed from it.

In the political order, this hierarchical world view means that authority comes from God and is transmitted in "descending" fashion through a hierarchical chain of authority.[46] Authority derives its validity and binding force not from any subjective act of consent or free acceptance, but from an objective moral order inherent in creation and intended by God.

It would appear that the logical institutional order suggested by such an outlook would be a single world-monarch, a Philosopher-King, characterized by superior holiness and wisdom, beneath whom are ranged lesser rulers in hierarchical fashion. However, in fact, in Western culture the functions of priest and king, which have been united in many other cultures, have been separated. Christ's words in the New Testament, "Render to Caesar the things that are Caesar's, and to God the things that are God's," im-

[46] The distinction between "descending" and "ascending" theories of the derivation of authority in medieval thought is made by Walter Ullmann, *Principles of Government and Politics in the Middle Ages* (London, 1961). Ullmann (see pp. 46-48) is one of the few writers on the Middle Ages to appreciate the significance of Dionysius for political theory.

plied a separation of the things of God and those of the political order. The development of the church as an organized body, independent of the empire during the periods of persecution, and later of isolation, meant that a fully articulated society could exist apart from, and to some extent in opposition to, the secular regime. St. Augustine's emphasis on the two cities, that of God and that of the world, while it did not identify them directly with the contemporary institutions of church and state, tended to confirm the already existing "diarchy,"[47] and the definitive statement by Pope Gelasius, "There are two powers by which this world is principally ruled," became the accepted theory, if not the practice, of most of the Middle Ages.

It is true that the Caesaropapism of Byzantium and the traditions of the Roman empire tended to ascribe certain sacerdotal functions to the emperor. It is also true that on the ecclesiastical side some of the papalists believed in the complete subordination of the temporal power to the papacy, and Boniface VIII cited Dionysius in support of the unitary thesis.[48] However, the hierarchical outlook is not incompatible with a belief in a dual structure of authority within the single *respublica Christiana*, as the analysis of the political theory of Nicholas of Cusa will demonstrate.[49] Within the two parallel hierarchies the same correspondences can be found, as well as a parallelism of structure between the one hierarchy and the other.

Along with the ideas of hierarchy and correspondence

---

47 The term is used by Luigi Sturzo, *Church and State* (London, 1939), p. 46.

48 "Nam secundum B. Dionysium, lex divinitatis est, infirma per media in suprema reduci." *Unam Sanctam,* in *Extravag. Commun.,* Lib. I, Tit. VIII, c. 1, in *Corpus Juris Canonici,* ed. Emil Friedberg, II (Leipzig, 1881), 1245.

49 See below, Chapter VIII.

which were to be prominent in *De Concordantia Catholica*, Cusanus also derived from the Neo-Platonic philosophers and Christian spiritual writers of the Middle Ages the method of the "negative theology," which was to be important both for his later philosophical development and for the recasting of his political thought after his transfer of allegiance to the papacy. He saw God not only as the source of authority and the creator of the universe which reflected His nature, but also as infinite, transcendent, and triune, capable of being known only through a higher form of cognition above sense experience and beyond rational categories of finite man. This view could also be combined with the hierarchical outlook, as it had been in the theology of Dionysius; but, as Eckhart's example indicated and Cusanus' subsequent development would demonstrate, it could be used to leap over and even to dissolve the elaborate chain which linked God to man in the traditional view.[50]

Hierarchical cosmology and negative theology—these were the doctrines which Nicholas of Cusa drew from the tradition of Christian Neo-Platonism. However, Cusanus was a canon lawyer as well as a philosopher and theologian, and therefore he was also influenced by a different set of theories deriving from Roman and canon law. To these we now turn in our examination of the sources of his political thought.

50 See below, Chapter X.

CHAPTER IV

. . .

THE LEGAL ANTECEDENTS

CANON LAW, CONCILIARISM, AND CONSENT

W H E R E earlier conceptions of both church and society had been traditional, integral, or sacral in character, the period from the eleventh century forward saw a new tendency to think of them not in mystical or sacramental terms, but as legal entities. With the development of the study of canon law, church writers attempted to define the relationships within the church in precise legal terms. This legalistic thought, influenced by the formulations of the Roman law, tended to work against the earlier organic, unitary, and hierarchic assumptions, and stimulated a more precise analysis of the relations of spiritual and temporal powers, of the pope and the council, the emperor and the empire, and the ruler and the ruled.

As the review of Nicholas of Cusa's life indicates, his university education, until he went to Cologne in 1425, was devoted to the study of canon law, culminating in the acquisition of the degree of Doctor of the Decrees (*Doctor Decretorum*) at the University of Padua in 1423. Moreover, it was as a canon lawyer that he first became involved in the Council of Basel and began the rise to prominence in church affairs which gave him the cardinal's hat and a reputation as one of the most prominent men in fifteenth century Europe. His writings on political theory are studded with references to the *Decretum* of Gratian and to the great canon lawyers, and nearly one fourth of his library is devoted to canon and civil law. Moreover, the conciliar controversy which was the occasion for most of his political writings was essentially a legal controversy concerning the respective rights of the pope and the council in the making and administering of church law. Although the study of Roman law had never completely died out and there were law schools in Rome, Pavia, and Ravenna earlier, the great impetus to the revived study of law came from the teaching of Irnerius at the University of Bologna early in the twelfth century.[1] The reintroduction of the study of Roman law was accompanied by the increasing systematization of canon law. Collections of excerpts from decrees of councils and popes had been made earlier, but Gratian's *Concordantia Discordantium Canonum* (c. 1140), gathering and harmonizing them under convenient headings, became the most influential work on church law ever assembled. The *Decretum* of Gratian, as it was usually called, was the text which the teachers of canon law used as the basis for their lectures, commentaries, and glosses. The best known of the Decretists, or commentators on the *Decretum*, were Huguccio (who wrote his *Summa* in 1190) and Joannes Teutonicus, whose comments became the *Glossa Ordinaria*, or standard gloss on the *Decretum*. The *Decretum* was never officially endorsed as church legislation during the Middle Ages, but it was studied in the universities and it exercised a great influence on canon law. Quotations from the *Decretum* were liberally used by both sides in any ecclesiastical controversy.[2]

1 Rashdall, *Universities*, I, 86-125.
2 For the history of canon law, see Feine, *Rechtsgeschichte*, vol. I, and J. B. Sägmüller, *Lehrbuch des katholischen Kirchenrechts* (Freiburg, 1909), pp. 149-164. The most important of the collections before the *Decretum* were the so-called *Pseudo-Isidorean Decretals*, a ninth century forgery which included the supposed Donation of Constantine (cf. E. H. Davenport, *The False Decretals*, Oxford, 1916), and the *Panormia* of Ivo of Chartres in the eleventh century.

In 1234 Pope Gregory IX in the bull *Rex Pacificus* sent to the universities of Paris and Bologna the definitive collection of papal legislation or *Decretals* with instructions that it was to be used along with the *Decretum* as the basis for the teaching of canon law. The Decretalists, or commentators on this collection, included Bernardus Parmensis, who provided the standard gloss, and Henricus de Segusio or Hostiensis, probably the greatest of the medieval canon lawyers. Gregory's collection was divided into five books, so that the next official collection, issued by Boniface VIII in 1298, was entitled the *Liber Sextus,* for which Joannes Andreae wrote the standard gloss. With the *Constitutions* of Pope Clement or *Clementinae,* formally issued in 1317, the official collections came to an end, although they were supplemented by the *Extravagantes* of Pope John XXII, and the *Extravagantes Communes* issued unofficially later in the century. All of these together formed what was later to be called the *Corpus Juris Canonici.*

The canon and civil lawyers who interpreted and taught the newly codified church law and the revived Roman law subjected to legal analysis the relationships within the church and empire which had formerly been left vague and undefined. A new source of political theory appeared—in the writings of lawyers about the structure and functioning of the church and civil society.

Until recently the theories of Roman and canon law have been reviewed as important influences in favor of the concentration of authority in the pope, the king, or the emperor. Yet both laws (the canon law borrowed many of its legal principles from Justinian's code and many lawyers held degrees in both laws) also contained passages which could be used as the basis of a theory of popular participation in government. The opening passages of Justinian's *Institutes,* while originally perhaps more rhetorical than legal in intention, implied theories of original natural freedom and (at least in the case of Rome) the popular origin of political authority, which influenced those who had learned to revere Roman law with a quasi-scriptural veneration. Wars, captivity, and slavery were considered contrary to nature, since "by the law of nature, all men from the beginning were born free."[3] The legislative authority of the Roman emperor was explained as the result of a single transfer of power from the people to the ruler (the *lex regia*) by which the people gave the emperor their right to make laws.[4] Implicit in these passages is a theory of original consent as the basis of governmental authority. If this consent is considered revocable, or if (as in Locke) it is only granted under certain conditions, then limits and control are set upon the political authority by the consenting party. However, the Roman lawyers did not discuss whether the Roman people could revoke the grant of power to the emperor. For them, the popular origin of authority was a constitutional myth without practical effect. The people were considered to have acted in corporate capacity only once, when they originally surrendered their power and authority to the ruler. It was only when the Roman law was revived in the Middle Ages that the *lex regia* was interpreted by Roman and canon lawyers as implying a residual authority in the people, which they could reassert if they desired.[5]

Additional examples could be cited to indicate how

[3] Justinian, *Institutes*, Book I, Title II, in Elliott and McDonald, *Western Political Heritage*, p. 284.

[4] Cf. C. H. McIlwain, *The Growth of Political Thought in the West* (New York, 1932), p. 128. "Quod principi placet habet legis vigorem, cum lege regia quae de imperio lata est, populus ei et in eum omne suum imperium et potestatem concessit" (*Institutes*, Book I, Title II).

[5] For discussion of this point, see A. J. Carlyle, *History*, II, 6off. Most of the controversy centered around whether the people could still make law through custom, once they had established the emperor as legislator.

certain expressions in an absolutist Roman law were forged by the medieval lawyers into instruments to impose restraints upon the rulers. Roman law had developed the conception of *universitas* or collectivity to enable cities and local groups to exercise juridical functions such as holding property or being represented in a legal action, and the Roman lawyers had discussed the rights of the *universitas* in relation to its head, rector, or representative *(procurator)*. The corporation theory of the medieval canon and civil lawyers developed this conception further, and distinguished between the rights of the corporation and those of its head or representative, delimiting the respective jurisdictions of each. Once the distinction between the *universitas* and its *rector* had been clearly made, the way was open for some degree of control of the head by the members, a conception which was foreign to earlier unitary and organic theories of social organization.[6]

A parallel development can be traced in the case of the Roman law maxim, "What touches all alike, must be approved by all" *(ut quod omnes similiter tangit, ab omnibus comprobetur)*. As originally stated in Justinian's Code (5, 59, 5, par. 3), it applied to the joint property rights of several guardians when some disposition of property was to be made. A similar maxim was used in the *Digest* with reference to water rights and the responsibilities of joint plaintiffs and defendants.[7] When Roman law was reintroduced into medieval Europe, this clause became the basis for requiring the head of a *universitas* to seek the consent of its members to matters which affected their interests in

---

6 See P. Gillet, *La Personnalité juridique en droit ecclesiastique* (Malines, 1927), esp. pp. 143-144.

7 *Digest* 39, 3, 8, cited in Gaines Post, "A Roman-canonical Precept, 'Quod Omnes Tangit' in Bracton," *Traditio*, 4:197-251 (1946). See also Yves M. J. Congar, "Quod Omnes Tangit ab Omnibus Tractari et Approbari Debet," *Revue historique de droit français et étranger*, 36:210-259 (1958).

the corporation. To this effect, it was quoted around 1200 by Bernardus Papiensis in his *Summa Decretalium* and repeatedly thereafter, finally being incorporated in the *Liber Sextus* edition of the canon law issued by Boniface VIII. The rule was regularly appealed to by the publicists and canonists of the fourteenth and fifteenth centuries. It stimulated detailed analysis of the rights of the members of a *universitas* to consent to actions of its *rector*, and it also was used as the basis for the consultation of the laity in the definition of matters of faith. In the secular world, it was cited by Frederick II in 1244, but its most famous use was by Edward I in the summons to the Model Parliament in England in 1295. From the thirteenth century it was repeatedly cited by the Italian city-states to assert the right of participation in legislation. Nearly all the conciliar writers used the clause to defend the participation of the council in church legislation, as the representative of the faithful.

Canon law also contained the elements of a theory giving the people a role in legislation. Discussion by the commentators on the *Decretum* was prompted by Gratian's statement in Distinction 4, chapter 3, that "laws are confirmed when they are approved by the custom of those using them."[8] Although this was in no way an assertion of popular sovereignty, the canonist discussion on this passage developed into a more general analysis of the relation of the *populus* to the law, and the conciliarists used it to claim a role for the laity in consenting to church law.

In the selection of church officers, by contrast, popular participation was diminished as a result of the legalization and institutionalization of electoral procedures. Through-

8 Cf. Luigi de Luca, "L'accettazione popolare della legge canonica nel pensiero di Graziano e dei suoi interpreti," *Studia Gratiana*, 3:195-276 (1955).

out the Middle Ages ecclesiastical officers were chosen, in theory at least, by election. A bishop was said to have been chosen by the clergy and people of the diocese, and until the eleventh century the pope was chosen in the same way. However, from the eleventh century there was a movement to restrict the election of bishops to ecclesiastics and, in particular, to the cathedral chapters. In the same century the election of the pope became the prerogative of the college of cardinals, the equivalent of the cathedral chapter in Rome. The *Decretum* itself, quoting the Second Lateran Council, restricted participation in episcopal elections to the cathedral chapter, and the Fourth Lateran Council in 1215 formally prohibited the participation of laymen in episcopal elections.[9]

The chapter could elect the bishop by unanimity (*per inspirationem*), but usually it acted by vote (*per scrutinium*). When the original myth of unanimous decision gave way to the requirement that elections were to be decided by the greater and sounder part, *major et sanior pars,* a problem was thereby posed as to the relative weighting of numbers and merit in the vote. Originally contained in the Benedictine constitution, the rule was applied to episcopal elections by the Fourth Lateran Council, which decreed that the bishop was to be elected either unanimously or by "the greater and sounder part" of the chapter.[10] Normally the judge as to whether the *sanior pars* had

---

9 C. 56, X *de electione,* I, 61 of the Decretals formally prohibits lay participation in church elections. The *Decretum* prohibition is located at D. 63 c. 1. Other sections dealing with the necessity of the election of church officers include C. 7 q. 1 c. 5 on election of bishops by the clergy and people; D. 61 c. 13 on the necessity of popular acceptance of bishops; and D. 66 c. 1, which is quoted from the Pseudo-Isidorean Decretals, and reflects the *quod omnes* clause when it says that archbishops should be appointed by those over whom they will preside.

10 C. 42, X *de electione,* I, 6, quoted in Feine, *Rechtsgeschichte,* p. 315, n. 9, and p. 317.

acted was the next highest officer in the church hierarchy. Yet, lacking any definite standard, the minority could argue that the *major pars* had not been *sanior,* and when this led to continued appeals from the majority decision it was decided (by Pope Gregory X) that a two-thirds vote would be sufficient to fulfill both requirements, a provision which was incorporated in the *Liber Sextus* at the end of the thirteenth century.[11] However, at the time of Nicholas of Cusa the minority at the Council of Basel could still claim that it was the *sanior pars.*

The elimination of the popular element from the election of the bishop was at least in part the result of the Christian belief in a special superior *character* in the clergy which required that the bishop be selected only by those in orders. However, the canons of the cathedral chapter were presumed to be acting on behalf of the other clergy of the diocese, and, in so far as the earlier notions of popular participation in the election of ecclesiastical dignitaries still survived, for the people as well. This rudimentary notion of presumptive representation received much more sophisticated treatment in the constitutions of the Dominican and Franciscan orders, which were governed by assemblies composed of delegates from the various houses of the order, who were endowed with limited and specific powers of representation.[12]

11 C. 9 *Liber Sextus* I, 6, quoted (inaccurately) in L. Moulin, "Sanior et maior pars," *Revue historique de droit français et étranger,* 36:514 (1958). The two-thirds rule had applied to papal elections since 1179.

12 See Sir Ernest Barker, *The Dominican Order and Convocation* (London, 1913); G. R. Galbraith, *The Constitution of the Dominican Order* (Manchester, 1925); and Maude V. Clarke, *Medieval Representation and Consent* (London, 1936), pp. 264ff. Barker's thesis on the influence of Dominican theories of representation on English parliamentary practice has been criticized by D. Pasquet, *An Essay on the Origin of the House of Commons,* trans. R. G. D. Laffan (Cambridge, 1925), pp. 20ff, and William A. Hinnebusch, *The Early English Friars Preachers* (Rome, 1951), pp. 489ff.

When this process had been completed, the bishop or abbot or other church officer began to face a corporate group which had elected him, the diocesan council or the cathedral or monastic chapter. With the aid of the texts of the Roman law, and in particular those referring to the rights of the *universitas,* these bodies began to claim for themselves certain rights in relation to the *rector* of the corporation, particularly a right of continuing consent on certain subjects which "touched all." The chapters demanded the right to be consulted *(consilium)* on certain administrative acts and dispensations, and to give or withhold their consent *(consensus)* on actions which substantially affected the property of the diocese or monastery. Once a corporate personality had been recognized, the bishop or abbot could not act arbitrarily since he was a *procurator* and not a *dominus* of the property of the diocese, that is, he was head of a corporate entity with limited control over church property. He could not dispose of it as he pleased, since the members of the chapter possessed the legal rights of a *universitas* against its *procurator.*[13]

By the end of the thirteenth century, the problems arising in the relations of bishop and cathedral chapter and in the self-governing ruling bodies of the monastic orders had stimulated the development of a body of law which discussed such political problems as consent, majority rule, and representation—and a corporate body in a special relationship to the ecclesiastical superior had been recognized which could check, at least occasionally, the power of rulers in the church.

Thus far, however, this thinking had not affected the papacy. Potentially, the corporation theory could also be applied to the pope in his relation to subordinate corporate

---

13 *Glossa Ordinaria* to *Decretum,* C. 23 q. 7 c. 3, quoted in Gillet, *Personnalité,* p. 93, n. 2. Cf. also Tierney, *Foundations,* pp. 106-131.

groups and to the church as a whole, defined as the *universitas fidelium,* a term already used by Hugh of St. Victor in the twelfth century. There were a number of chinks in the papal armor which could be used to assert some control by the church as a corporate entity over its head. The openings were provided by the text of the *Decretum,* the *Decretals,* and the glosses upon those documents which were familiar to every student of canon law.

In the first place, an instrument existed for the corporate representation of the whole church: namely, the general council. The early church after its emergence from the catacombs had defined church doctrine by means of councils, often called and presided over by the emperors. The four great councils of Nicea (325), Constantinople (381), Ephesus (431), and Chalcedon (451), were to be recognized "like the four evangelists," said a letter by Pope Gregory the Great, reproduced in the *Decretum.* The reformed papacy after the Cluniac revival in the eleventh century held councils called by the pope and presided over by his legate at Lyons, the Lateran (four times), and Vienne. Thus there was a tradition that important decisions on faith and reform were made by the general council.

The council could be considered as representing the church from two possible points of view. In the first place, there was the old tradition preserved in Gratian's *Decretum* that the church officers were chosen by the *clerus et populus,* thus admitting a popular element in the election of church officers. More important, nearly all the canonists defined the church as the congregation of the faithful, *congregatio fidelium,* making no distinction between the clergy and the laity. The term did not have any corporate connotation as it was first used, but the development of corporation doctrine, and its combination with the belief that the council represented the church, made it possible to consider the council as a corporate organ representing the entire body of the faithful, both the clergy and the laity, and capable of enforcing limitations on the pope as *rector* of the corporation.[14]

Distinct from this, but also anticipated in Gratian, is another view of the council, not as a representative of all the members of the church but as an assemblage of the bishops—what Hirsch calls "episcopalism," as distinct from true "conciliarism."[15] According to this view, which was based on the scriptural grant of the power of binding and loosing to all the apostles and not just to Peter—all the bishops including the pope received equal power from Christ, and from the point of view of divine grant of authority the pope was only a *primus inter pares,* whose purpose was to delimit jurisdictions and maintain church unity *(propter tollendum schisma).*[16] As the discussion of the episcopalism of Dionysius the Areopagite has shown, this theory of church government antedated the systematizing of canon law. However, it can be combined with the corporation theory so that the council is considered as a corporate body of all the bishops, which can act to control its administrative head, the pope.

14 Tierney, *Foundations,* pp. 202-203, lists the instances of the use of *congregatio fidelium* as a definition of the church. Among those who used it were Thomas Aquinas *(Summa Theologica,* I, q. 111, a. 2) and Hugh of St. Victor. Even the later papalist, Turrecremata, mentions it as a definition of the material cause of the church. See Gillet, *Personnalité,* pp. 52ff, and Gewirth, *Marsilius of Padua,* I, 260, n. 2.

15 K. Hirsch, *Ausbildung,* p. 3. The relevant texts of the *Decretum* include D. 21 c. 2 and C. 24 q. 1 c. 18.

16 Gratian, of course, was not an episcopalist. He distinguished between the sacramental power in which all bishops are equal and the power of jurisdiction in which the pope was supreme. However, when later canon lawyers discussed the bishop's power of jurisdiction, they derived it from election by the chapter rather than consecration by his ecclesiastical superior—paving the way for the conciliar assertion of the derivation of papal power from election and consent. For discussion, cf. Tierney, *Foundations,* pp. 31ff and 126ff.

Besides the council, the church constitution at this time included another organ which might be used to limit the pope, the college of cardinals. The cardinals, since they elected the pope, were particularly well situated to control him, at least by attaching conditions and extracting promises at the time of election. Hostiensis, writing on the *Decretals* in the middle of the thirteenth century, described the cardinals as parts of a single *collegium* related to the pope in the same way as the cathedral chapter and the bishop are related to each other. However, Hostiensis did not provide for any way in which the cardinals could act against the pope, although, like Aegidius Romanus fifty years later, he did admit that the authority of the church reverted to the college of cardinals if the papacy was vacant.[17]

Although there were two possible institutions to apply limitations to papal power, the general council and the college of cardinals, canon law as codified in the *Decretum* stated that the pope was above human judgment, and this seemed to rule out the possibility that either the council or college of cardinals could take any action. However, there were references in canon law to limitations on papal power which could be used to justify action against the papacy. The *Glossa Ordinaria* mentioned the council as the appropriate body to decide on a disputed papal election (gloss on D. 79), precisely the case which later gave rise to the Conciliar Movement. Moreover, some canonists of the twelfth and thirteenth centuries, when they discussed the papal right of dispensation, asserted that it could not be used against the general state *(generalis status)* of the

17 See Tierney, *Foundations*, pp. 68-84, for the Decretist theory of the role of the cardinals, and pp. 149-153 for Hostiensis' views. The latter are also discussed by him in "A Conciliar Theory of the Thirteenth Century," *Catholic Historical Review*, 36:415-440 (1951).

church. Probably most significant of all was the qualification which the *Decretum* added to its statement of papal immunity from judgment: "[Papa] a nemine est judicandus, nisi deprehendatur a fide devius" (D. 40 c. 6). The *Decretum* referred to the cases of Anastasius, Marcellinus, Liberius, and Honorius, as heretical popes, and the canonist commentaries progressively widened the notion of heresy until papal liability to judgment was extended to include any notorious crime because it "scandalizes the church."[18]

Following the *Decretum,* everyone granted a theoretical limit on papal authority, at least in the case of heresy, but there was little reason at this time to assert a role for the council or college of cardinals in enforcing it. Huguccio in the twelfth century seems to have granted the college of cardinals at least a declaratory role in the judgment of public heresy or notorious crime. Probably most influential was the statement of Joannes Teutonicus in the *Glossa Ordinaria* that in matters of faith *synodus major est papa,* and the English canonist, Alanus, seems clearly to have held to the doctrine that the council is superior to the pope in matters of faith.[19]

However, when the dispute between Boniface VIII and Philip the Fair gave rise to a mass of controversial literature, the arguments of the earlier canonists became potent

18   See J. Lebreton and J. Zeiller, *History of the Primitive Church,* vol. II (New York, 1949), for details on the four heretical popes. The Vatican Council in 1870 did not consider these examples as arguing against the doctrine of papal infallibility, since none of these popes was speaking *ex cathedra,* as defined by the council. The general argument of the paragraph is drawn from Tierney, *Foundations,* pp. 47-67. See also his later article, "Pope and Council: Some New Decretist Texts," *Medieval Studies,* 19:197-218 (1957).

19   The comment of Huguccio on D. 63 of the *Decretum, Nam et cardinales possunt deponere papam pro heresi,* is quoted in Walter Ullmann, *Medieval Papalism* (London, 1949), p. 157. Tierney, *Foundations,* pp. 66-67, gives the references to Teutonicus and Alanus.

political weapons. Both sides accepted the possibility of papal heresy, but the propapal writers held that a heretical pope would cease *ipso facto* to be pope and would be self-judged. This not very satisfactory interpretation of the plain meaning of Gratian was necessary since the previous extensions of the content of the charge of heresy had opened the door to a general superiority of the council to the pope, once the possibility of its passing judgment on him was admitted. The papalists also tried to undercut the conciliar argument by insisting that since, according to the *Decretum,* the pope must call the council, it could not be convoked to judge him unless he voluntarily submitted.[20]

On the antipapal side, in 1297 the Colonna cardinals appealed to the universal council to determine whether Boniface VIII was a legitimate pope, and in 1303 the followers of Philip the Fair accused Boniface of a variety of heresies and called for a council to pass judgment upon him.[21] These cases were based on contemporary canonist doctrine, but they still did not go beyond the two specified cases of disputed elections and papal heresy. The first fully articulated theory of conciliar supremacy appears in *De Potestate Regia et Papali,* written in 1302 by a French Dominican, John of Paris.

While John was not a canon lawyer, it was largely out of canonistic doctrines that he developed his theory. His contribution to conciliar theory was to combine the canonistic notion of residual authority in the college of cardinals or the council with the accepted belief that the pope could be called to account for heresy, or, in some writers, for

[20] Citations from Augustinus Triumphus and Alvarus Pelagius are given in Lewis, *Medieval Ideas,* II, 616. Cf. also N. Iung, *Alvaro Pelayo* (Paris, 1931), pp. 178-181.

[21] John T. McNeill, "The Emergence of Conciliarism," in *Medieval and Historiographical Essays,* ed. James L. Cate and Eugene N. Anderson (Chicago, 1938), pp. 284 and 289-290.

scandalous sin or injury to the general state of the church, and to set it in the general framework of the legal categories of corporate action, consent, and representation which had previously been developed with reference to diocesan government and the religious orders. Just as the head of any ecclesiastical corporation, such as the bishop and his diocese or the abbot and his monastery, does not, he said, have *dominium* or the right to do as he pleases (*ad libitum detrahere seu distrahere*) with the property of the *universitas*, but only the right to use the goods of the community for the purposes required by his office (*secundum exigentiam sui status*), so the pope is only the *dispensator* of the property of the church and can only use it for the requirements of the church (*ad necessitatem vel utilitatem ecclesiae communis*).[22] At a later point, he rephrased the same notion in philosophic terms when he applied the Aristotelian concept of final causality to papal election, noting that *ex parte causae finalis,* the pope had been elected for the common good of the church and he could be removed if he did not fulfill this purpose.

If the pope violates the trust placed in him to work for the interests of the church (*ad aedificationem et non in destructionem*), he can be deposed in the same manner as a bishop or abbot who is guilty of neglect of his office. Here John cites the gloss on Gratian's Distinction 40, chapter 6, which provided for papal deposition in cases of scandalous sin as well as heresy.

For John of Paris, the pope is simply an administrator whose function is "to dispose of ministers and determine

<hr/>

22 John of Paris, *De Potestate Regia et Papali,* chap. vi, in Simon Schard, *De Jurisdictione, Autoritate, et Praeeminentia Imperiale, ac Potestate Ecclesiastica* (Basel, 1566), pp. 155-157. For commentaries see Tierney, *Foundations,* pp. 157-178; R. Scholz, *Die Publizistik zur Zeit Philipps des Schönen* (Stuttgart, 1903), pp. 275-336; J. Riviere, *Le Problème de l'église et de l'état au temps de Philippe le Bel* (Louvain, 1926), pp. 281-300.

jurisdiction" in order to "prevent confusion . . . and to preserve the unity of the church." It is true that at one point he states that the papacy is necessary "so that there can be one superior in spiritual matters through whose decision controversies are settled," which would seem to imply some power to define articles of faith, but he seems to believe that even this power is administrative in character.[23]

In addition to establishing certain limitations on the papal office, which, if exceeded, could lead to deposition, John of Paris also was obliged to combat the hierarchical papalist view that the papal office was above human judgment, since the pope received his power directly from God and all other offices in the church were granted through him. Once again, the *Decretum* is the source of John's argument that, as far as their power or orders is concerned, all bishops including the pope are equal, receiving their power directly from God and not by way of any papal mediation. John cites Distinction 21 of the *Decretum*, which quotes Cyprian's declaration that all the apostles have received their power of binding and loosing *pari consortio* directly from Christ. Since the bishops are successors to the apostles, John argues, they too have received equal power directly from Him. There are only two sacramental grades in the church hierarchy, priests and bishops, and all other ranks—archbishops, primates, patriarchs, and popes —are only jurisdictional divisions, pertaining to certain geographical areas but not imparting any special and indelible *character* to those who hold them. Once again, John applies to the papacy the theories which the thirteenth century canonists had developed concerning the derivation of the powers of the bishop when he asserts that papal

23 John of Paris, *De Potestate*, chap. xiii, p. 177, chap. x, p. 165, chap. iii, p. 150. "Necesse est unum esse superiorem in spiritualibus per cuius sententiam controversiae terminentur."

powers of jurisdiction are derived from election and consent. The pope's sacramental power is similar to that of all other bishops and cannot be taken away from him, but his "jurisdictional power can be increased or diminished or destroyed and taken away."[24]

After establishing the existence of certain limitations on the pope and showing that the papacy did not receive any direct divine grant of orders as pope, John then moves to a consideration of the possible instruments that can be used to enforce limitations on papal power. Again utilizing his legal background, he says that the pope's power, like that of kings and bishops, is derived both from God and from the people. "While the papacy in itself is from God, nevertheless it is in this person or that, by human cooperation, that is, by consent of elector and elected." From this original consent, John then derives a consequent power of deposition: "as there is a type of marriage between prelate and church by consent of elector and elected, so it can be dissolved in the event of disagreement."[25]

The church which exercises this control on the pope is variously defined in John's theory. He notes that the term *ecclesia* can be taken to stand for all priests, the *congregatio clericorum,* or more generally for all the faithful, the *communitas fidelium.*[26] There is no attempt in the treatise to connect the laic and the sacerdotal conceptions of the nature of the church, and when John goes on to discuss the relationship of the college of cardinals to the pope, he derives its power at one point from the fact that it acts

24 John of Paris, *De Potestate,* chap. xxiv, p. 222.
25 John of Paris, *De Potestate,* chap. xxiv, p. 219. (See also chap. xi, p. 168.) "Igitur licet papatus sit a solo Deo in se, tamen in hac persona vel illa, est per cooperationem humanam, scilicet per consensum electi et eligentium. . . Sicut sit conjugium quoddam inter praelatum et ecclesiam per consensum eligentium et electi, ita per dissensum dissolvitur."
26 John of Paris, *De Potestate,* chap. xvii, p. 190.

"in place of the whole clergy," and at another point "in place of the whole clergy and whole people."[27]

The college of cardinals is in John's view competent to enforce restrictions on the power of the pope, since it acts for the whole church in electing the pope, and can so act also in deposing him. John does recognize that some canonists would restrict this right to the general council, but he seems to think of the council's role in restraining the pope as restricted to the definition of heresy, followed by admonition, and, if necessary, deposition of an heretical pope.[28] He also recommends an advisory council, elected from the church provinces, although it is not clear whether this is intended as a reformed college of cardinals or a new representative body.[29]

The secular ruler also has a function, in John's theory, in bringing the pope to account. He can act on the cardinals or the people to bring about the deposition of the pope and can use force to see that no one obeys the pope if he persists in public sin. However, the first actions should be taken by the cardinals, who should warn the pope of his error; the ruler can act only after his aid has been sought by the cardinals.[30]

Just as the secular ruler can act only indirectly upon the people or cardinals to reform the church, so in John's theory the pope can act against an heretical ruler only by urging the people to depose their ruler on grounds of heresy. The pope has no direct authority to depose secular rulers, in John's theory; the deposition takes place only

27 John of Paris, *De Potestate,* chap. xiv, p. 183, chap. xxiv, p. 216.
28 John of Paris, *De Potestate,* chap. vi, p. 157, chap. xxiv, p. 221, chap. xxiii, p. 215.
29 John of Paris, *De Potestate,* chap. xx, p. 202.
30 John of Paris, *De Potestate,* chap. xiv, pp. 181-183.

because the people want a Catholic ruler.[31] Similarly, the secular ruler's action to reform the church is taken, not because he is the ruler, but because he is a Christian, with special obligations as a Christian to assist and protect the church.

According to the theory of John of Paris, the pope's power is a limited one, derived from God through the clergy and people, normally as represented in the college of cardinals. If he abuses this power, he can be restrained by the cardinals or, in cases involving definitions of articles of faith, by the general council. The secular ruler, in his capacity as a member of the church, should assist in the reform of the church when necessary.

The theory of John of Paris contains nearly all the elements which go to make up the later conciliar theory, but, although the council's jurisdiction has been extended, there does not seem to have been any attempt to make it an integral part of the regular governing mechanism of the church. The councils remain an emergency device to restrain the pope when the college of cardinals is not functioning or not effective in restraining him.

The first attempt to assert a continuing part for the councils in the government of the church came in 1311 with the publication of Gulielmus Durandus' *De Modo Celebrandi Concilium Generale.* Durandus was Bishop of Mende in France, and nephew of a famous canon lawyer

31 Because John of Paris denied that the pope had any power over the civil ruler except through the people, interest in his work has been revived in recent years by John Courtney Murray, S.J., in his writings on Church-State theory. See, for example, "Contemporary Orientations of Catholic Thought on Church and State in the Light of History," *Theological Studies,* 10:177-234 (1949), and "The Problem of the Religion of the State," *American Ecclesiastical Review,* 124:327-352 (1951).

of the same name. He wrote his treatise at the request of Pope Clement V in preparation for the Council of Vienne. While it cannot be demonstrated that Nicholas of Cusa read John of Paris (although many of his arguments bear a marked similarity to those of John), an annotated copy of Durandus' work is still preserved in the cardinal's library at Kues.[32]

The overall theses which Durandus attempts to establish in his treatise are (1) the subordination of the pope to church law as made by the general council, and (2) the independence of the bishops from papal intervention. To do this he uses canon law and church history, quoting from the *Decretum* and from the records of early popes and church councils to exalt the position of the bishops and councils and to diminish that of the pope.

Durandus urges the pope to maintain the laws which have been decreed by the councils acting on the inspiration of the Holy Spirit (*instinctu Spiritus Sancti*). Dispensations should only be given, he says, in cases of clear necessity, and "no law against previous councils may be made or granted without the assembly of a general council, since according to the rule of both laws, what touches all should be approved by all." This procedure is to be used in all cases concerning the general state of the church, and whenever new legislation is to be adopted.[33]

---

32 Marx, *Verzeichnis*, no. 168, p. 155. I have used the 1531 Paris edition which is divided into books and rubrics as well as folios. All three references will be given in the footnotes. Durandus is discussed in Haller, *Papstum*, pp. 60-66, and Scholz, *Publizistik*, pp. 208-23.

33 *Instinctu Spiritus Sancti* is used three times in Book I, rubrics 2 and 3, folios 4 and 5. It recurs in Book III, r. 31, f. 61. The *quod omnes* reference appears in Book I, r. 4, f. 7. "Et quod contra dicta concilia et jura nihil possent de novo statuere vel concedere nisi generali consilio convocato, cum illud quod omnes tangit, secundum juris utriusque regulam, ab omnibus debeat communiter approbari." The "both laws" referred to are Roman and canon law. Cf. discussion earlier in this chapter.

Having established the revolutionary position that all general church legislation must be made by the general council, Durandus then provides for regular meetings of that body every ten years. He also recommends that legislation for the church provinces be made by provincial councils to meet twice yearly.[34]

These councils are to be meetings of bishops, and to justify their authority Durandus attempts to establish the equality of all bishops with regard to the power to define church doctrine. In rapid succession, he cites what were to become the stock arguments of the antipapal writers: Distinction 21 of the *Decretum* on the equal power of all the bishops (already used by John of Paris), a quotation from St. Cyprian on the unity of the episcopate, and Augustine's interpretation of the text of Matthew 16:19 as Christ's recommendation of Peter's confession of faith, and not the establishment of any special primacy.[35] When Durandus goes on to outline a system of appeals to neighboring bishops in the event of controversies (rather than to the pope), it appears that he is developing a complete episcopalist system.[36]

However, he does not and cannot go this far in a treatise written for the pope at the beginning of the fourteenth century. While he attempts to establish the legislative subordination of the pope to the council, his thought remains thoroughly hierarchical in other respects. A hierarchy like that in heaven has been instituted, he says, to bring about agreement among men *(propter concordiam humani ge-*

34 The recommendation on provincial councils appears in Book II, r. 1, f. 15, and again in r. 11, f. 18, while the decennial general councils are described in Book III, r. 27, f. 59.

35 Durandus, Book I, r. 4, f. 9. Similar points asserting the equality of all bishops as successors of the apostles are also made earlier in the same rubric in folio 8, and later in Book II, r. 7, f. 16, and Book III, r. 27, f. 58.

36 Book II, r. 11, f. 18.

neris) and to prevent division in the church of God (*ne schisma fieret in ecclesia Dei*). "All creatures can not be governed and live in the same rank; the example of the heavenly choirs teaches us that as there are angels and archangels they are not equals but differ in authority and rank the one from the other . . . While this world exists, men will be over men, demons over demons, angels over angels."[37]

Although Durandus does not cite Dionysius the Aeropagite, the dependence is clear, but, unlike Dionysius, Durandus accepts a special position for the pope as head of the ecclesiastical hierarchy. When he describes the Roman church at the start of the third book, he calls it "the head of all the others, the lord and judge of all churches, whose rector, when he is orthodox, can not be judged by anyone."[38] He does not seem to regard the council primarily as an instrument to be used against the pope, except in the single generally accepted case of heresy. His purpose is to emphasize the independent derivation of the powers of the bishops and their right to consult with the pope on the making of laws for the church. He is ready to accept a special position for the papacy as *primus inter pares*, but not the utilization of that position to destroy the traditional rights of the bishops.

What is new about his theory is his proposal that the council, comprising both the pope and the bishops, become

37 Book I, r. 4, f. 8. "Quia vero quaeque creatura in una eademque qualitate gubernari vel vivere non potest, celestium militiarum exemplar nos instruit, quia dum sunt angeli, sunt archangeli et liquet quia non sunt equales sed in potestate et ordine differunt alter ab altero. . . Dum mundus iste durabit homines praesunt hominibus, demons demonibus, angeli angelis." This passage seems to have been influenced by Aegidius Romanus, *De Ecclesiastica Potestate*, ed. Richard Scholz (Weimar, 1929), Book II, chap. xiii, pp. 120-127.

38 Book III, r. 1, f. 52. "Romana ecclesia caput est omnium aliarum . . . domina et judex est aliarum cujus rector catholicus non judicatur a quoquam."

the regular legislative organ for the making of general laws of the church. This, together with his linking of the council with consent and the inspiration of the Holy Spirit, is the element in his thought which seems to have most influenced Nicholas of Cusa in the development of his theories.

Like the corporate theories of John of Paris, the elements of Durandus' theory are drawn almost exclusively from the canon law, and in particular from Gratian's *Decretum*, but he lays more emphasis on the historical and scriptural examples in Gratian than on the purely legal conception of the relation of the corporation to its head. Moreover, for Durandus the council's role in church government is justified not because it represents all the people or even all the priests in the church, but because it is composed of equal bishops with special powers of orders, derived by succession from the apostles.

Thirteen years after Durandus wrote his work, the most important book of political theory in the fourteenth century was published—the *Defensor Pacis* by Marsilius of Padua. Marsilius was trained in medicine, but he quotes canon law when it can be used to support his position. In contrast to the other conciliarist writers, there is an almost total absence of references to the *Decretum* of Gratian, and little use of later collections, partly because Marsilius was attempting to deny their validity. When he refers to church law and practice, he ordinarily uses the earlier collection of the so-called Pseudo-Isidorean Decretals, especially when he attempts to substantiate his theory of the structure of the early church.

Marsilius does not attempt to go into the subtleties of the corporation theory in order to develop his conceptions of government. However, he uses the term *universitas* to describe the whole body of citizens or of the faithful in his theory, and there are traces of canon law discussions of voting procedures in his definition of his all-powerful *legislator* as the *universitas civium* or its *valentior pars* . . . *considerata quantitate personarum et qualitate.* Although Marsilius appeals to Aristotle in support of his doctrines, there is at least as much medieval legal theory as Aristotelianism in the *Defensor Pacis.* While his naturalistic view of the state in the first book is a mark of Aristotelian influence, the central position of consent to law has no counterpart in Aristotle but is anticipated in some of the discussions of the Roman and canon lawyers.[39]

To prove that all lawmaking should be done with the participation and consent of the entire body of citizenry Marsilius uses three principal arguments. He declares (1) that individual prejudice will be less likely to operate when all participate in lawmaking; (2) that the citizenry is more likely to obey an obligation which it has placed upon itself; and (3) "what affects the benefit or harm of all ought to be known and heard by all"[40]—an echo without specific reference of the Roman law *quod omnes* clause, discussed earlier.

With these principal arguments, Marsilius then goes on to claim for the legislator the right to control the government (*pars principans*) and to make all coercive law. When in the second part of the book these principles are applied to church organization, a similar conclusion follows—the

---

[39] The *Defensor Pacis* is available in Latin editions by C. W. Previte-Orton (Cambridge, 1928) and Richard Scholz (2 vols., Hanover, 1932-1933). These Latin editions have been compared with the recent English translation by Alan Gewirth, *Marsilius of Padua*, vol. II (New York, 1956). The term *valentior pars* appears in Dictio I, chap. xii, v. 3, and is discussed in Gewirth, *Marsilius*, I, 184. On the relation of Marsilius' consent theory to Aristotle, see Paul E. Sigmund, "The Influence of Marsilius of Padua on XVth Century Conciliarism," *Journal of the History of Ideas*, 23:392-402 (1962).

[40] Marsilius, D. I., chap. xii, v. 7. "Quae igitur omnium tangere possunt commodum et incommodum, ab omnibus sciri debent et audiri."

universitas fidelium, that is, all believing Christians, must make church law. But first, Marsilius must refute the hierarchical view that the church officers, receiving their power from God, are exempt from regulation by the *universitas fidelium.*

In doing this, he does not deny altogether the supernatural powers of the priesthood. He is prepared to grant that by the laying on of hands God imprints on the soul a sacerdotal *character* which gives the priest the power to consecrate the Eucharist and bind and loose from sin (the power of orders). However, beyond this he is not willing to go, and every priest can ordain other priests. All other ranks in the church for Marsilius are administrative in nature (*tribuit solum ordinationis iconomicae in domo Dei seu templo potestatem quandam*). The church hierarchy is only necessary *ad scandalum et scisma evitandum.* This applies even to the papacy. The monarchical constitution of the church is simply a matter of convenience.[41]

Marsilius attempts to prove that according to the original constitution of the church all the apostles were equal in power, citing the statement about the grant of power *pari consortio* with Peter. However, he draws it not from the *Decretum,* as the other conciliarists did, but from the Pseudo-Isidorean Decretals. The primacy of Peter he attributes to reverence by the other apostles for his age and virtue. Rome received its present position of prominence because its first bishop was St. Peter or St. Paul or both, because of its illustrious saints and martyrs, and because, since it was the center of coercive rulership at the time, the other churches consented to Rome "as it were by election" (*quasi electione*).[42]

41 D. II, chap. xv, v. 7 (the entire chapter is important for Marsilius' conception of the church hierarchy), and chap. xviii, v. 8.
42 D. II, chap. xxii, v. 16.

Like all other church offices, the papacy is subject to the control of the *universitas fidelium* which acts through the general council composed of all Christians "or their weightier part *(valentior pars)* or those to whom authority has been granted by the *universitas* of faithful Christians." This council is composed of both priests and laity, and is convened by the "faithful [i.e., Christian] legislator without a superior," although the pope or a majority of the churches may request a council.[43] It alone represents the apostles and the early church, and it is under the direction of the Holy Spirit guiding its deliberations to keep it from error in matters of faith. Decisions on matters of doctrine are taken by unanimous vote of the priests, but, in the event of disagreement among the priests, the *valentior pars* of the faithful present will prevail.[44]

The council has the power to define all doubtful passages of Scripture which are to be rules of faith, and it also assigns all church offices, and attaches coercive penalties where church law has secular consequences. The council alone can excommunicate, canonize saints, regulate fasting, approve religious orders, and elect and depose the pope. The council in Marsilius' theory is an all-powerful legislature with complete control of church affairs, giving orders to the church hierarchy on penalty of immediate deposition. Original consent has been transformed into continuing participation in lawmaking, and a radically new conception of the church has been derived from Marsilius' argument about the necessity of popular participation.

The three writers discussed so far, John of Paris, Durandus, and Marsilius, drew on canon law in different

---

43 Marsilius describes the composition and voting procedure in the council in D. II, chap. xx. The role of the *legislator fidelis* in convening the council and its general powers are treated in chap. xxi.

44 D. II, chap. xix, v. 2, and chap. xxvii, v. 21.

ways. John used it to derive the theory of papal power from consent, and to develop a theory of the pope as the head of an ecclesiastical corporation consisting of the whole church. For Durandus, it provided historical examples of an episcopalist organization of the church under a periodic legislative council. Marsilius drew his original inspiration from the Aristotelian conception of a self-sufficient community sharing in participation in government, but he used examples drawn from earlier canon law collections and developed a theory of legislation which undermined the claims of the papalists to hierarchical rulership. The council representing all Christians was supreme. Little was left of the special role of the priesthood and virtually nothing at all of the episcopacy and the papacy.

William of Occam was a contemporary of Marsilius, who also received the protection of Lewis the Bavarian and wrote in Lewis' defense in his struggles with the papacy. Conciliarism was an important element in the emperor's antipapal program, and the Appeal of Sachsenhausen, issued in 1324, specifically called for a general council against the pope. Occam wrote a large number of political works in defense of conciliarism, three of which, the massive *Dialogus,* the *Octo Quaestiones de Potestate Papae,* and the *Breviloquium de Potestate Papae,* are especially important sources for his political and sociological theory.[45]

[45] The *Dialogus* is to be found in M. Goldast, *Monarchiae Sancti Romani Imperii* (Frankfurt, 1668), II, 396-957. It also is printed as volume I of the Lyons edition of Occam's *Opera,* recently reissued in a facsimile edition (London, 1962). The *Octo Quaestiones* is also in Goldast, but a better edition of this work was produced by J. G. Sikes, *Guillelmi de Ockham Opera Politica,* I (Manchester, 1950), 1-223. A second edition has recently been published (Manchester, 1962). The *Breviloquium* has been edited by L. Baudry (Paris, 1937) and is perhaps the best summary of Occam's personal position, which is sometimes difficult to discern in the balancing of pro's and con's in the *Dialogus.* Occam's political theory is discussed

None of Occam's works are to be found in Cusanus' library, and his direct influence on Nicholas' theories, both in the areas of political philosophy and metaphysics, seems to have been negligible. He is discussed here because of his influence on the other conciliar theorists, especially Henry of Langenstein and Pierre d'Ailly, and because of the effect of his thought on the intellectual life of the fourteenth and fifteenth centuries, particularly in the universities.[46]

It is difficult to place Occam in the canon law tradition which has been thus far considered as the principal formative influence in the development of conciliarism. It is true that he views the council as superior to the pope and that there is a characteristic conciliarist tendency in his thought to increase the role of the laity and of the secular ruler in the conduct of church affairs. However, he breaks with the corporatist element of canon law theory in his doctrine of infallibility. Where the usual practice had been to locate the infallibility, which all granted was inherent in the church, either in the council as representative of the *congregatio fidelium* or in the pope or *sedes Romana* as endowed directly by divine grant with the gift of preserving the church from error, William in the *Dialogus* is willing at least to cite the arguments (already explored by some canonists before him) for the position that the pope and

---

from the point of view of the *Breviloquium* in A. Hamman, *La Doctrine de l'église et de l'état chez Occam* (Paris, 1942), and in Richard Scholz, *Wilhelm von Ockham als politischer Denker* (Leipzig, 1944). See also Max A. Shepard, "William of Occam and the Higher Law," *American Political Science Review*, 26:1005-1023 (1932), and 27:24-38 (1933); John B. Morrall, "Ockham's Political Philosophy," *Franciscan Studies*, 9:335-369 (1949); E. F. Jacob, "Ockham as a Political Thinker," *Essays*, pp. 85-105; Francis Oakley, "Medieval Theories of Natural Law, William of Ockham and the Significance of the Voluntarist Tradition," *Natural Law Forum*, 6:65-83 (1961) (criticizing Shepard).

46 "No later reformer was uninfluenced by his ideas," which are "nearer to the *De Concordantia Catholica* of Cusanus than to the radicalism of the *Defensor Pacis*" (Jacob, *Essays*, p. 87).

all but one of the bishops, or all the clergy, or all men, or even all those who had attained the use of reason, could fall into error, leaving the infallibility of the church to one woman (and here he cites the case of the Blessed Virgin after Christ's death), or even only as a potentiality (*habitus*) in baptized infants. The infallibility of the general council is specifically rejected, although with some qualifying introductory phrases. The council is only a part of the church, and although it represents the church it does not necessarily enjoy the church's prerogative of infallibility. Since the true faith may be preserved in one member of the church, only when everyone without exception accepts a council's decrees can one be certain that they are infallible. (Just how little children who may be the only bearers of the true faith are to show whether they do or do not consent to a conciliar decree is difficult to conceive.)[47]

Aside from his peculiar position on infallibility, Occam tends to share the outlook of most of the conciliar thinkers. While, unlike Marsilius, he grants that the papal primacy is of divine origin, "it is up to men to designate a particular person as pope, and to decide who will elect him and who will correct him if he needs correction."[48]

The clearest example of legal influence comes when he

[47] Occam discusses the possibility that the true faith may inhere in only one woman, in the *Dialogus*, Part I, Book V, chap. xxv, p. 429; in little children, Book V, chap. xxxv, p. 506. The possibility that all men or all the clergy may be in error is discussed in chap. xxxii, p. 503. The council must have the unanimous consent of the faithful to its decrees, in Part I, Book II, chap. xxv, p. 429. In the *Breviloquium*, Book VI, chap. iv, p. 165, he says that the pope and all the bishops "except perhaps one" could be heretics. Occam prefaced his remarks in the *Dialogus* with statements by the Disciple and Master, indicating that they did not share the positions that they were about to set forth, but were only presenting some of the reasons for and against them.

[48] *Dialogus*, Part III, Tract I, Book II, chap. xx, p. 806. "Nam ad homines pertinet ordinare quis assumi debeat ad ipsum et qui debent eligere et qui debent assumptum corrigere si correctione indigeat."

states that all the Romans have a right to elect the pope because "no one should be set over a *universitas* of mortal men unless by their election and consent,"[49] and cites the *quod omnes* maxim to prove his point. The pope like all bishops should be chosen by election and consent in his diocese or by those to whom the diocese has entrusted the task of election—in this case, the college of cardinals.

Once he is elected, the pope's power is limited. He can do whatever is necessary for the preservation of the faith and even dispense with canon law where this is necessary —the power of *epieikeia* or equity, described in Book V, chapter 10, of Aristotle's *Nicomachaean Ethics*.[50]

However, the *necessitas* doctrine in Occam's hands is a two-edged sword, and it is used more often to reduce the power of the papacy than to extend it. In this context Occam develops his concept of *libertas Christiana*, in accordance with which the pope cannot impose heavier burdens on the faithful than are absolutely necessary to salvation. Otherwise, the New Law would be more burdensome than the Old Law, and Christians would be slaves not freemen. A sort of "Occam's razor" is thus applied to papal claims to eliminate anything which cannot be related directly to the end of salvation.[51]

---

49 *Ibid.*, Part II, Tract II, Book III, chap. vi, p. 934. "Universitati mortalium nullus praefici debet, nisi per electionem et consensum eorum."

50 For Occam's treatment of *epieikeia*, see the *Dialogus*, Part III, Tract I, Book I, chap. xvi, p. 786, and Part III, Tract I, Book II, chap. xxi, p. 809. Discussions of *necessitas* appear in the *Breviloquium*, Book II, chap. xvii, pp. 52-54, and in *Octo Quaestiones*, Q. I, chap. xvii. For references to *epieikeia* by Thomas Aquinas and other medieval writers, see Gerd Heinz-Mohr, *Unitas Christiana* (Trier, 1958), p. 363, n. 42-44. On the canonist origin of Occam's *necessitas* doctrine and many other aspects of his theory, see Brian Tierney, "Ockham, Conciliar Theory, and the Canonists," *Journal of the History of Ideas*, 15:40-70 (1954). See also C. C. Bayley, "Pivotal Concepts in the Political Philosophy of William of Ockham," *Journal of the History of Ideas*, 10:199-218 (1949).

51 The doctrine of Christian liberty appears very often in Occam's

The most important limit on papal power for Occam is the possibility that the pope may fall into heresy. The pope is only one part of the infallible church, he says, and there are numerous examples of heretical popes in the past, including that of John XXII, the antagonist of Lewis the Bavarian (William's protector). If the pope is a heretic, he must be subject to judgment, just as any bishop would be. This judgment is to be carried out by a general council which is defined as *"diversae personae gerentes auctoritatem et vicem universarum partium (qui) ad tractandum de communi bono rite conveniunt."*[52]

Occam also discusses the canon law provisions that the councils are to be called only by the pope. Normally (*regulariter*), he says, the pope calls the council, but if the pope is a heretic, then the college of cardinals or the "congregation of the Romans" must take action to depose the pope and to choose a successor. If they do not act, then all the faithful can act on the basis of the evident state of necessity to elect representatives to a general council. The council should include both laity and clergy, and elections should be carried out by cathedral chapters and the secular parliaments. "Since the church is not the Pope or the congregation of the priests but the congregation of the faithful," representatives of the laity, and even women, should participate in the council, for "what touches all ought to be discussed and approved by all." If necessary for the welfare of the church, the initiative in convocation of a council can be taken by any Catholic, but a special responsibility devolves on the emperor since canon law

---

works. See, for example, *Dialogus,* Part III, Book I, chap. v, p. 776, and *Breviloquium,* Book II, chap. iii, p. 19.

[52] *Dialogus,* Part I, Book VI, chap. lxxxv, p. 603. The examples of popes Marcellinus, Symmachus, Liberius, and Anastasius are referred to in the *Dialogus,* Part I, Book V, chap. ii, p. 469.

declares that "where ecclesiastical power is lacking, resource is always to be had to the secular arm."[53]

Occam never attempts to resolve the difficulty created by his earlier denial of infallibility to the general council, which seems to imply that there is no special reason that a council should be better situated to decide on matters of faith than the pope. While he had prefaced his remarks on infallibility with a denial that the speaker actually believed that a council would be in heresy, Occam's arguments on the inadequacy of the representation of the whole church by the council are never answered. The denial of infallibility to the council would be in keeping with the individualism of his metaphysical theories.[54]

The doctrine of a limited power derived from the people and enforceable by deposition is also applied to the secular ruler by Occam. The Roman emperor received his right to rule from the people voluntarily submitting to his rule. The present emperors are elected by all the people "since the electors . . . are to elect the emperor as representatives of all the princes and peoples of Germany, Italy, India, Africa, Greece and other provinces which are legally subject to the kingdom and empire of the Romans, acting, as it were, in place of all."[55]

---

[53] *Octo Quaestiones,* Q. 1, chap. xvii, p. 60, ". . . ubicumque deficit ecclesiastica potestas, semper recurritur ad brachium seculare." See also *Dialogus,* Part I, Book VI, chap. lxxxv, pp. 603ff, and *Breviloquium,* Book V, chap. iv, pp. 135-136, for an individualist solution to the problem of papal heresy. (Any Christian by simple cognition can know when the pope decrees something which is heretical, although in cases where the expert theologians would be expected to know better, it is their duty to judge him.)

[54] For a complete discussion of Occam's ideas on representation, see G. de Lagarde, "L'Idée de représentation dans les oeuvres de Guillaume d'Ockham," *Bulletin of the International Committee of Historical Sciences,* 9:425-451 (1937). On the relation of Occam's metaphysics to his political theory, see articles by Max A. Shepard and Francis Oakley cited above in note 45.

[55] *Octo Quaestiones,* Q. VIII, chap. i, p. 192. "Et principes electores

If the emperor commits a notorious civil crime, he can be deposed by the electors, or by the Roman people who originally delegated to them the right of election. If his crime is religious, that is, heresy, the pope can declare him a heretic, as in the theory of John of Paris, but the actual sentence and execution must be carried out by the electors or the Roman senate and people.[56]

William of Occam developed several new concepts which were later used by the conciliarists. His doctrine of Christian liberty and his emphasis on election and consent in both church and state placed limits on pope and emperor which could be enforced if the *congregatio fidelium* or *populus* conceived of itself as capable of acting upon the ruler. Occam's doctrine of *necessitas,* an emergency power in the ruler, and inherent in the community, to depart from the letter of the law because of urgent necessity, was also to prove very useful to the later conciliarists when they attempted to justify departures from the canon law, particularly the crucial canon law requirement that councils be convoked by the pope alone.

Although John of Paris, Durandus, Marsilius, and Occam had already developed the principal elements of the conciliar theory, it was only after the divisions in the college of cardinals in 1378 had produced two popes, one at Rome and the other at Avignon, that the doctrine of a general superiority of the councils received widespread acceptance. The best-known early works upholding the conciliar solution to the schism were the *Epistola Con-*

. . . habent eligere imperatorem repraesentantes in hoc omnes principes et populum Germaniae, Italiae, Indiae, Africae, Graeciae, et aliarum provinciarum, quae de jure regno et imperio Romanorum sunt subjectae, quasi vice omnium eligendo." See also *Breviloquium,* Book IV, chap. iii, p. 107.

56 *Breviloquium,* Book VI, chap. ii, pp. 156-160.

cordiae of Conrad of Gelnhausen, and the *Epistola Concilii Pacis* of Henry of Langenstein.[57] Gelnhausen's *Epistola Concordiae* written in 1379 shows strong influences of William of Occam's *Dialogus* upon its argumentation, and even upon its wording, but no credit is given to that work. In support of the superiority of the council, Gelnhausen cites the example of the early church and repeats a variation of the *quod omnes* maxim, "What touches all should be discussed by all or by their representative."[58] He adds the usual citations from the *Decretum* concerning papal heresy (the gloss on Distinction 40 concerning papal deposition, and the references to the heresies of Popes Anastasius and Liberius in Distinctions 19 and 17). Then he defines the council in a fashion very similar to that of Occam. "Concilium generale est multarum vel plurium personarum rite convocatarum, repraesentatium vel gerentium vicem diversorum statuum ordinum et sexuum et personarum totius Christianitatis venire aut mittere valentium et potentium, ad tractandum de bono communi universalis ecclesiae in unum locum communem et idoneum conventio seu congregatio."[59]

A comparison with Occam's definition shows that Gelnhausen has added the requirement that the council be "properly convened" (*rite convocatarum*) and has referred to the different ranks and *sexes* represented. (The require-

57 Gelnhausen's work may be found in E. Martène and U. Durand, *Thesaurus Novus Anecdotorum*, vol. II (Paris, 1717), cols. 1200-1225. Langenstein is reproduced in *Joannis Gersonii Opera Omnia*, ed. L. E. du Pin, vol. II (Antwerp, 1706), cols. 809-840. The two authors are discussed in most histories of conciliarism, but no special monographs have been published on their theories, although August Kneer, *Die Entstehung der konziliaren Theorie* (Rome, 1893), is concerned primarily with their works.
58 Gelnhausen, *Epistola Concordiae*, col. 1207. ". . . ut quod omnes tangit ab omnibus vel vice omnium tractetur."
59 Gelnhausen, *Epistola Concordiae*, cols. 1217-1218.

ment that women be represented is another mark of Occam's influence.)

For Gelnhausen, as for Occam, the church is composed of all the faithful and not just the priests, and, like Occam, he grants the possibility that the Christian faith could be preserved in one man or woman, as in the case of the Virgin Mary after Christ's death. Once again, there is no attempt to harmonize the belief in the infallibility of the general council as representative of the whole church with the acceptance of the possibility that all the members of the church except one could be in error.

The principal contribution of Gelnhausen to the development of conciliar theory was his use of the Aristotelian doctrine of *epieikeia* to solve the problem of convocation of the general council. Canon law said that the pope was to call the council—but what was to be done if the pope was a heretic or if there was doubt as to who was pope? Gelnhausen answered that *epieikeia* or equity enjoined that an exception be made to the general rule, in keeping with what would certainly have been the intention of the legislator. However, as in Occam, the use of *epieikeia* was limited to cases of necessity or a rational and urgent cause. The pope normally called the council into session and only in special cases could the council be called by someone else. A council which came into session without the pope's consent, in cases other than those of necessity, was not a *concilium* but a *conciliabulum*.[60]

Henry of Langenstein uses similar arguments in his *Epistola Concilii Pacis*, written in 1380. He also uses *epieikeia* to justify calling a council without the pope's consent in cases of necessity, and he cites the *quod omnes* maxim and the same references to canon law discussions of

60 Gelnhausen, *Epistola Concordiae*, col. 1208. This distinction is also used by Nicholas of Cusa in both his conciliar and post-conciliar writings.

papal heresy. One major difference between the two is that Langenstein not only recommends the use of the general council for ending the schism and in cases of papal heresy, but goes on to say that "even if this schism had not taken place, a general council has been necessary for a long time, in order to reform the church in many other disorders and deviations enumerated below."[61] Instead of an emergency procedure justified by papal heresy, the death of all the cardinals, or a schism, Langenstein asserts the general superiority of the council to the pope for purposes of reform.

A second important difference in Langenstein in his discussion of the method of election of the pope and the theory of representation which it implied. Noting that methods of election of the pope have varied, he discusses the problem that would arise if the cardinals were all to die or were unwilling to choose a new pope. Election then reverts, he says, *primarie* to the *universitas* of bishops and, if the bishops cannot act, to the *universitas* of priests, *consentiente populo*.

That the bishops or priests have a representative role in relation to the people is demonstrated by Langenstein's use of the phrase *congregatio fidelium* as one possible definition of the general council. However, he adds that since the participation of all the faithful is no longer possible, a more useful (*expedientior*) method is the election by the bishops of representatives from every country to form the general council.[62] Langenstein's book concludes with a

---

61 Langenstein, *Epistola Concilii*, col. 825. "Esto quod hoc schisma non evenisset, adhuc ad reformationem Universalis Ecclesiae in plurimis aliis exorbitationibus et deviationibus inferius enumerandis opus fuisset diu Concilio generali."

62 Langenstein, *Epistola Concilii*, cols. 826-828. Hirsch, *Ausbildung*, p. 71, discusses whether Langenstein was a conciliarist or an episcopalist in his theories. In view of the above, he seems to be both.

plea for twice-yearly provincial councils (also part of the program of Durandus).

Although there are works by Henry of Langenstein in Cusanus' library, the *Epistola Concilii Pacis* is not contained there. Yet many of the ideas in *De Concordantia Catholica* are similar to those of Langenstein. Both books quote extensively from the records of the Council of Toledo. Both call for frequent provincial councils for purposes of reform, and in both the bishops hold a special position, although ultimately the church is conceived as a gathering of all the faithful.

The influence of William of Occam is also very clear in the writings of Pierre d'Ailly, the French cardinal whose public career almost exactly parallels the Western Schism. His doctoral disputations at the University of Paris in 1380 repeated the ideas of Occam's *Dialogus* in unmistakable fashion.[63] The church is defined as the *congregatio fidelium,* and is infallible, although the pope can err. All members of the clergy can lose the faith, it can remain in one lay person, and even the general council is capable of error.

D'Ailly's most important work of conciliar theory, and the one which influenced Nicholas of Cusa directly, was *De Potestate Ecclesiastica,* written much later (1417) after the deposition of Pope John, the Pisan pope, at the Council of Constance.[64]

63 See du Pin, *Gersonii Opera,* vol. I, cols. 662-693, and discussion in Hirsch, *Ausbildung,* pp. 82-84, and Jacob, *Essays,* p. 93; Jacob mentions an abbreviation of Occam's *Dialogus* made by d'Ailly at the Council of Constance.

64 Printed as *De Ecclesiae, Concilii Generalis, Romani Pontificis, et Cardinalium Autoritate,* in du Pin, *Gersonii Opera,* vol. II, cols. 925-960. The work is listed as no. 165 in the library at Cues, and it is possible

Occam's influence is still evident in this work, but it is also clear that d'Ailly had read and utilized John of Paris. Like the two earlier theorists, d'Ailly goes back to the early church to learn of its original constitution. He distinguishes the various powers of the original apostles, and comes to the conclusion that all the apostles were equal except as to "the power of disposition of ministers to determine their jurisdiction." Peter, however, is greater than the others in administration (*major administratione*) and he and his successors have special rights over the whole church and its property, as *universalis dispensator* but not as *dominus*. Christ intended that there be a hierarchy in the church with the pope at its head, but the offices in this hierarchy are to be filled by election.

So far, d'Ailly has not said anything strikingly different from the other conciliarists. It is when he comes to the question of the election of the pope that he makes his distinctive contribution to conciliar theory. On the one hand, he says, the pope is head of all the faithful, and should be elected by the whole church since "those over whom he is to rule have the right of electing the one ruling over them, for no one ought to be given to them against their will."[65] However, he is also bishop of a particular church, the *ecclesia Romana,* and the Romans have some claim to

that part of the manuscript was transcribed by Nicholas himself. See Marx, *Verzeichnis,* p. 151, where the date of composition is erroneously put at 1442 instead of 1417. (He may have read MCCCCXVII as MCCCCXLII.) Works on d'Ailly include Paul Tschackert, *Peter von Ailli* (Gotha, 1877); Louis Salembier, *Le cardinal Pierre d'Ailly* (Cambrai, 1932); and John P. McGowan, *Pierre d'Ailly and the Council of Constance* (Washington, 1936). See also discussion in Morrall, *Gerson and the Great Schism,* pp. 112-119, and Francis Oakley, "The 'Propositiones Utiles' of Pierre d'Ailly," *Church History,* 29:398-403 (1960).

65 D'Ailly, *De Autoritate,* cols. 930-931. ". . . illi quibus est praeficiendus, habent jus eligendi praeficiendum eis. Unde nullus debet eis dari ipsis invitis." D'Ailly does not specifically mention Distinction 61 of the *Decretum* of which this is a paraphrase, but it must have been familiar to his audience.

choose their bishop. He resolves the difficulty by saying that, since it is hard to assemble all the faithful in the whole church, or even their representatives, the right of electing the pope has been transferred to the Roman people, who in turn have transferred their right to the Roman clergy and ultimately to the college of cardinals. However, when the council can be convened, the right of election reverts to it as representative of the whole church. The distinction made here between the pope as head of the whole church and of the *ecclesia Romana* was to be used by Nicholas of Cusa to solve the problem posed by the existence of contradictory canon law texts on the relationship of the pope and council.

D'Ailly was himself a cardinal, and it could be expected that he would devote some time to defending the position of the cardinals, particularly since they had come in for some criticism at Constance as a comparatively recent (eleventh century!) innovation not really necessary to the constitution of the church. D'Ailly attempts to prove that the apostles before they left Jerusalem assisted Peter in the same way that the cardinals assist the pope in ecclesiastical administration in Rome. In addition to this rather weak parallel, d'Ailly also attempts to justify the cardinals' position from political theory, quoting Aristotle on the virtues of a mixture of monarchy, aristocracy, and democracy as the best form of government. "Thus it is clear that the best government for the church would be one in which several people are elected from each province under one pope and these would be the cardinals who together with and subject to the pope would rule the church and limit the plenitude of power."[66] The idea of the cardinals as

---

66 D'Ailly, *De Autoritate*, col. 946. ". . . sic etiam manifeste videtur, quod esset optimum regimen ecclesiae, si sub uno Papa eligerentur plures de omni et ab omni provincia et tales deberent esse cardinales, qui cum

representatives of the church provinces was borrowed from d'Ailly by Nicholas of Cusa, although he did not express a similar enthusiasm for mixed government. The democratic element in d'Ailly's mixed constitution is the general council representing the church as a whole. Here, as in the case of many of the conciliarists, it is not clear whether d'Ailly conceives of the council as a gathering of representatives of all the faithful (as in Marsilius) or only of the pope and bishops (as in Durandus). D'Ailly is aware of this confusion when he says, "Some hold that the power to judge, legislate, and define belongs to the bishops and upper prelates . . . others, all who want to be present at this council to bring about the unity of the church."[67]

The tension between the equalitarian and the hierarchical outlook toward the council is also brought out in the next paragraph where d'Ailly notes that "to many" it seems better that, in the voting system used at the council, attention should be paid not only to numbers but also to status (*dignitatem*). It is possible to resolve the conflict between the two views, as d'Ailly does earlier in the case of the election of the Pope, by saying that the bishops in some sense represent the faithful (thus reducing episcopalism to conciliarism), but d'Ailly does not specifically do this.

D'Ailly embraces an intermediate position between the papalist assertion of the plenitude of power and the coun-

---

Papa et sub eo ecclesiam regerent et suam plenitudinem potestatis temperarent." D'Ailly also cites without credit the Old Testament example used by Thomas Aquinas in his *Summa Theologica*. The idea of the cardinals as representatives of the provinces of the church is also developed in d'Ailly's *De Reformatione* in du Pin, *Gersonii Opera*, vol. II, cols. 903-916.

67 D'Ailly, *De Autoritate*, col. 941. "Nam quibusdam videtur quod auctoritas judicandi, statuendi, et diffiniendi, pertinet ad episcopos seu majores praelatos. . . Alii vero dicunt . . . omnes qui ad effectum unius ecclesiae vellent huic Concilio interesse."

cil's demand that it be acknowledged as superior to the pope. In best scholastic fashion, he distinguishes between the plenitude of power residing ultimately (*finaliter*) in the whole church, representatively in the general council, and in a lesser way (*non aequaliter*) in the *ecclesia Romana* as representative of the whole church. The pope, he says, also shares the plenitude of power, but as a servant of the whole church (*ministerialiter*).

D'Ailly does not devote much attention to the problem of the convocation of the general council. "Necessity," he says, would demand that the cardinals call the council without the pope, and if they refuse, "the rest of Christendom" can convoke it. This council can overrule the pope, who is capable of error. Here the usual canon law citations are given, notably the gloss of Distinction 40 of the *Decretum*, proving that the pope can be judged by the church if he is guilty of heresy or of a notorious crime.[68]

D'Ailly was basically a conservative churchman faced with the problem of establishing the theoretical basis for the restoration of unity to a divided church. To justify the deposition of Pope John, he must maintain a type of superiority of the council to the pope, but at the same time he does not wish to alter the constitution of the church (particularly the rights of the cardinals) nor to limit the papacy excessively. Thus he has the pope presiding over the council ("unless a manifest cause, based on divine law, prevents this") and he views the *ecclesia Romana* as the *pars principalis* of the general council with a special superior quality above all other churches. Of all the conciliarists, he is probably closest both in general tone and in specific argumentation to Nicholas of Cusa.

The distinction which d'Ailly made between the *ecclesia*

68 D'Ailly, *De Autoritate*, cols. 935, 960, 953, 956.

Romana and the universal church is also important in the theory of Dietrich of Niem, an administrator at the papal court at the time of the Councils of Pisa and Constance.[69] The *ecclesia Romana* for Dietrich is not the pope and cardinals, as it is usually defined, but includes pope, cardinals, bishops, prelates, and ecclesiastics—thus, it seems, the whole clergy. The clergy can and has erred, and is subordinate to the whole church. It acts as the executive agent of the whole church without any greater power than the universal church has given it. The pope is head of the church, but "an angel can not be pope and therefore the pope as pope is a man and as a man is pope, and as pope can sin and as man can err." He can be deposed for "evil living, public scandal, heresy, and any mortal sin which scandalizes the universal church."[70]

Dietrich discusses the problem of the convocation of the council in the face of papal opposition. He agrees that "where the pope is not suspect or where there is no question of the unity of the head of the church," it is up to the pope to call the council, but if there is any question of trying the pope, it is up to the "bishops, cardinals, patriarchs, secular princes, communities, and the rest of the faithful" to do so. At another point, he says that primary responsibility for the convocation of a council rests with

69 Recent work on Dietrich is summarized in Jacob, *Essays,* chap. ii, pp. 24-43. The definitive biography is Hermann Heimpel, *Dietrich von Niem* (Münster, 1932). His major work of conciliar theory, *De Modis Uniendi et Reformandi Ecclesiam in Concilio Universali,* has been edited by Heimpel (Leipzig, 1933) with the 1410 and 1415 versions in parallel columns. Roger Bauer, in "Sacrum imperium et imperium germanicum chez Nicholas de Cues," *Archives d'Histoire,* 21:224 (1954) has noted the influence of Dietrich on Nicholas of Cusa.

70 Niem, *De Modis* (Heimpel ed.), pp. 8, 21, and 42. "Quia ergo angelus papa esse non potest: ergo papa ut papa est homo et ut homo sic est papa et ut papa potest peccare et ut homo potest errare."

the emperor as *advocatus ecclesiae,* and secondarily with the kings.[71]

In his desire to save the church from evils of which he is acutely aware, Dietrich is the most extreme advocate of a kind of *raison d'état* for the church. "Not only secular princes but farmers and laborers and the lowest of the faithful should be ready to expose themselves to death if necessary for the sake of the salvation of the whole flock . . . Deceit, fraud, arms, violence, power, promises, gifts, money, and even prison and death may be used to procure somehow the most holy union of the church and the agreement of the faithful."[72]

In arguing for the supremacy of the council over the pope, Dietrich occasionally quotes from the *Decretum,* but he usually manifests an extreme hostility to canon law and such canonical practices as reservations, provisions, and exemptions. His primary inspiration seems to have been Occam, but he quotes frequently from Marsilius as well. He never specifically identifies his sources, although at one time he refers to Marsilius as "another great modern theologian."[73]

Unlike the other conciliarists, Dietrich also refers to

71 Niem, *De Modis,* pp. 9, 36, 58, 88, 90, 100.
72 Niem, *De Modis,* pp. 10, 33. ". . . non solum principes seculares, sed rustici et laboratores, et quicumque quantumcunque etiam minimi fideles, debent occurrere et morti, si oporteat, se exponere pro totius gregis salvatione . . . dolis, fraudibus, armis, violentia, potentia, promissionibus, donis et pecuniis, aut tandem carceribus et mortibus convenit sanctissimam unionem ecclesiae et conjunctionem quomodolibet procurare." For a discussion of "reason of church," see C. J. Friedrich, *Constitutional Reason of State* (Providence, 1957), p. 6. A garbled version of the above quotation is used by Arthur Koestler to introduce the second part of *Darkness at Noon* (New York, 1941, p. 95).
73 For examples of Occam's influence, see Niem, *De Modis,* pp. 38, 80, and 100. The reference to Marsilius appears on page 61, and other quotations from the *Defensor Pacis* occur on pages 21, 60, 63, and 64. See discussion in Sigmund, "The Influence of Marsilius," pp. 393-395.

examples from the history of the relations of the Holy Roman Empire to the papacy, especially to the reigns of Otto I and Henry II. In this he was followed by his countryman, Nicholas of Cusa.

If d'Ailly represents the adaptation of Occam by a prominent churchman, and Dietrich the influence which Marsilius still exerted even after church condemnation, the writings of Cardinal Francesco Zabarella are the best summing up of the remedies which were found in the canonist tradition for the grave problems of division within the church. Zabarella taught canon law at the University of Padua from 1394 until 1411, and his nephew, Bartholomew, taught the same subject when Cusanus was pursuing his doctoral studies. His *Commentary on the Decretals* was almost certainly studied by Nicholas of Cusa during his years at Padua. Zabarella's *Treatise on the Schism (Tractatus de Schismate)* is the commentary on Book I, title vi, ch. 6, of the Decretals, but it was also known apart from the commentary itself.[74]

More than any other conciliar theorist, Zabarella emphasizes consent as the basis for rulership in both church and state. The pope has been chosen by consent of the whole *universitas* of the church. The *congregatio fidelium* acts through a representative council made up primarily of bishops and upper ecclesiastics who represent and have the consent of all the faithful. Although they are not members of the council, in cases involving the definition of articles of faith the laity also ought to give their consent, since "what touches all ought to be approved by all, as is

[74] The *Tractatus* is printed in Schard, *De Jurisdictione*, pp. 688-711. Summaries of Zabarella's theories appear in Tierney, *Foundations*, chap. iv, pp. 220-237, and Ullmann, *Origins*, pp. 191-231. There are also older biographies by August Kneer (Münster, 1891) and Gasparo Zonta (Padua, 1915).

the rule in the *Liber Sextus.*[75] The council acts through its *major pars,* since "whatever the majority of the *universitas* does, the whole *universitas* is said to have done . . . As the majority of the *universitas* of Catholics think, the rest should think and hold because it is taught by the Holy Spirit."[76]

Zabarella solves the problem of convocation of the council by resorting to the emperor, who takes action on behalf of the *populus Christianus* "since jurisdiction and power over the whole world have been transferred to him."[77] *Epieikeia* is not mentioned, since it seems obvious to Zabarella that when the church needs help the emperor should step in and take the necessary action.

So far, Zabarella has only treated the problem of reunion of the church in the situation of divided jurisdiction in which the papacy was, as he put it, "quasi-vacant," but what about the case of a single undisputed pope? Writing before the end of the schism and before the adoption of the reform decrees of Constance, Zabarella proposed that the council take action not only to end the schism but also to ensure that no future pope would usurp the powers of his inferiors. Moreover, the council should at any time act to depose the pope if he is guilty of heresy or injures the general state of the church.

Like d'Ailly, Zabarella was a cardinal, and, as one might

75 Zabarella, *Tractatus,* p. 702. ". . . quod omnes tangit ab omnibus approbari debet, ut est regula 'quod omnes' Libro Sexto." Carlyle, *History,* VI, 165, gives additional citations from Zabarella basing rulership on consent.

76 Zabarella, *Tractatus,* p. 700. ". . . quicquid major pars universitatis facit, tota universitas fecisse dicitur . . . ex quo major pars universitatis Catholicorum sic sentit, caeteri debent sic sentire et opinari quod a Spiritu divino ducatur." Zabarella (pp. 688-689) also uses the phrase *valentior pars* in discussing who should come to the council but disagrees with "the philosophers" (clearly Marsilius is meant) who define the council to include all the faithful rather than "the bishops and other prelates."

77 Zabarella, *Tractatus,* pp. 689, 691.

expect, he develops a legal analysis of the position of the college of cardinals in relation to the pope. The college is considered as a *universitas,* and Zabarella claims for the cardinals the rights of any members of a *universitas* to be consulted on matters affecting the general state of the church. The pope and cardinals are head and members respectively of the *ecclesia Romana,* and if there is disagreement between them a general council of the larger *universitas,* the *ecclesia universalis,* should be convoked. The college of cardinals may assist in the convocation of a council when necessary, but it is generally held (*receptum est*) that the cardinals cannot depose the pope, despite their power to elect him.[78]

The church as Zabarella describes it is a hierarchy of corporations in each of which the members retain certain legal rights against the head. They act through representatives to control abuses and fill vacancies in their rectorships. The highest *universitas,* that of the *congregatio fidelium,* has the plenitude of power, *tamquam in fundamento,* and this is expressed (*explicatur*) in the pope as its principal minister, but this power can never be completely surrendered. At any time the *universitas* can act to change its head for sufficient cause, "since the power of the people is greater than that of the ruler."[79]

Zabarella represents the culmination of the canonist tradition in the church which viewed the pope as the elected agent of the legal corporation, the *congregatio fidelium,* subject to its control and enjoying a specific mandate to work as administrator (*dispensator*) of the goods and offices in possession of the church. The central position of consent in his theory, and the view that the church

---

78 Zabarella, *Tractatus,* pp. 701-702, 707.
79 Zabarella, *Tractatus,* p. 709. ". . . major est potestas populi quam magistratus ipsius." Cf. also p. 703.

is a system of corporations with mutual rights and obligations, contrasts vividly with the direction which the contemporary civil law was taking in Europe, where absolutism was more and more exalted and legal theorists were maintaining that people had transferred all power to the ruler irrevocably and could not exercise any control over his actions.[80] In Germany, of course, there was always the procedure of election to remind the electors of the possibilities for control of the emperor. In the case of the church, canonical elections recalled to the faithful that the designation of the pope and of church officers was not exclusively divine but also involved an important human element. Moreover, every canon lawyer was aware that election by the cardinals was a relatively recent development, that procedures for choosing the pope had varied from one century to the next, and that the emperor had taken a very active part in the conduct of church affairs during the period between the age of Constantine and the rise of the Hildebrandine papacy. The canon law provided the raw materials with which the conciliarists worked, and it was no accident that the leading conciliarists were churchmen trained in canon law.

Although the dominant influence in the conciliar movement was legal and canonistic, the older hierarchical and sacerdotal tradition was represented by the writings of Jean Charlier de Gerson, successor of Pierre d'Ailly as Vice-Chancellor of the University of Paris. He attempted to harmonize conciliar thought with the hierarchies of Dionysius the Areopagite, while including a liberal admixture of Aristotle where Dionysius did not fit his purpose. His best-known works are *De Auferibilitate Papae ab Ecclesia*

---

80 Cf. Myron Gilmore, *The Argument from Roman Law* (Cambridge, 1941), and Walter Ullmann, *The Medieval Idea of Law* (London, 1946).

and *De Potestate Ecclesiastica*. Neither is represented in the library at Kues, and it is possible that Cusanus did not read these works, although, as noted earlier, it is certain that he read Gerson's *Mystical Theology*. Yet Gerson's thought contains striking similarities to that of Cusanus, particularly in his attachment to the idea of hierarchy.[81]

Gerson had little use for the standard canon law defense of the rights of the church against the pope. Although critical of Marsilius, he used similar argumentation when he derived the power of the church to control the pope from the natural right of the community to decide its own rulers and to change those rulers if it saw fit.[82] Moreover, like d'Ailly, he believed that the best constitution was not a monarchy but a mixed government in which the pope represented the monarchical, the cardinals the aristocratic, and the council the "timocratic" element.[83] It is possible also to see an Aristotelian teleological element in Gerson in his constant emphasis on the purpose of the grant of power to the pope *ad aedificationem* and not *ad destructionem*.[84] However, there is nothing strikingly new about this, since it is a paraphrase on St. Paul which had been repeated by all the conciliarists since John of Paris.

Combined with these arguments from natural law and

81 Du Pin, *Gersonii Opera*, vol. II, contains *De Auferibilitate* (cols. 209-224) and *De Potestate Ecclesiastica* (cols. 225-256). Excerpts are translated in Lewis, *Medieval Political Ideas*, II, 403-415, and in Carlyle, *History*, VI, 158-164, and a new edition of Gerson's *Oeuvres complètes*, edited by Palémon Glorieux, is now in progress (Paris, 1960). Secondary works include Carl Schäfer, *Die Staatslehre des Johannes Gerson* (Bielefeld, 1935), and Morrall, *Gerson*. For Gerson's biography, see James L. Connolly, *John Gerson, Reformer and Mystic* (Louvain, 1928).

82 Gerson, *De Auferibilitate*, consideratio 11 in du Pin, *Opera*, vol. II, col. 216, quoting Aristotle's *Politics*, Book V. See also *De Potestate*, cons. 9, du Pin, *Opera*, vol. II, col. 238. Gerson quotes canon law only once in each of the two works.

83 Gerson, *De Potestate*, cons. 8, col. 237; cons. 12, col. 248; cons. 13, col. 254.

84 Gerson, *De Potestate*, cons. 1, col. 227, and cons. 11, col. 244.

Scripture were hierarchical conceptions derived from the writings of Dionysius. For Gerson, the Holy Spirit is the soul of the church infusing the various grades of the hierarchy with life. Contrary to Occam, he maintains that the church can never live on in a single lay person. Christ established the bishops and they can never die out, since without them there would be no one to pass on the Holy Orders established by Christ. Not content with disagreeing with Occam, Gerson specifically attacks Marsilius for denying the divine origin of the papacy.[85]

However, the members of the church hierarchy, although they receive their orders from God, are chosen by election. Papal legislation is approved by the consent of the church, and even the monarchical constitution of the church was established "with the consent of the whole primitive church or of the General Council."[86]

Gerson borrows from Dionysius the threefold purpose of the ecclesiastical hierarchy—to illuminate, perfect, and purify all lower ranks, "leading the lowest to the highest through the intermediate ranks." The ecclesiastical hierarchy imitates the heavenly hierarchy with the pope and cardinals representing the top rank, the patriarchs, archbishops, bishops, and priests in the middle ranks, and in the lowest group the *populus* and ordinary religious.[87]

In the general council only the bishops and higher prelates have the right to vote, although others may participate in the discussions which concern them. The hierarchic nature of Gerson's thought comes out once again when he

[85] Gerson, *De Auferibilitate*, cons. 4-8, cols. 211-213, and *De Potestate*, cons. 1, col. 227.

[86] Gerson, *De Auferibilitate*, cons. 6, col. 212; cons. 16, col. 221; *De Potestate*, cons. 9, col. 238.

[87] Gerson, *De Potestate*, cons. 5, col. 233, and cons. 9, col. 239. In an earlier sermon (quoted in Morrall, *Gerson*, p. 66) Gerson speaks of the papal curia as "ad similitudinem hierarchiae angelicae ordinanda."

defines the general council in a manner significantly different from that of Occam and Langenstein:

> Concilium generale est congregatio legitima auctoritate facta ad aliquem locum, ex omni statu hierarchico totius ecclesiae Catholicae, nulla fideli persona quae audiri requirat exclusa, ad salubriter tractandum et ordinandum ea quae debitum regimen ejusdem ecclesiae in fide et moribus respiciunt.[88]

This definition combines Gerson's emphasis on the church hierarchy with his belief in the participation of all in the deliberations of the council. He anticipates Cusanus in trying to combine the older hierarchic elements derived from the Neo-Platonic tradition, with the legal and Aristotelian influences calling for universal participation and consent (even if only indirectly) in church law and government.

Before the process of legal analysis of the relations of the various offices in the church had prepared the way for the assertion of the theory of conciliar superiority, the older sacral-traditional view had regarded the church as a unity, a mystical entity which was not subjected to the close scrutiny and dissection of the legal mind. The members of the hierarchy, and the pope at its head, were there by divine appointment. They represented the church, as the king or emperor represented the temporal community, in the sense that they personified it, and there was no conception of any organized body representing the community independent of its leader. Relationships were personal ones and both the church and the secular realm were regarded as indivisible. It was unthinkable that one part would act against another in the same body.

When as the result of the development of the study of

88 Gerson, *De Potestate*, col. 249.

Roman and canon law the conceptions of the church and of the empire changed from those of a traditional or sacramental order to a more rational-legal approach, this habit of looking at church and society in a unitary fashion began to break down. Roman law discussed the community action to transfer power to the ruler, and the medieval lawyers analyzed the nature of this transfer and the relations of the *populus* and their ruler. They also discussed the possibilities of corporate action through the *universitas,* and of consent by all whom a given action affected (the *quod omnes* principle). These concepts were developed by the medieval canon lawyers in their discussions of the relationships of the bishop and the cathedral chapter, and this formed the background for similar discussions of the relations of pope and council.

In addition to developing Roman law corporation theory, canon law specifically sanctioned church action against the pope in the case of papal heresy. It also contained numerous references to the necessity of election to church office, which contrasted with the increasingly frequent contemporary practice of papal appointment.

This canon law background provided the material for the development of the theory of corporate church action against the pope by the conciliar writers. In some cases, the theory was expressed in precise canon law terms as in John of Paris and Zabarella. In others, it also received reinforcement from the medieval Aristotelian doctrines of community participation in lawmaking, as in Marsilius and Gerson. At times it took the form of a theory that the pope was one among many bishops as in Durandus, and at other times the papal office and the council's authority were derived from all the faithful who made up the church. Sometimes the two theories were connected, as when it was said that the bishops in their participation in the council represented all the faithful. But the constant element in all conciliar theory was the belief in the right of the community to elect and remove its ruler and to participate in some sense in the making of the law to which it was subject.

In the development of their theories two principal problems faced the conciliarists. The canon law stated that the councils must be called by the pope, and one could hardly expect the pope to call a council to act against himself. To deal with this difficulty, Occam and the later conciliarists used the adage, "Necessity has no law," and the Aristotelian conception of *epieikeia* to prove that the emperor or any Christian could call the council if there was an urgent need. The second problem was that of the composition of the council once it was called into session, and here the "episcopal" and the "democratic" conciliar theories came into conflict, since the former wished to restrict the meeting to the higher clergy, while the latter sometimes called for the participation of representatives of the laity.

This was the state of conciliar theory at the time that Nicholas of Cusa wrote his *Concordantia*. He had the practical example of the success of the Council of Constance in restoring unity to the church. He also had a formidable array of theoretical concepts of consent, election, and representation with which to build his theory. At the same time, he was also aware of an earlier philosophical and theological tradition, that of hierarchy and functional interdependence, and it was from these two principal traditions that he attempted to construct his theory.

CHAPTER V

. . .

DE CONCORDANTIA CATHOLICA

CONCORD AND HIERARCHY

ALL THE writers considered in the last chapter, with the possible exception of Marsilius, were primarily concerned with church government. However, in the course of the development of their theories on the structure and authority of the church, they discussed such topics of general interest to the political theorist as the emergency powers of the ruler (Occam), the virtues of a mixed constitution (Gerson and d'Ailly) and the right of those subject to a law to participate in its formulation (the *quod omnes* principle, cited by nearly all the conciliar theorists). In fact, most of the political theory produced in the Middle Ages was really ecclesiastical theory, since the questions which gave rise to the theorizing were problems concerning the church. This is understandable in view of the near-monopoly of the church on education and the fact that the best minds of the age were attracted to service with the church, where careers were more open to talent than anywhere else on the medieval scene.

Yet this is not enough to explain the predominance of questions relating to the structure and functioning of the church in medieval political thought. Figgis somewhat overstates it when he says, "In the Middle Ages, the church was not a state, it was *the* state,"[1] but it is true that the

---

1 Figgis, *Gerson to Grotius*, p. 5.

medieval conception of the organization of society was very different from modern conceptions. It is very difficult therefore to use the modern terms "church" and "state" when dealing with their medieval antecedents. In medieval theory, there was a single composite Church-State, with two administrations, one for spiritual matters and one for temporal concerns. The relations between these two hierarchies were a subject of continuous controversy, but no one doubted that the over-all framework within which they acted was a *respublica Christiana,* or Christian commonwealth, created by, and directed to, God. The respective roles of God's vicars on earth (the term *vicarius Dei* was applied both to pope and emperor) were not always clear, but their common subordination to the Triune Creator was not a matter of dispute.

The confusion surrounding the medieval conception of the church is illustrated by the ambiguity of the term in *De Concordantia Catholica.* Nicholas described the subject of the first of the three books into which the work is divided as "the union of believers which is called the church," *ecclesia.* The second book he entitles the *sacerdotium,* the priesthood which is described as the soul of the church, and the third discusses the empire, *sacrum imperium,* which is its body. The *ecclesia* in this context is equated with the whole of Christian society as Nicholas knew it, and what in modern parlance would be called the church is what Cusanus refers to as the priesthood. Yet, for reasons which have only become clear as a result of recent investigations of the manuscript history of the work, Nicholas is not consistent on this point. The first book is largely concerned with problems of the structure of ecclesiastical authority, and the parts of the second book which were included in the first draft often use the term *ecclesia* where a more consistent usage would require the use of *sacerdotium.*

DE CONCORDANTIA CATHOLICA

The division of the work brings out a characteristic of medieval theory which helps to explain the reason for the study of medieval ecclesiology by students of political theory. Theories of the structure and legitimation of the church were not as sharply differentiated from those concerned with the temporal order as they were later to become. The best form of government was best for both *regnum* and *sacerdotium,* and arguments developed for one set of institutions were by a process of transfer often applied to the other. In a society which assumed uniformity of religion, the church hierarchy was not one voluntary organization among many, but the entire culture and society as organized for spiritual purposes. When this organization was threatened by a constitutional crisis such as the Western Schism and the Conciliar Movement, the resulting controversy drew not only from the resources of revealed religion, the Scriptures and the fathers of the church, but also from philosophical and legal theory in general. The theories which the controversy produced had a relevance for both the spiritual and temporal orders. Later when the empire or the nation-states faced similar crises, they could draw upon the conciliar theorists for suggestions on such questions as the nature of government, of law, of society, and of their relation to man and to the cosmos. The analysis of *De Concordantia Catholica* is undertaken on the assumption that the work is more than a study in the constitutional history and doctrine of the church. It is an attempt at a grand synthesis of the thought of Greece, Rome, and the Christian Middle Ages, as they are relevant to the proper ordering of the two authorities of united Christendom, threatened by divisions both in the spiritual and the temporal orders.

Although the various parts of the *Concordantia* were written at different times, the work seems to have come down to us with little effort at correction, polishing, or the elimination of irrelevancy or repetition. As Cusanus admits, it appears a bit "confused and rough," and it was evidently written in considerable haste.[2] The style is not difficult but it is lacking in grace or distinction of expression. Nicholas was conscious of this failing, attributing it to the difficulties of all Germans with the Latin language.[3] He sometimes discusses problems at great length and then abruptly changes the subject. Quotations and references to the church fathers are repeated again and again with no indication that Nicholas realizes that he has already used them, and sometimes, particularly in the final book of the work, he reproduces long and often highly rhetorical quotations from early medieval councils which seem to bear very little relation to the central argument. Yet for all its irrelevancies and disorder, De Concordantia sums up the main currents of medieval thought at a time when the world which that thought had dominated was passing from the scene.

The dominant note of De Concordantia Catholica, as the title indicates, is the search for universal harmony in a world which seemed, as Cusanus viewed it, to be "rushing to its end."[4] This harmony was not only to be sought in church organization. The ideal order in the church was part of a larger order in the universe, in civil society, and in man. For all its diversity, Nicholas believed that the world had within it certain unifying principles on the basis

---

2 The reference to the work as written "confuse et ruditer" appears in DCC, Book II, chap. xxxiv, p. 308. For the manuscript evidence see literature cited above in Chapter II, note 22.

3 DCC, preface, p. 2.

4 DCC, Book II, chap. xxxiv, p. 308. For references to signs of the end of the world see Book I, chap. xii, p. 72. Later in his life, Nicholas predicted on the basis of a mathematical scheme that the end of the world would take place early in the eighteenth century.

of which society was, or should be, ordered. This conception of a universal order and harmony, a higher unity in diversity, was by no means original with Nicholas. Whether it is the transcendental universe of forms of Plato, the immanent order of ends in the Aristotelian teleology, the higher law of the Stoics, or the divinely created rational universe of Thomistic Christianity, the assumption that the universe is basically harmonious and intelligible runs through nearly all of ancient and medieval thought. Although it may be argued that the Old Testament God had elements of the irrational in His activities, the loving God of the New Testament, particularly as developed by the church fathers, was also a rational God who created a purposive universe.

This belief in an ordered universe was further developed, by the Neo-Platonic and theological writers surveyed in Chapter III, into a belief in a hierarchical order consisting of parallel or corresponding sets of relationships at various levels of being. *Concordantia* would result when this ideal order had been achieved.

The term *concordantia* was used with reference to church organization by Cyprian, and Nicholas quotes his reference to *unitas in concordantia*. However, as noted in an earlier chapter, the principal sources for Cusanus' conception seem to have been Augustine and Raymond Lull. Like Augustine's goal of *concordia ordinata*, Cusanus' *concordantia* was an attempt to find the principles of order and harmony implanted in the universe by a beneficent Creator. More specifically, Cusanus seems to have borrowed his definition of the term and his conception of a resolution of differences and contraries from Lull, whom he knew through his teacher at Cologne, Heimericus de Campo.[5]

[5] The reference to Cyprian's letter to Antonianus (erroneously referred to as Novatian) is made in *DCC*, Book I, chap. vi, p. 57. Augustine's word

While Cusanus' philosophical and religious interests were probably primarily responsible for his choice of *concordantia* as the central concept of his major political work, the canon law probably also had some influence. Gratian's *Decretum* was actually entitled *Concordantia Discordantium Canonum*—from its attempt to reconcile seemingly contradictory legal precedents. However, it is not surprising that it is difficult to single out a single source for *concordantia,* since the search for a principle of order and harmony is present in most medieval thinkers. It runs through all of Nicholas' thought from his earliest writings through his metaphysical works, such as the *Docta Ignorantia* (the "coincidence of opposites" unifying contradictories) and *De Conjecturis,* which discusses "concordance" and "difference" as tools of philosophical analysis, to his later philosophical and theological works, such as *De Pace Fidei,* the attempt to bring out the common or unifying elements in the many religious faiths in the world.

Concordantia has this meaning of unity in diversity in Cusanus' definition in the opening chapter of the work, as it applies to the "union of believing people"—"that by reason of which the Catholic church is in agreement in one and many—in one Lord and many subjects."[6] The content of this agreement of the one and many is developed in the course of the work in a scheme of social and religious organization which is a synthesis of two bases of social and political organization—that of hierarchy and that of consent to law and government. The first has as one of its

---

was *concordia,* not *concordantia,* but in one instance Nicholas uses *concordia*—Book I of *DCC,* chap. iv, p. 45, "Necesse est ergo concordiam illam esse in uno et pluribus, in uno capite et pluribus membris." On Lull's influence see Chapter III above, especially note 40.

6 *DCC,* Book I, chap. i, p. 31. "Concordantia enim est id, ratione cuius ecclesia catholica in uno et pluribus concordat, in uno Domino et pluribus subditis."

principal sources the Neo-Platonic world view transmitted to the Middle Ages in the writings of Pseudo-Dionysius and the commentaries on Plato's *Timaeus* and *Parmenides*. The other conception, that of consent, is strongly influenced by ideas drawn from Roman and canon law.

The Neo-Platonic tradition leads to a theory of hierarchy and inequality; the legal tradition, to one of equality. The one emphasizes reason in nature; the other, the human will (not necessarily the individual will, but at least the corporate will). Hierarchy is objective and immutable. Consent is subjective and flexible. In the one case, legitimacy comes from above; in the other from below.[7] When these two traditions are brought together in Nicholas of Cusa's social ideal of *concordantia,* the result is a hierarchy of diverse orders and functions, united by the consent of its members. Both the ecclesiastical and the secular rulers carry out their functions with the consent of their subordinates through a natural hierarchy, based in the case of the ecclesiastical authorities on consecration, and, in the civil order, upon the possession of a natural superiority of reason and wisdom.

The social order is thus unified in two ways. On the one hand, there is the principle of an objective standard in accordance with which the different functions or offices are allocated in a hierarchical fashion. On the other, there is the consent or agreement of all the members to the social order of which they are a part. When a principle of order and the consent of all have brought about unity in diversity, *concordantia* is the result.

The first of the three books of *De Concordantia Catholica* is devoted primarily to Cusanus' conception of the place

7 This distinction is similar to but not identical with that of Gierke between the view of society as an institution *(Anstalt)* and a fellowship *(Genossenschaft),* the one derived from canon law and the other from Germanic folk-law.

of the *ecclesia* in the hierarchical and triadic order of the universe. From the opening chapter it shows a close dependence on the Neo-Platonic tradition. The political and social system is linked to a grander scheme which unites all created things with their Creator in a hierarchy of ascending value. Heaven and earth are joined, and politics and sociology blend into cosmology and theology. "From the one peaceful King of infinite concordance flows a sweet and spiritual harmony in different grades and series to all subordinate members united with Him so that the one God is all things in all things."[8]

The conception of God as *omnia in omnibus* appears often in Cusanus' later writings. It is derived ultimately from St. Paul's First Epistle to the Corinthians (I Cor. 15:28) and is frequently found in Neo-Platonist works. The use of the verb *fluere* to describe God's creative action is a mark of Neo-Platonic influences, since in the Plotinian theory of emanation, creative power *flows* from the One to subordinate beings. The same term is also used by the theologians to describe the relationship of head and members of the Mystical Body, thus linking the organic theories of Christian theology with the Neo-Platonic theories of emanation.

As Nicholas describes it, the chain of Being begins with God and descends through the angels to man—another threefold division. God draws all things to Himself as a magnet. He is the Light, and all created things are shadows or reflections of that infinite light. The further distant a thing is from God the less perfection and the less "reality" it has. His power *(virtus)* penetrates to the lowest creature

---

8 *DCC,* Book I, chap. i, pp. 31-32. "Et ab uno infinitae concordantiae rege pacifico fluit illa dulcis concordantialis harmonia spiritualis gradatim et seriatim in cuncta membra subjecta et unita, ut sit unus Deus omnia in omnibus."

without in any way losing its creative properties. All things are dependent on God, and at the same time at an infinite distance from Him. Yet no matter how distant, God's creative activity is present in its full intensity.[9]

When Cusanus comes to discuss the various ranks and orders in the hierarchies of heaven and earth, he again utilizes a threefold division, since "all created things show the figure of the Trinity."[10] Nearest to the Triune God are the threefold orders of the angels, each of which is divided into three choirs. Below the lowest of nine choirs of angels begin the nine spheres around the earth. On earth itself, all nature is divided into rational, sensate, and vegetative—"and here there are choirs and orders on the model of those of the angels."[11] In heaven, in purgatory, and on earth is the church which is defined as "rational spirits and men who are united with Christ, although not all in the same manner, but hierarchically."[12] In heaven it is the church triumphant, in purgatory the church sleeping, and on earth the church militant.

Just as man on earth is composed of body, soul, and spirit, the church militant comprises the sacraments as the spirit, the priesthood as the soul, and the faithful as the body. The sacraments illumine and purify; the priests

9 *DCC*, Book I, chap. ii, pp. 35-37, and ch. 7, p. 61. The attempt to find a way of knowing this omnipresent, creative, but infinitely distant God is the subject of *De Docta Ignorantia*.

10 This Augustinian doctrine of the "vestiges" of the Trinity in creation is further developed in *De Docta Ignorantia*. The division of the three books of *De Concordantia Catholica* itself reflects the threefold division of man into body, soul, and spirit. The use of threefold divisions in Nicholas of Cusa has been exhaustively treated in Rudolf Haubst, *Das Bild des einen und dreieinen Gottes in der Welt nach Nikolaus von Kues* (Trier, 1952).

11 *DCC*, Book I, chap. ii, p. 37. ". . . et in ea ordines et chori ut in angelica."

12 *DCC*, Book I, chap. ii, p. 38. ". . . ex rationabilibus spiritibus et hominibus, qui cum Christo uniuntur, licet non omnes pariformiter, sed gradatim."

purify and are purified; and the faithful are purified and do not purify.[13] As in any triadic hierarchical order outlined by Dionysius, the middle term, the priesthood, mediates and transmits the power that it receives from the rank above (in this case, from the sacraments) to the rank below (the faithful).

Within each of these ranks in turn there is a hierarchical order. The Eucharist is the highest-ranking of the sacraments, but since the church had enumerated seven sacraments and not three, this was as far as Cusanus could go with his schema on the subject. The priesthood is also divided on the model of the celestial choirs into nine ranks. The bishops, priests, and deacons form the first triad, all of them with the power of dispensing the sacraments. Below them are the subdeacons, acolytes, and exorcists, who have less sacramental power. The lowest order comprises the readers, porters, and tonsured clergy, who do not possess these powers as yet.

The nine ranks which Cusanus has outlined so far conform to the traditional major and minor orders and recall the hierarchical divisions of Dionysius the Areopagite. As in his hierarchies, they are triadic in form and the highest rank mentioned is that of bishop.[14]

The theory of the equality of all bishops as to orders or power to consecrate was by now a commonplace of conciliar

13 *DCC,* Book I, chap. vi, pp. 54-55. Cusanus refers here to Dionysius' *Ecclesiastical Hierarchy,* but the scheme may be derived from intermediaries such as Eriugena, Albertus Magnus, and Bonaventure. The comparison of the priesthood with the soul of the church may be drawn from Gregory of Nazianzen, whom Cusanus cites in a later work (cf. Haubst, *Das Bild,* p. 151, n. 19). The division into body, soul, and spirit appears in St. Augustine—*De Anima,* in *Opera Omnia,* vol. X (Paris, 1838), col. 720A— and in the writings of the twelfth century Cistercians.

14 Subdeacons are usually considered among the major orders. In Dionysius' system the priesthood was subdivided into bishops, priests, and ministers, and the people divided into monks, faithful, and catechumens.

theory. Using the *Decretum*, John of Paris, Durandus, and the other later conciliarists had cited Augustine and Cyprian to prove that all the apostles and their successors, the bishops, had received the same power of orders—although their hierarchical position in church government might vary.

Nicholas of Cusa characteristically goes beyond the quotations in the *Decretum* to the original works of Cyprian and quotes him directly to support an almost mystical view of the episcopate by which, "through a kind of concordance which is in one and many," the church is under coequal bishops sharing in the unity of the whole without being in any way subordinated to one another.[15]

Yet other conclusions about the structure of the church hierarchy could be drawn from the *Decretum*. It is full of references to the divinely established primacy of Rome and the necessity of obedience to the Roman church. Rome is described as the mother of churches, whose decrees are not to be resisted.[16]

The commentators on the *Decretum* had resolved the problem of reconciling the equality of all the bishops and the primacy of Rome by distinguishing between the power of orders and the power of jurisdiction. As to sacramental powers, all bishops were equal, but as to jurisdiction, Peter and his successors were superior to the others.

Without acknowledging his indebtedness to the canon lawyers or the conciliar theorists, Nicholas utilized a somewhat similar division to answer the difficulty of reconciling the equality of all bishops and the supremacy of the pope. Immediately after outlining the *ordines religionis*, as he calls them—the nine ranks in the church ranging from

---

15 *DCC*, Book I, chap. vi, p. 57, and chap. x, p. 67.
16 *Decretum*, D. 19 c. 1-2, D. 21 c. 2-3, 9, D. 22 c. 1-2.

bishop to tonsured cleric—he moves in the next chapter
to a completely new hierarchical scheme, based on ruling
and pastoral responsibilities *(praesidentialitas et pastoralis
cura)*. Once again there are nine ranks, but this time we
begin with the pope, followed by the patriarchs and archbishops. Next comes a second threefold rank, comprising
bishops, archdeacons, and deans. Finally there is the lowest
rank possessing *virtus regitiva,* which consists of priests,
deacons, and subdeacons. Peter (the pope) has a *praesidentia regitiva* "in order that there may be unity in concord . . . so that having established a head, the occasion for
schism may be removed. Hence just as there is one episcopate, so there is one *cathedra* and ruling power established
by hierarchical grades."[17]

Thus there is a double hierarchy in the church. There
is a sacramental hierarchy (based on the power of orders)
which culminates in the rank of bishop, as in the earlier
theories. But there is also a governmental or administrative
hierarchy, and in this the pope is supreme.

However, for the relationship of either of these hierarchical constructions to the church or to the general
council we must look elsewhere than to the first book of
De Concordantia Catholica. In Book I, Nicholas never even
mentions the council. It is true that he has endeavored to
prove that all bishops are equal, and it was on this basis
that Durandus and d'Ailly developed their episcopalist
theories of conciliar supremacy. However, Cusanus' principal effort in Book I is to describe the hierarchical structure of the universe and the part played by the *ecclesia* in
the larger plan. Even here, he could have followed Dionysius in making the episcopacy the highest rank. Yet, charac-

---

[17] *DCC,* Book I, chap. vi, p. 57. ". . . unitas in concordantia . . . ut
capite constituto scismatis tollatur occasio. Unde sicut episcopatus unus,
ita una cathedra et una praesidentia gradualiter et hierarchice constituta."

teristically, he tries to have it both ways. The bishops are supreme in the sacramental hierarchy, but when it comes to the government of the church he begins with the pope, not the bishops or the general council. The council's role in church government only becomes clear with the development of Cusanus' theories of consent and representation in the second book of *De Concordantia Catholica*.

The prominent position of the pope in the opening book of *De Concordantia Catholica* foreshadows the later change in Cusanus' loyalties from support of the council to that of the pope. From the beginning, the pope had an important position in his theory. Nicholas was never a thoroughgoing conciliarist in the sense of advocating popular sovereignty in the church, and his transfer of allegiance to the papacy did not involve a substantial alteration of his theory of the church.

Cusanus conceived the structure of the ruling authority in the civil order, the body of the church, to be an exact parallel of that of the ecclesiastical order. There is no question in *De Concordantia Catholica* of a hierocratic subordination of emperor to pope. Both receive their power directly from God, and the empire is a *sacrum imperium,* the legitimacy of which is in no way dependent on the action of ecclesiastical authority. The parallel hierarchy in the civil order is described in the third book in a much less elaborate and complete fashion than the hierarchies of Book I. This paucity of material devoted to the structure of the civil society is understandable, for although the emperor was present at the Council of Basel, and although *De Concordantia* is jointly dedicated to him and to Cardinal Cesarini, the work was originally written as a contribution to the solution of the difficulties which had arisen between the council and the pope, and the third book was added later.

In the ecclesiastical hierarchy, the various gradations were determined by the grant of Holy Orders (the sacramental hierarchy) or by the allocation of jurisdiction (the hierarchy of rulership). Presumably, although not necessarily, these differences were based upon the possession of varying degrees of sanctity. In the civil hierarchy, Nicholas follows Plato, Aristotle, and the church fathers (there is a long quotation from St. Ambrose), in saying that the basis is wisdom *(sapientia)*.

As Nicholas puts it in the preface to the third book, "Almighty God has fixed a certain natural servitude for the stupid and ignorant in accordance with which they readily trust the more intelligent, so that they may thus be directed by their assistance."[18]

This statement indicates how far is Cusanus' political thinking from modern democratic conceptions. The political order is an order based on nature and natural differences. The ruler exercises his authority because he possesses more wisdom than his subjects, and legislation is initiated by the wise. Yet this rationalistic elitism is combined with an altogether different set of ideas which makes *De Concordantia Catholica* more than one more footnote to Plato—the conception of consent as the basis of legitimate authority and the ground of political obligation.

In describing the structure of the civil order, the body of the church, Nicholas follows very closely the structure which he outlined earlier for the *sacerdotium*. Like the pope at the head of the ecclesiastical hierarchy, the emperor presides over a parallel temporal hierarchy embracing all of Christendom. He derives his authority independently of the church and has a divinely intended function, the

---

18 *DCC*, Book III, Preface, p. 315. "Sed cunctipotens Deus stultis et fatuis quandam naturalem servitutem adiunxit, per quam facile credant sapientibus, ut sic ipsorum adiutorio gubernentur. . ."

care of the temporal needs of his subjects. "Everything which is derived from God is necessarily ordered. And so in this order, there is one ruler of the world exercising his authority over the others in the plenitude of powers, who, in his own sphere, the temporal hierarchy, on the model of the sacerdotal hierarchy, is the equal of the Roman pontiff, always keeping in mind the difference between the spiritual and the temporal."[19] Below him are the kings of Europe, over whom he has a type of religious overlordship, even when they do not recognize his temporal supremacy, by virtue of his duties as *advocatus ecclesiae* to enforce church law throughout Christendom. This parallels the structure of papal authority in the church. Just as the pope's responsibility is greatest in his diocese, less in his archdiocese or metropolitanate, still less in his patriarchate, and weakest in the whole church, so the emperor is primarily responsible for the subjects immediately subordinate to him, then for those subject to princes who are his vassals, and finally for those "whose kings and princes are not subject to him, but, while recognizing his primacy, claim parallel places for themselves."[20] Beneath the emperor and kings are the dukes, marquesses, counts, and local rulers *(rectores)* continuing down to "the simple lay people who are figuratively the feet of the body." Each of the secular rulers corresponds to a member of the church hierarchy (dukes to archbishops, counts to bishops, and so forth). In a later chapter, the authorities in the empire assembled in

---

19 *DCC*, Book III, chap. i, p. 327. "Omnia enim, quae a deo sunt, ordinata necessario sunt. Est itaque in catholica ecclesia in hoc ordine unus in plenitudine potestatis ceteris supereminens mundi dominus, qui Romano pontifici suo modo in hac corporali hierarchia ad instar ipse in sacerdotali regulariter par esse dicitur servata differentia, quae inter spirituale et corporale exsistit."

20 *DCC*, Book III, chap. vii, p. 361. ". . . quoad subjectos per medium regum et principum proprie sibi non subjectorum sed lateralia loca sibi vindicantium et eum primum omnium recognoscentium."

council are grouped into three ranks, parallel to the structure of ecclesiastical authority outlined earlier. "In the first rank are kings and electors of the empire, its patricians. Second are dukes, provincial governors, prefects, etc. Third come marquesses, landgraves, and similar ranks."[21]

The influence of the Neo-Platonic hierarchies is much diminished in the third book of *De Concordantia Catholica*. Marsilius, whom Nicholas read as he was finishing Book II,[22] completely dominates the preface (although he is never mentioned by name), and most of the later discussion is devoted to the problem of reform of the institutions of the empire. Yet, at the end of the entire work there is a return to the unified and hierarchical world view of the early Middle Ages. In the last chapter of *De Concordantia*, Cusanus develops an elaborate analogy between the functional interrelations of the parts of the human body and the interaction of the parts of the church and empire.[23]

Returning to the threefold classification used in Book I —body, soul, and spirit—he develops the organic analogy much further. As the soul is present in every part of the body, so the priesthood is present in every part of the empire. The priesthood in the head is the pope, in the eyes and ears the patriarchs. The archbishops are compared to the soul in the arms, the bishops in the fingers, and so on, down to the rural clergy, the soul in the feet of the commonwealth.[24]

---

21 *DCC*, Book III, chap. xxv, p. 421. "Primi ordinis sunt reges et electores imperii, patricii. Secundi sunt duces, praesides, praefecti et huiusmodi. Tertii marchiones et lantgravii et similes."

22 See *DCC*, Book II, chap. xxxiv, p. 298, for the reference to "Marsilius de Padua quem post omnem collectionem istius voluminis vidi."

23 *DCC*, Book III, chap. xli, pp. 466-73. As has been shown in a previous chapter, the Neo-Platonic theory of hierarchy is linked to the use of the organic analogy. The subordination of the various ranks to God at the summit of the hierarchy is similar to the dependence of the members of greater or lesser dignity upon the head of the organism.

24 *DCC*, Book III, chap. xli, pp. 467-468. Footnotes on these two pages

Revealing his knowledge of the human circulatory system, Cusanus compares the arteries to the commandments of God and the veins to conciliar decrees, "and as the smaller veins nourishing certain individual parts of the body can not bring life, strength, and spirit, unless they flow from the common source, so all provincial and local statutes must conform to the principles of canon law."[25]

Similar elaborate analogies are drawn for the empire. The body is composed of bone, nerves, and flesh. The imperial laws are the nerves radiating from the brain. The bones are the fatherland and the flesh is the ever-changing membership of the body politic "which often on account of weakness, ignorance, or sickness has human failings."[26]

Perhaps the most exaggerated use of the analogy is Nicholas' comparison of the process of lawmaking with the intake and digestion of food. The emperor's privy council, like the teeth, tastes and chews on the proposal. Then if it finds it good, it passes it to the stomach, the Great Council, which digests it, separating the pure from the impure. The nourishment thus derived goes to the judges who, like the liver, distribute the health-giving law to every member. Fortunately for the reader's sensibilities, Nicholas stops here.

While this may appear to be stretching the organic

---

in the Heidelberg edition derive these analogies from Vincent of Beauvais and ultimately from John of Salisbury.

25 *DCC*, Book III, chap. xli, pp. 469-470. "Et sicut parvae venae certa particularia membra rigantes non habent nisi ad communem fontem continuentur vigorem vivificativum et animae delativum, sic oportet omnes provincialium ac particularium locorum statuta conformitatem ad communes canones absque contradictione habere." Cusanus' collection of medical works appears as no. 222 in the library at Kues (Marx, *Verzeichnis*, p. 219).

26 *DCC*, Book III, chap xli, pp. 470-471. "Carnes vero transitoriis hominibus qui saepe ob mollitiem, ignorantiam, vel infirmitatem humaniter delinquunt.

analogy a bit far, it illustrates Cusanus' preoccupation with unity and interdependence of function in both church and empire. The two hierarchies of ecclesiastical and civil authority cooperate as parts of a single organism working together as body and soul under the temporal and spiritual headship of emperor and pope. All the members are related to each other in interdependence and subordination in a perfectly ordered and harmonious *ecclesia,* the union of believers on earth.

CHAPTER VI

. . .

CONSENT

THE BASIS OF LAW
AND GOVERNMENT

I N T H E theory outlined so far, it would be difficult
to find any basis for classifying Nicholas of Cusa as a
conciliar theorist. The cosmological and theological arguments which he employed could stand by themselves as
a theory of the nature and legitimation of authority. Both
church and empire were governed by a hierarchical order
which received its legitimacy from above—from God. The
emperor as well as the pope ruled by divine right, and it
was by virtue of the emperor's religious function that the
head of the *sacrum imperium* was considered to have jurisdiction over all of Christendom. The connecting link between the theological hierarchies of the first book of *De
Concordantia Catholica* and the conciliarism which follows
is provided by the single political doctrine for which
Nicholas of Cusa is best known as a political theorist—
consent as the basis for political obligation.

It has been suggested that the prominent place of consent in his theory may be related to the legal case which
Nicholas was arguing at the time he wrote *De Concordantia*.[1] His client, Ulrich von Manderscheid, had been
elected by the cathedral chapter of the archdiocese of Trier
(although not without considerable intimidation by the

---

1 Vansteenberghe, *Nicolas*, p. 56, and E. Meuthen, "Nikolaus von Kues
und der Laie," pp. 119-120.

local nobility) and he was claiming the archbishopric in a dispute with the appointee of the pope. If it were established that papal appointments were illegal unless preceded by a proper ecclesiastical election, Manderscheid's case could be considered won.

However, while the manuscript evidence seems to point in this direction, *De Concordantia* is more than a mere *livre de circonstance*. The doctrine of consent, while novel in the central position which it holds in his theory of law and government, is drawn from a long tradition in ancient and medieval thought, and, as the review of conciliar thinkers has already indicated, consent was playing an increasingly important role in political and legal theory at the end of the Middle Ages.

The dominant tendency in ancient and medieval political theory had been to justify rulership on the basis of Platonic rationalism. One should obey the ruler because of his superior wisdom or sanctity, observing the natural law by which inferior obey superiors. An objective natural and rational order justifies government, and if a ruler possesses superior knowledge and training it is only natural and in accordance with the objective order of the universe that he should rule, whether or not he has sought to elicit the consent of his subjects. In this tradition, consent plays only a very secondary role. At best it is a method of eliciting compliance with minimum difficulty, rather than a source of moral justification for government. Even Aristotle, who defines citizenship as participation in government, holds that the rule of the wise and good (aristocracy) or of the "one best man" is the best form of government.[2]

The belief that rulership is based upon the consent of

2 Cf. Aristotle, *Politics,* Book III, chap. xii, v. 13, chap. xvii, v. 5, chap. xviii; Book IV, chap. xi; Book VII, *passim.*

all is much more a characteristic of medieval legal theory than of its philosophy. Of the well-known medieval philosophers writing before the fourteenth century, only Duns Scotus gives a prominent position to consent in his discussion of the derivation of political authority.[3] Yet as early as the twelfth century the canon lawyers were engaged in subtle discussions of the mode and legitimacy of election and consent for both spiritual and temporal rulers.[4] As the review of conciliar theory before Cusanus has indicated, the conciliarists such as John of Paris, Marsilius, and Zabarella used the canonistic categories and doctrines and with slight alterations transformed them into theories of conciliar supremacy in which consent played an important part.[5] Nicholas of Cusa, trained in the canon law, derived his consent theory from these sources as well.

In the fourteenth chapter of the second book of *De Concordantia* Nicholas states his theory of the justification of government by consent. After quoting Gratian's *Decretum* to prove that all legislation is based on natural law, Nicholas concludes that, since natural law is derived from reason, those who are more rational ought to rule. He then proceeds to add a very important qualification to what had

---

[3] Georges de Lagarde, *La Naissance de l'esprit laique*, III (Paris, 1942), 332, n. 113, quotes a passage from Duns Scotus' *Opus Oxoniense* (III, d. 15, para. 2) stating that "political authority over others which rests in one person or in the community can only be justified by the common consent of that community." (Although Cusanus must have studied some of the writings of Scotus when he was at Cologne, he never refers to him in *De Concordantia*. The library at Kues contains the *Opus Oxoniense;* cf. Marx, *Verzeichnis*, no. 79, p. 80.)

[4] For an example, see the argument of the twelfth century canonist, Huguccio, quoted in S. Mochi Onory, *Fonti canonistiche dell'idea moderna dello stato* (Milan, 1951), p. 151.

[5] Cf. the judgment of Gewirth *(Marsilius,* I, 60): "Where the antecedent tradition had held that the test of valid human laws and of just government are to be found in their conformity to the rational criteria of the natural law, and their being directed to the common benefit, Marsilius makes the people's 'consent', 'election', or 'will', the decisive factor."

been standard Platonic theory on claims to political authority. The rule of the wise should be over consenting subjects.

> Therefore since all are by nature free, then every rulership whether it is by written law or by living law through a prince, which restrains the subjects from evil and directs their freedom to good through fear of punishment can only come from the agreement and consent of the subjects. For if, by nature, men are equally powerful *(potentes)* and equally free, a true and properly ordered authority of one common ruler who is equal in power can only be naturally constituted by the election and consent of the others.[6]

One writer on medieval theory has derived this passage from the writings of the church fathers, but on the basis of Cusanus' background and training it seems more likely that the major influence on his theory of consent came from Roman and canon law.[7] Where there is a reference to Augustine or Ambrose, it is usually a quotation from the *Decretum* of Gratian, as for example the statement, "There is a general agreement of human society to obey their rulers" (originally found in St. Augustine), which is quoted from the *Decretum* in support of the doctrine of elective consent, immediately following the above passage.

Other citations from Gratian adduced by Cusanus to support government by consent include canon law refer-

6 *DCC*, Book II, chap xiv, p. 161. "Unde cum natura omnes sunt liberi, tunc omnis principatus sive consistat in lege scripta sive viva apud principem, per quem principatum coercentur a malis subditi et eorum regulatur libertas ad bonum metu poenarum, est a sola concordantia et consensu subiectivo. Nam si natura aeque potentes et aeque liberi homines sunt, vera et ordinata potestas unius communis aeque potentis naturaliter non nisi electione et consensu aliorum constitui potest."

7 Gewirth, *Marsilius*, I, 215, n. 15. Although Cusanus' degree was in canon law *(doctor decretorum)*, he was also familiar with the main doctrines of the civil law. See, for example, the discussion of the references to Roman law in Cod. Cus. 220 (Nicholas' transcription in 1423 of lectures on judicial procedure in church courts) in Krchňák, "Die kanonistischen Aufzeichnungen," p. 78.

ences to the necessity of election of bishops and archbishops, and numerous discussions of the type of quasi-
matrimonial consent existing between the bishop and his
church.[8] Nicholas also refers to the distinction which he
had utilized in the first book between the power of orders
in which all bishops are equal and that of administration
in which the pope is supreme. In the second book, however, he uses it as an argument for the derivation of papal
authority from consent. Possibly borrowing from John of
Paris, Nicholas recalls that the great thirteenth century
canon lawyer, Hostiensis, had derived the power of orders
directly from God, but had maintained that the power of
administration required among other things *(partim)* the
consent of the subordinates. In the case of the pope (and
Nicholas quotes the *Liber Sextus* on this) this consent is
given by the college of cardinals on behalf of the whole
church, while for the emperor (and here there is a reference to the canonist, Joannes Andreae) the electors give the
consent of the people.[9]

Yet the canon law references cited do not state directly
the doctrine of natural freedom and equality on which
Nicholas bases his theory of consent. One source for this
may have been Roman law, since Cusanus' statement that
all men are "by nature equally free" resembles the passage in Justinian's *Institutes,* "By the law of nature, all
men from the beginning were born free." The parallelism
of the text with that of Cusanus and the probability that
the youthful *doctor decretorum* would be familiar with the
opening chapters of the *Institutes* are arguments for Roman
law as one influence on his theory of consent derived from
equality.

8 See especially the references to the *Decretum* quoted in *DCC,* Book
II, chap. xviii, pp. 199-200, and chap. xxxii, pp. 276-278.
9 *DCC,* Book II, chap. xiii, p. 151; Book III, chap. iv, p. 345.

The Roman law text of the *lex regia* was also utilized by Nicholas to prove the derivation of the emperor's authority from popular consent. It was familiar to the canon lawyers from the discussion in medieval Roman law commentaries of the nature of the original transfer of authority from the people to the emperor, a controversy to which Nicholas refers in his discussion of the empire. As noted above, the principle, "What touches all should be approved by all," which appears in various forms in Nicholas' discussion of consent, was also ultimately derived from Roman law.[10]

The basis for consent in Nicholas' theory goes beyond mere citation of Roman and canon law texts. More fundamentally the appeal is to natural law. It is nature which has created all men free and equal, just as it has given some more wisdom than others. Nature requires that the wise rulers be chosen by the election and consent of their subjects. The doctrine of natural equality and liberty, as old as the Stoics, becomes the cornerstone of Cusanus' conciliarism and his philosophy of political obligation.[11]

The argument from nature in Cusanus' theory is used in two different directions. The hierarchical structure of the universe and the unequal distribution of reason among men are the natural bases for social hierarchy and the rule of the wise. Yet there is also a natural equality of moral freedom, and possibly of physical power, from which is derived the requirement of consent to government. The possibility of a conflict between the two claims to legitimacy is avoided because the universe is purposive and har-

[10] *DCC*, Book III, chap. iv, p. 352. A slightly altered version of the *quod omnes* clause, derived from Gratian, also appears in Book II, chap. xxxii, pp. 276-277.

[11] Principal references are *DCC*, Book II, chap. xi, p. 143, and chap. xviii, p. 199, as well as Book III, chap. iv, p. 346. For other discussions of natural law as the basis of all other laws, see Book II, chap. xiv, p. 160, and repeated references in the preface to Book III.

monious, and "by a certain natural instinct, the rule of the wise and the subjection of the ignorant are brought into harmony by common laws of which the wise are the authors, protectors, and executors with the agreement of all the others, concurring to this in voluntary subjection."[12]

When he discusses natural law, Nicholas ignores the elaborate system of distinctions developed by St. Thomas in the *Summa Theologica* (I^a II^{ae}, q. 90-97). For Cusanus as for the canonists, the natural law is bracketed together with the divine law. "Against this conclusion (the necessity of consent to law), no prescriptive right or customary usage can prevail, since they can not violate natural and divine law, from which this conclusion is drawn." "Every ecclesiastical order has rulers, who are ultimately subject to one ruler, but all those rulers, according to divine and natural law, must be established by consent."[13]

As Nicholas conceives it, the consent of the faithful forms the precondition for the grant of authority by God to the ecclesiastical superior who rules in union with Christ, the

12 *DCC,* Book III, preface, p. 317. "Et sic naturali quodam instinctu praesidentia sapientum et subiectio insipientum redacta ad concordiam exsistit per communes leges, quarum ipsi sapientes maxime auctores, conservatores, et executores exsistunt, aliorum omnium ad hoc per voluntariam subiectionem concurrente assensu."

13 *DCC,* Book II, chap. xi, p. 143 and chap. xviii, p. 199. "Et contra hanc conclusionem nulla prescriptio vel consuetudo valere potest, sicut nec contra jus divinum et naturale, a quo ista conclusio dependet." ". . . omnis ordo ecclesiasticus rectoribus utitur, in quibus demum ad unum devenitur, isti autem rectores per consensum jure divino et naturali constitui deberent." For other instances of the coupling of natural and divine law, see Book II, chap. xxxii, p. 281, chap. xxxiv, p. 304, and Book III, chap. iv, p. 346. Cusanus follows the canonist usage which practically identifies the *jus divinum* with the *jus naturale,* the one being the divine archetype of the other. This contrasts with the sharp distinction both as to origin and content which St. Thomas Aquinas draws between the two types of law. For numerous examples of the canonist attitude, see Ullmann, *Medieval Papalism,* pp. 40-42. A possible influence on Cusanus' thought on the subject is a work by his teacher, Heimericus de Campo, *Collectio posicionum iuris naturalis divini et humani philosophice doctrinalium,* now in the library at Kues (cf. Marx, *Verzeichnis,* no. 106, 9, p. 106).

head of the body of the church. When he discusses the relationship of God, as the source of all authority, and the people who give their consent to a ruler, he uses the Aristotelian categories of act and potency, matter and form, in a way which once more demonstrates the complete parallelism in his thought between the basis of rule in empire and papacy.

> It is an admirable observation that all power both spiritual and temporal or corporeal rests potentially in the people, although, for the power to rule to be established, the form-giving radiance must be granted from above to set it into being, since all power is from above (I speak of rightly ordered power). This is rightly so, just as the earth is the raw material from whose potentialities heavenly influences draw forth the various vegetable and sensible beings.[14]

The grant of authority by God follows the choice by the people so that the ruler receives his authority both from above and below. This is the way in which Nicholas and other medieval thinkers reconcile two apparently opposed opinions—the theological doctrine that the ruler's power comes from God, and the legal derivation of the ruler's authority from the people. The concordant mean position *(medium concordantiae)* is that "rulership is from God through men and councils, by elective consent."[15]

The consent theory of Cusanus is not only based on legal

14 *DCC*, Book II, chap. xix, p. 205. "Et pulchra est haec speculatio, quomodo in populo omnes potestates tam spirituales in potentia latent quam etiam temporales et corporales, licet ad hoc, quod ipsa praesidentialis potestas in actu constituatur, necessario desuper concurrere habeat radius formativus, qui hanc constituat in esse, quoniam omnis potestas desursum est—et loquor de ordinata potestate—recte, sicut terra est faex elementorum de cuius tamen potentia mediante influentia caelesti varia vegetabilia et sensibilia educuntur."

15 *DCC*, Book II, chap. xxxiv, p. 293. See also page 306 of the same chapter. On the two sources of legitimacy in medieval thought, see Ullmann, *Principles,* and Kantorowicz, *King's Two Bodies, passim.*

or natural law sources. It is also influenced by theological and philosophical concepts which are not drawn from the canonistic or natural law tradition. Although we have already identified the principal theological and philosophical influences on Cusa as hierarchical in nature, and subversive of the principle of consent as the basis of political obligation, there are also elements in Cusanus' theology which are used to justify his emphasis on consent.

Consent is mentioned in Book I of *De Concordantia* even before Cusanus tries to develop his conciliar theory. Here the analogy of matrimonial consent is used to describe the consent of the man who is resolved to do God's will.[16] This harmonious acceptance of God's will is the basis of Cusanus' theological conception of consent. Twice Nicholas quotes the Pseudo-Isidorean Decretals to prove that "God is present where there is simple consent without deformity." The very fact that many people agree or consent to a given ruler or action is a sign that God is inspiring them in their action. The church councils too are characterized by consent, if they are divinely inspired, and where they have disagreed, inspiration ceases, for "where there is dissent, there is no council."[17]

Consent establishes "a spiritual matrimonial union" like that between Christ and His church. This theological conception of consent to law and government is characterized by a harmonious unity marking the presence of the Holy Spirit, a mystical agreement which is the proof that the assembled group has come to the right decision. Probably *consensus,* the English transliteration of the Latin word which Nicholas uses, is a more accurate rendering of this

16 *DCC,* Book I, chap. iv, p. 46.
17 *DCC,* Book II, chap. x, p. 138, and chap. xix, p. 205. "Ibi enim est Deus, ubi simplex sine pravitate consensus." *DCC,* Book II, chap. i, p. 93. "Qui enim sibi dissentiunt, non agunt concilium."

unanimous agreement. The hierarchical outlook could be combined with it without difficulty. While Plato, for instance, never considered consent as a source of legitimacy, he believed that, given the proper conditions, the citizens of his ideal state would agree unanimously on what was to their own good. Dissent was a sign of moral and intellectual failing on the part of the citizen, and the dissenter had to be re-educated or removed. Consent, as unanimous consensus, would result from the conformity of the system to objective justice.

The emphasis on consensus and unanimity is also characteristic of a traditional society which is not aware of, or not willing to recognize, alternative modes of thought and action. Yet with the development of legal theory a new conception of consent was emerging in Western Europe, particularly in economic relations. Decisions on the disposition of property by corporate groups in the churches, municipalities, and guilds were taken by majorities and minorities, and a different mode of thought was developed which was reflected in the application of the rules of election, consent, and representation to the lower ranks of the church and ultimately to the entire *universitas fidelium*.

De Concordantia Catholica contained elements both of the integralist and the legalistic views of consent. Nicholas seems to be approaching a doctrine of majority rule in the church when he says, "Wherefore the body of priests, although it is transitory, mortal, and subject to error in its members, is never in error as a whole, where always a majority *(major pars)* remains in the faith and law of Christ."[18] A similar conception with perhaps some allowance for a weighted vote also appears in his discussion of

[18] DCC, Book I, chap. viii, p. 63. "Quare corpus sacerdotale, licet caducum et mortale et deviabile in membris, non tamen in toto, quando semper maior pars in fide et lege Christi permaneat. . ."

the empire. "When, by common consent, the welfare of the community is discussed, the majority of the people, citizens, and illustrious men *(heroicorum)* will not fail from the right course at the proper time."[19] Yet, in his discussion of the council, he insists that the minority formally endorse the decision of the majority after the vote so as to produce the required unanimity, especially in the definition of doctrine.[20] Always in the back of his mind was the theological belief in the action of the Holy Spirit working to inspire the harmonious agreement of head and members in both church and empire. Reflecting the divergent traditions which were combined in his thought, and the ambivalence present in the council for which he was writing, Cusanus' consent theory was both a legal conception involving majorities and minorities and head-counting and a theologically inspired theory of unanimous consensus. The theological aspects of his consent theory are very important in assessing the reasons for the later change of position to the side of the pope in 1437.

There are other elements in Cusanus' theory besides canon law and theology. The influence of William of Occam and of Marsilius are evident in the following passage, which combines with the Roman law doctrine of original liberty Marsilius' view of law as regulative of external acts and Occam's doctrine of Christian liberty as a restraint on the ruler's right to impose obligations on his subjects.

For those who were previously completely free submit themselves to a ruler whom they have placed over themselves by

19 *DCC,* Book III, preface, p. 314. "Dum communi consensu res pro conservatione rei publicae tractantur, maior pars populi civium aut heroicorum a recta via ac pro tempore utili non deficiet." The term *heroici* seems to have been borrowed from a discussion of the Roman republic in Marsilius, *Defensor Pacis,* Dictio I, chap. ix, v. 10.
20 *DCC,* Book II, chap. xv, p. 170.

election. . . . Although all power is from above . . . in order for it to regulate and compel free Christian men to external action, right rule requires their free subjection, since, by the law of Christian faith and by natural law, they may not be compelled beyond the limits of liberty.[21]

Once the principle that legitimacy comes from consent is established, the next problem is how to put the principle into practice. Here Nicholas develops an elaborate program by which he attempts to expand and extend certain existing practices to an over-all system of consent to law and government. In prescribing what was necessary for reform of church and empire, he could then claim that what he was doing was returning to the old ways which had fallen into disuse, rather than attempting to institute any radical innovations. In this, his proposals are typically medieval in their approach, and on every occasion he is ready to make compromises with existing reality rather than call for radical reform of the type that Marsilius, for instance, had demanded. For all the implicit radicalism of his consent theory, Nicholas is essentially a conservative in his approach to governmental institutions, attempting to combine into one harmonious whole all the elements of the often antithetical traditions which preceded him. When events proved that the structure which he had erected could not bear the burden he had laid upon it, he abandoned it, and recreated out of the same elements a theory which led to very different institutional conclusions.

In *De Concordantia,* specific procedures and institutions

21 *DCC,* Book II, chap. xxxiv, p. 304. "Qui enim prius liberrimi erant eligendo super se praesidem se ei subiciunt. . . Quamquam omnis potestas desursum sit . . . ut ipsa extrinsece in actum prorumpere possit homines liberos Christianos regulando vel cogendo, tunc recta regula praerequirit subiectionem liberam eorum cum ipsi ex lege fidei Christianae et naturali jure non artarentur extra terminos libertatis."

are recommended for the expression of the people's consent. It is first expressed by election of the rulers in both church and empire by the representatives of the people. In the case of the pope, election is carried out by the cardinals who act as representatives of the church provinces. Elections are to be held in each of the lower ranks as well. The curates should be elected or at least appointed with the consent of the people. The clergy with the consent of the laity should elect the bishops. The bishops with the consent of the clergy should elect the archbishops or provincial metropolitans. The metropolitans are to choose their legates "who are called cardinals" to assist the pope, and the cardinals with the consent of the metropolitans choose the pope. The whole program is supported by numerous references to Gratian's *Decretum,* but, needless to say, this was a somewhat idealized version of what actually happened in the selection of the church hierarchy.[22]

The emperor is chosen by the electors, "representing the German people and the others who were subject to the empire at the time of Henry II."[23] Although Cusanus allowed for a hereditary monarch, a system which could also conform to the principle of consent by the election of a king "with his successors," his clearly expressed preference was for a new election for each ruler, "by all or a

22 Elections were carried on, although not in exactly the hierarchical fashion recommended by Cusanus. The most notable divergence from his scheme was the selection of the cardinals, who, then as now, were simply appointed by the pope. Bishops were elected by the cathedral chapters and not by the entire clergy of the diocese. For the description of the entire hierarchical program, see *DCC,* Book II, chap. xviii, pp. 200-201. See also chap. xxxii, p. 281, for the three requirements for the selection of bishops: election by the clergy, consent of the pope, and approval by the metropolitan.

23 *DCC,* Book III, chap. iv, p. 348.

majority, or at least by the leaders who by their consent represent the others."[24] The ultimate right of election, however, belongs to the whole people, who have transferred it to the college of cardinals or to the imperial electors, as the case may be. They can take back the right to make law and depose the ruler at any time, if they wish. "The people have transferred, that is, conceded, power to the emperor, for they have kept for themselves the power to withdraw it. . . It is the common opinion of scholars that the Roman people can take away from the emperor the power to make laws, because the emperor has this power from the people."[25]

What is true of the emperor is also true of the pope. He too can be deposed, and not only for heresy but also for neglect of duty or even for reasons of convenience (*quando inutiliter administraret*).[26]

So far, there seems to be no opportunity for controlling the ruler short of deposition, a rather extreme measure not likely to be utilized in normal circumstances. However, the requirement of consent applies not only to the selection of the ruler, but also to the passage of laws for the whole commonwealth, although here Nicholas is much more ready to introduce important qualifications which considerably diminish the force of his theory.

In the case of the church, the influence of Durandus is evident when Cusanus states that universal statutes ought to be made by universal councils, "since, according to divine

24 *DCC,* Book III, preface, p. 322. ". . . non est melior quisquam statuendi modus, quam per novam electionem omnium aut maioris partis, vel saltem eorum procerum, qui omnium vices ex consensu habent."
25 *DCC,* Book III, chap. iv, p. 352. ". . . et hoc est commune omnium peritorum dictum, potestatem condendi leges populum Romanum ab imperatore tollere posse, quoniam ab ipsis potestatem habet." For the various opinions concerning the character of the transfer of power from the people to the emperor, see Carlyle, *History,* vol. II, chap. vii.
26 *DCC,* Book II, chap. xviii, p. 197.

and natural law, the power to enact legislation depends on common consent." At numerous other points in the treatise, he insists that laws and conciliar decrees can only have force *(vigor, robur)* if they have consent.[27]

Nicholas is aware that this is not the practice in the church of his time, but he cites the canon law doctrine requiring that a law be accepted and approved by usage in order for it to be true law. It is the actual observance by the church which determines which of the conflicting conciliar decisions and church laws will be observed, he says. In the case of papal legislation, the pope has acquired this function *ex longa consuetudine* by tacit consent of the church.[28]

A similar radicalism in theory and conservatism in practice is observed when Cusanus speaks of legislation in the empire. From his argument from natural equality in the second book of the *Concordantia,* and from some of the opening passages of the third book, he seems to be advocating a doctrine of majority rule in making laws. Adopting the argument of Marsilius (without, however, mentioning his source), he asserts:

> Legislation ought to be adopted by all or a majority of those who are to be bound by it. . . What touches all ought to be approved by all. . . Nor can there be any possibility of being excused from obedience to a law when each one has imposed it on himself.[29]

27 Consent is said to give force to law in *DCC,* Book II, chap. viii, p. 130, chap. x, p. 137, chap. xii, pp. 143-144, chap. xiii, p. 160, and Book III, chap. xviii, p. 396. The quotation is from Book II, chap. xi, pp. 142-143, and a similar statement appears in chap. x, p. 137.

28 *DCC,* Book II, chap. xi, pp. 139 and 143. Cf. article by Luigi de Luca cited in Chapter IV, note 8.

29 *DCC,* Book III, preface, p. 318. "Legis autem latio per eos omnes qui per eam stringi debent aut maiorem partem aliorum electione fieri debet . . . quod omnes tangit ab omnibus approbari debet. . . Nec potest excusatio de obedientia legum sibi tunc locum vindicare, quando quisque sibi ipsi legem condidit." Cf. Marsilius, *Defensor Pacis,* D. I, chap. xii, v. 6.

Yet in the same discussion, Nicholas proposes that the laws be made by the rationally superior to whom the less intelligent will consent "by a natural instinct," assuring that the lower orders will submit freely to rule by their betters, and by obeying their laws give tacit consent to them, just as in obeying the emperor the people give their tacit consent to the choice of the imperial electors.[30] The reliance on tacit consent and natural subordination assures that the bold theory announced at the outset is not to become a program of radical democracy.

When there is express consent to law, it is given through synods and councils at various levels in each hierarchy. In the church "there are different types of synods, because they have different ranks from local councils through various intermediate levels up to the universal council." "The only real canonical laws are those which have been adopted by synods because these synods represent, according to their rank, a province, a country, or the whole church."[31]

There is a corresponding structure in the empire. The emperor chosen by the electors acting as representatives of the whole people must govern according to laws made by the imperial council, corresponding to the *concilium universale* in the church. The same thing is true of all rulers, since "it is fitting that whatever concerns the whole commonwealth be legislated and decided in a council of the leaders and lords of both estates; and the king should execute these by the agreement of the council. For this

---

30 *DCC*, Book III, chap. iv, p. 352.
31 *DCC*, Book II, chap. i, p. 93. "Est autem varia synodus, quoniam graduationes suas habet a particulari usque universalem per media varia." *DCC*, Book II, chap. xi, p. 140. "Ex quo habetur quod recte illa sunt canonica statuta quae sunt synodice constituta, quoniam synodus repraesentat secundum suam qualitatem aut provinciam aut regnum aut universalem ecclesiam."

order is the rule according to which the subjects wish the power of the king to be directed."[32] As in the church, for the ruler to change the law he must convene the council, although, like the pope, the emperor or king has the power to grant dispensations. To consent to these dispensations and to advise him, the ruler should also have a daily council of advisers, paralleling the function in the church of the college of cardinals.[33]

Nicholas does not discuss the arrangements at lower levels of the empire. However, it seems likely that from the parallelism of structure which is at the heart of Cusanus' constitutional conception for church and empire, he would favor an arrangement similar to the system proposed for lower ecclesiastical offices—local, regional, and provincial councils—were it not for the disfavor with which this would be regarded by the German nobility.

The voting procedure in the councils is not outlined in detail, but, in keeping with Cusanus' hierarchical conceptions, special weight would be given to more important representatives. In the church council, Cusanus warns that "discretion, prudence, and authority ought to be duly weighted, lest the judgment of the ignorant whose number is infinite outnumber the votes of the wise."[34] In the empire, the *ratione vigentes* would draw up laws which would receive the consent of all or the *major pars* of the less intelligent. When Nicholas is writing under the influence of Marsilius, the *major pars* becomes the *valentior*

[32] *DCC*, Book III, chap. xii, p. 375. "Unde opportunum est in concilio utriusque status primatum et praesulum cuncta universalia rem publicam tangentia statui et ordinari. Illius vero sic per concordiam constituti exsecutor rex esse debet. Quoniam est ipsa constitutio regula secundum quam subjecti potestatem regis ordinatam esse volunt."

[33] *DCC*, Book III, chap. xii, p. 376.

[34] *DCC*, Book II, chap. xvi, p. 172. "Discretio et prudentia et auctoritas merito ponderari debet, ne fatuorum judicium, quorum infinitus est numerus, numero vota sapientum vincat."

pars or weightier part, and although he does not add Marsilius' qualification, *qualitate et quantitate,* this is implied in the context.[35] Probably a large part of the population would not be represented at all, their tacit consent to legislation being assumed. (Later the preponderance of the lower orders at the Council of Basel was one of the factors in Cusanus' shift of allegiance.)

In *De Concordantia Catholica* the theory of consent to law and government has been combined with earlier philosophical and theological ideas to produce two parallel hierarchies of rulers and councils in church and empire. At the top of each is the *caput,* the emperor or pope, advised by a daily council and subject to laws made by a universal council. Below each of these are lower rulers, each elected by his own council and subject to laws which the council has made. The rulers are chosen because of a natural or supernatural superiority which has been recognized and accepted by their subjects. At any point, if they are guilty of maladministration they can be deposed, but under normal circumstances the subjects defer to the wisdom and knowledge of their rulers, and give their consent to the laws which are made by the wiser among them in representative legislative councils. "The diversity of rank and rulers and subjects works for the well-being of the commonwealth so that, since the lower show reverence for their superiors, and the rulers demonstrate their love for those under them, a real harmony emerges from this diversity and the responsibilities of each office are carried out."[36]

---

[35] *DCC,* Book III, preface, p. 315. Cf. Marsilius, *Defensor Pacis,* D. I, chap. xii, v. 3-5, and chap. xiii, v. 2.

[36] *DCC,* Book II, chap. xxxii, p. 277. "Diversitas enim ordinum praepositorum et subiectorum pro conservatione rei publicae ordinata est ut dum reverentiam exhibent minores potioribus et potiores minoribus dilectionem, vera concordia ex diversitate contexeretur et recte officiorum generaretur administratio."

This theory differs from later consent theories in a number of ways. While based on a subjective element, consent, it assumes an objective order to which that consent must be given. The modern (and Aristotelian) conception of a variety of political forms, adapted to history and circumstances, is absent from Nicholas' thought. Consent is to be given to a fixed political and ecclesiastical order, which is part of the natural order of the universe, designed by God. The people have no right to choose their form of government although they may choose between individuals to occupy the ruling positions.

Cusanus' theory is not a theory of individualism like that of John Locke, for example. Consent is given by corporate groups rather than by individuals in a state of nature or facing an absolute monarch who personifies the sovereign power. The individual is not considered in abstraction from his social life but is always viewed in relation to his hierarchical status in the social and ecclesiastical orders. To someone far down in those hierarchies, consent may mean nothing more than tacit acceptance of an hereditary monarch and customary laws, and, although the members of the universal councils or imperial diets may be said to have rights against the pope or emperor, notably that of deposition and refusal of consent to unjust laws, the concept of rights inherent in the individual (apart from the one right of consent, express or tacit) is lacking from Cusanus' theory.

Above all, the right of revolution, especially in the sense of a violent overturn of the whole social order, is notably absent, and Nicholas is especially strong in his strictures against those who break their feudal oaths in order to make war on their lords. The only limit on the ruler is possible deposition by his council in cases of abuse of power, and this limit, for historical reasons, is stated much more explicitly in the case of the pope than in that of the emperor. As the history of the Council of Basel indicates, this could be a rather effective threat in certain special circumstances, but was normally such an extreme remedy as to be virtually useless.

The claim of the right of participation in lawmaking for the council could also be a very important restraint on the ruler, but Nicholas vacillates on the question of consent to law and ultimately seems to accept tacit consent or agreement through customary observance of a law as tantamount to the consent which he requires for a valid law.

If constitutionalism is defined as "effective restraints on governmental action,"[37] Nicholas of Cusa's proposals might be the basis for a constitutional system. The rulers would be elected (for life) and would be subjected to removal by representative assemblies which would also be charged with making the laws to be executed by the rulers. While this would be closer to the modern British than to the American constitutional system (since the executive, the emperor, pope, or other ruler, would also participate in the representative councils), in the event of disagreement between the ruler and council, the council could depose the ruler.

In addition to constitutional elements derived from consent, the hierarchical elements in Cusanus' theory also contain some notion of restraint on power. Local activities would be regulated by local rulers and assemblies, regional affairs by their own executive and legislative organs, and so on, up to the emperor and his great council. A similar type of federal decentralization would also be applied to the church.

Yet Nicholas' proposal is a mixture of existing institu-

[37] Carl J. Friedrich, *Constitutional Government and Democracy* (Boston, 1950), p. 26.

tions and proposed radical reforms. The councils which were central to his system were in fact made up not of elected representatives but of persons who held their positions by reason of heredity or ordination to ecclesiastical office by a superior authority. The hierarchical order which he proposed could and often did degenerate into feudal anarchy. Consent became tacit acceptance, representation became hereditary and appointive, controls on the ruler unenforceable, and Cusanus' constitutionalism illusory.

Nicholas was not primarily interested in establishing an elaborate system of controls on the ruler. What he hoped for was spontaneous agreement, a harmonious concord of ruler and ruled, head and members, working together in a spirit of free cooperation. In his thought there is no conception of an intrinsic need for institutional checks as a permanent part of the system, and what restraint on power there is, is dictated by a moral *a priori*, the notion of *libera subjectio*, not by any belief in the virtue of institutionalized limits on power. In fact, if there is continued dissent or disagreement, this is a sign that there is something fundamentally wrong with the system—that the Holy Spirit has left it, that it is no longer achieving divinely inspired agreement. Nicholas of Cusa's ideal is a free union of wills consenting to two hierarchies of ever-widening corporative units, each composed of mutually interacting head and members working together in harmony to produce the *Concordantia Catholica*.

CHAPTER VII

. . .

THE CONSTITUTION
OF THE CHURCH

IN FACT, for the last fifty years there had been anything but harmony and concord in the church. Two, and later three, popes had each claimed supreme authority, and only the action of the Council of Constance had terminated the schism. The choice of a single pope did not end the dissension because, in ending the schism, the council issued decrees which declared that it was superior to the pope and called for the convocation of general councils at stated intervals in the future. The Council of Basel, called in pursuance of these decrees (but also because of the dangers of the Hussite heresy in Bohemia) met in 1431 in the presence of the papal legate, Cardinal Giuliano Cesarini. Shortly after its convocation the pope attempted to dissolve it.

De Concordantia Catholica was written in the period of dissension between the pope and the council, and, for all its praise of the ideal of harmonious cooperation of the various organs of the church, it was compelled to define the precise jurisdiction of the universal council and its relationship to the pope. The Council of Constance had successfully deposed the competing claimants to the papacy. The Council of Basel was successfully resisting an attempt by Pope Eugene to dissolve it. In these circumstances, Nicholas of Cusa in developing his conciliar theories could not avoid answering the questions posed by these developments. Is the council superior to the pope?

Can it depose him? Can it infallibly define church doctrine even in the pope's absence? Is the pope the only one who can call a council? Once called, can it continue over his opposition or even his active attempts to dissolve it?

The composition of the council itself had to be examined. Various voting procedures had been utilized at Constance and Basel, and different ranks of the laity and clergy were present in Basel. It had to be decided which of them could speak and vote on conciliar questions The place of the pope and of the papal legate or legates in the council also had to be determined.

The place to look for guidance on these essentially legal questions, for Nicholas as for most of the conciliarists before him, was the canon law. Gratian's *Decretum,* although never an official collection of canon law, was his source for the law and practice of the church.

The *Decretum* provided ammunition for both sides in the conciliar controversy. On the one hand, it described the pope as head of the church whose decisions could not be disobeyed. The first see *(prima sedes)* was to be judged by no one. The pope called the council, and his presence in it was necessary.[1] On the other hand, the apostles (and their successors) were described as holding the same honor and power as Peter. Cyprian's doctrine of a single episcopate governing the church was quoted, as was Pope Gregory the Great's denial that the title of "universal bishop" should be applied to himself. The *Decretum* also included Augustine's interpretation of Christ's promise to build his church on "this rock" as a reference not to Peter but to Christ, in whom Peter had expressed his faith. Even the power of the keys ("I will give thee the keys of the king-

---

[1] See the *Decretum,* D. 12 c. 1; C. 3 q. 6 c. 9; D. 21 c. 7; and D. 17 c. 2-6. Other propapal statements appear in D. 19 c. 5; D. 22 c. 7; and C. 9 q. 3 c. 6.

dom of heaven") had been interpreted by St. Augustine and many canonists who followed him as a grant to the whole church, not to Peter alone. Most important of all was the statement that the pope could be judged if *deprehendatur a fide devius*—a case which had been extended by the canon law commentators to any situation where the pope scandalized the church.[2]

It seems that, like Holy Scripture, the *Decretum* was capable of being quoted to support many different positions. The problem set for Nicholas of Cusa was how to reconcile these contradictory statements and establish a synthesis of the papalist and the conciliarist positions which would satisfy both sides—but which, since he was writing for the council, would be basically conciliar in tone.

In the earlier chapter on Cusanus' ideas on hierarchy, we have seen that in Book I of *De Concordantia* he attempted to combine the idea of the equality of all bishops and the supremacy of the pope by distinguishing between a hierarchy based on Holy Orders—the power to dispense the sacraments—and a hierarchy based on *presidentia regitiva,* the power to rule and assign various offices—what the canonists had called the power of jurisdiction. The reason for the establishment of this hierarchy of rule with the pope at its summit was always given in conciliar theory as the avoidance of schism—*propter tollendum schisma,* a phrase taken from a letter of St. Jerome.[3] This would seem to imply some role in defining doctrines of faith, since most divisions were precisely over this issue. However, the conciliarists used it to prove that the pope's role was merely that of allocation of duties and general adminis-

2 *Decretum,* D. 21 c. 2; C. 2 q. 7 c. 35; C. 24 q. 1 c. 18; C. 11 q. 3 c. 87; and especially D. 40 c. 6.
3 The first letter of St. Jerome to Jovinian, cited in *DCC,* Book I, chap. vi, p. 57. This was a commonplace of conciliar theory, since the first part of the quotation speaks of Peter as elected by the other apostles.

tration. The pope is *major in administratione,* but he does not have the power to define matters of faith.

This is Nicholas' first argument for the superiority of the council to the pope. Recalling the episcopalist theories of Durandus discussed earlier, he says that as far as the direct grant of power by God is concerned, the highest sacerdotal grade in the church is that of bishop, and the pope has no special position in the council except a primacy of honor. The council is a meeting of all bishops including the pope, the Bishop of Rome. "The supreme council is the council of the whole Catholic church where all bishops in harmony assemble either in person or by representatives, or at least all bishops have been called and have the possibility of attending."[4] This is the body which defines church law, makes policy, and can (as at Constance) elect the pope.

This is the theory put forward in those parts of *De Concordantia Catholica* in which Nicholas emphasizes the distinctive character of the priesthood and episcopacy. It relies upon the records of early councils, and especially on the quotations of theories contained in the *Decretum.* The argument is based on hierarchy rather than consent, but the hierarchy goes no further than the rank of bishop, and the pope is an administrative agent of the council of equal bishops.

4 *De Auctoritate Presidendi in Concilio Generali (DAP),* ed. Kallen, p. 22. This work was written in February 1434, a few months after the completion of *De Concordantia Catholica.* There is no reason not to take it together with *De Concordantia* as forming a single body of theory. The original text of the definition is ". . . supremum concilium est universalis totius catholice ecclesie, ubi conveniunt cum potestate per se vel legatos consentientes omnes episcopi, vel saltem vocati sunt et possunt interesse." *DCC,* Book II, chap. i, pp. 93-94, quotes the canon law definition of the council as composed of "the pope and his legate with all the bishops." Cf. also Book III, chap. xiv, p. 385, where Cusanus restricts the council to bishops and those allowed by them to participate.

The episcopalist approach is also followed in Cusanus' short work, *De Auctoritate Presidendi in Concilio Generali (On the Authority to Preside at the General Council)*, where he argues that while the papal legates must be seated as part of the council, and, as a recognition of the honor of the papal chair, may also be given the power to chair meetings in the sense of deciding the order of business and speeches *(presidentia directiva, ordinativa, et ministerialis)*, they do not have any authority over the meeting nor can they make any judicial or punitive decisions *(presidentia auctoritativa et judicativa)*.[5]

According to the episcopalist conception, the church is a federation of virtually independent bishoprics which form a single episcopate. The bishops meet periodically to decide on doctrine and church laws. For the intervals between meetings, one of these bishops has been chosen by them, just as the apostles chose Peter at the foundation of the church, to exercise certain administrative and executive functions, described by Cusanus as "the avoidance of schism" and the representation of the unity of the church.[6]

A second argument which Nicholas uses for the superiority of the council to the pope is the argument from consent. Government, to be justified, must be based upon the express or tacit consent of the governed, and universal church laws should have the consent of the universal church. Peter was chosen head of the apostles by Christ with the consent of the apostles. The pope also receives his power by consent of the church. If the church wished, it could decide that Trier rather than Rome should be the head of

5 *DAP*, p. 12.

6 *DCC*, Book I, chap. xi, pp. 68-69; Book II, chap. xiii, pp. 149-51, and chap. xxxiv, p. 302. Note that in summarizing his position at the end of chap. xii of Book II, Nicholas asserts that the pope is "primus super alios" and does not use the usual episcopalist formulation, "primus inter pares."

the church, but Rome was chosen because of its administrative importance, its age and divine privilege, and because so many apostles and martyrs had died there.[7] The council is the fullest expression of the consent of the faithful to church law and to papal rule. In the event that that rule is abused, it is also the instrument through which that consent can be withdrawn by deposition.

Here the Council is regarded not as an assembly of bishops possessing special orders but as the embodiment of the consent of the *congregatio fidelium.* However, unlike Marsilius and Occam, Nicholas never draws from his doctrine of universal consent the doctrine that the laity should participate and vote in the council. The members of his council are still priests, not subject to the control of laymen. When Nicholas defines the universal council as the congregation or assembly gathered together *(congregatio sive ecclesia congregata)* from all the members of the universal Catholic church, he is careful to explain that the laity will be excluded as participants, except as witnesses to decisions on dogma. The council is made up of priests and bishops gathered together directly or through representatives *(actu vel virtualiter).*[8] If government and law are to be made with the consent of those under them, it is difficult to defend the exclusion of the laity from the councils. However, the priests could in some sense be said to

7 *DCC,* Book I, chap. xvi, p. 87; Book II, chap. xiii, p. 152; Book II, chap. xvii, p. 179, chap. xxxiv, p. 305. Cf. the argument of Marsilius, *Defensor Pacis,* Dictio II, chap. xxii. What the *divinum privilegium* comprises is never made clear. If it is in some sense divine protection from error, this would undercut the argument that the church could choose any city as its head.

8 In the opening pages of Book II, Nicholas defines the council as composed of the pope and bishops. In later sections of the book, however, he is willing to admit other priests. They should not be admitted *indifferenter.* Only chosen and learned ecclesiastics (like himself) are to be allowed to participate. See *DCC,* Book II, chap. xvi, pp. 171-172, and Book III, chap. xvii, pp. 392-393.

represent the laity since, in Cusanus' theory, the priests are to be chosen with the consent of the laity. He quotes Cyprian's opinion that the *plebs* should have the power to elect and refuse priests, and insists that priests should at least be appointed with popular consent, in the sense that no one should be appointed to whom the people are opposed.[9]

Of course, if Cusanus takes the view that only those in Holy Orders are capable of making decisions on church doctrine, it is very easy to defend the exclusion of the laity. In essence, this is what he is saying when he calls the priesthood the soul of the church, constituted by the Holy Spirit to rule it. However, this hierarchical justification of rulership does not correspond with his doctrine of legitimacy from consent.

Since most of the members of the church, both clergy and laity, were excluded from the council, a theory of representation was necessary to explain the identification of the council with the church. Nicholas must also have known that Occam, in his *Dialogus,* although granting infallibility to the church as a whole, had specifically denied it to the council, precisely because he did not believe that a representative could exercise all the powers of the person represented. In addition, the papalists had their own theory of representation, according to which the pope represented or personified the church in a mystical way which made it impossible to conceive of the church or the council as ranged against him. In order to argue from the natural law requirement of consent to the superiority of the council, Nicholas had to develop a theory of representation to explain why the general council was the best expression of the consent of the whole church. The theory which he

9 *DCC,* Book II, chap. xviii, p. 200, chap. xxxii, p. 278.

developed to do this becomes very important later for an understanding of his change of position in 1437.[10]

The first time Cusanus discusses representation is in Book I, after he has developed the theory of the equality of all bishops and the unity of the episcopate. The bishop represents his diocese *per unionem,* since the church is in the bishop. The bishop symbolizes and represents his flock as a public person *(persona publica).*[11] Similarly, Peter confessed his faith in Christ and received the power of the keys and the promise of infallibility ("the gates of hell shall not prevail against thee") as a representative and "figure" of the church. As first of the apostles he represented and embodied *(gerebat personam)* the church.[12] In all these cases, representation is defined as personification of the body represented.

In the eighteenth chapter of Book II, there is a lengthy discussion of the representative character of the pope and the council in relation to the church as a whole. The Augustinian conception of the pope as the "figure" of the church is repeated, but now the pope is said to represent the church "in a very confused fashion" *(confusissime).*

10 For discussion of representation theory in Nicholas of Cusa's writings, see Kallen's introduction to *DAP,* especially pp. 73-80. His interpretation of Cusanus' representation theory as embodying the canonist conception of representation as delegation (the German *Stellvertretung),* rather than the older theories of representation as impersonation *(Vergegenwärtigung),* is challenged by Josef Koch in *Nikolaus von Cues und seine Umwelt,* in *SBH* 1944-48, no. 2 (Heidelberg, 1948), p. 24, n. 5. As subsequent discussion will indicate, both theories are reflected in Cusanus' writings. On the distinction between "delegation" and "impersonation" theories of representation, see Jacob, *Essays,* pp. 17-18; Tierney, *Foundations,* p. 126; and de Lagarde, "L'Idée de représentation."

11 *DCC,* Book I, chap. vi, pp. 58-59, chap. xv, p. 79. The same expression is applied to the emperor in Book III, chap. iv, p. 348.

12 *DCC,* Book I, chap. xi, p. 69, chap. xiii, p. 74, chap. xv, p. 78; Book II, chap. iii, p. 104, chap. xviii, p. 193, chap. xxxiv, p. 293. The interpretation is that of the *Decretum,* C. 24 q. 1 c. 6, where Augustine is cited. In DCC, Book III, chap. xxxiv, p. 293, the original text from Augustine is quoted.

Moreover, the pope is not absolutely infallible, while the universal council represents the church more clearly (*certius*), "and it is always better in judgment than the single pontiff who is a more uncertain representative."[13] Why is the council more representative than the pope? It contains other hierarchical ranks than the highest, for example, the patriarchs, cardinals, and archbishops, and "the more specific the headship, the more certain is the representation."[14] Thus, the pope is only remotely representative of the whole church, but he represents more certainly the groups closer to him. He represents his patriarchate better than he does the whole church, his province and diocese still better, and his clergy and diocese best of all. In accordance with the same theory, the council is superior to the pope because it better represents the consent of the whole church. It has more of the specific headships (*praesidentiae particulares*) in it, and so gives a closer approximation to the representation of the church than can the pope by himself.

In these passages Cusanus utilizes an integralist conception of representation as impersonation (the ruler in a certain way personifies his subjects) rather than the later legal theories of delegation (the representative is specifically chosen to take the place of others). The council is not superior to the pope because it is made up of representatives chosen by others to take their places, but because a larger number are present of those who "figure" or "personify" the lesser hierarchical groupings in the church. This is a different conception from the modern theory of

13 *DCC*, Book II, chap. xviii, p. 194. ". . . eius judicium . . . semper maius est iudicio unici Romani pontificis confusissime figurantis." See also *DAP*, p. 28, where the representation of the church by the pope is said to be *remotissima* and that of the council *proxima*.

14 *DCC*, Book II, chap. xviii, p. 199. ". . . quanto particulior est praesidentia, tanto certior repraesentatio."

representation involving election and control of representatives. The church officers "bear the public person" in the sense of being personally identified with all those below them, in a manner akin to Burke's view of virtual representation.[15] (Louis XIV's *l'état, c'est moi* comes to mind, and if it were not so flagrant an anachronism one would be tempted to suggest an analogy with Hitler's sense of identification with the German *Volk*.) The theory only needed the addition of a bit of Neo-Platonic philosophizing about absorptive hierarchy to provide a rationale for the papalist position which Nicholas soon assumed.

There are evidences of delegation theories of representation in the *Concordantia* as well. When Nicholas speaks of the councils, he notes that they are made up of the *praesides,* the heads of the various hierarchical ranks, and of the *legati,* apparently some type of elected representative of various communities in the church. The term *legati* is also applied to the college of cardinals. They are said to take the place of all the faithful (*aliorum omnium vices gerunt*) in electing the pope, and they represent the metropolitans of the church provinces in the day-to-day work at Rome, assisting the pope as *legati* or *vices provinciarum,* advising him "in deciding difficult decisions," and approving dispensations from church law.[16]

Presumably, on this basis, the cardinals are to be

15 Letter to Sir Hector Langrishe, quoted in Alfred de Grazia, *Public and Republic* (New York, 1951), p. 43. ". . . a communion of interests and sympathy in feelings and desires between those who act in the name of any description of the people and the people in whose name they act, though the trustees are not chosen by them."

16 *DCC*, Book II, chap. xxxiv, p. 292 and 305, chap xviii, pp. 199 and 205, chap. xxi, p. 236, chap. xxv, p. 245. Similar expressions are used with reference to the imperial electors, e.g., Book III, chap. iv, pp. 345-346. On the use of the term *legati*, see Garrett Mattingly, *Renaissance Diplomacy* (Boston, 1955), chap. ii. As applied to the cardinals the term may be borrowed from d'Ailly, although no reference is made to his works.

answerable to the heads of the provinces, since they are specifically said to take their places at Rome. At least, utilizing this theory of representation, there is a greater likelihood of the development of responsibility to the electors than in the older theory according to which the ruler, even sometimes chosen originally by election, then personifies the community. In the older theory, he does not represent the community in the sense of taking its place, he *is* the community personified, and there is no separate source of limits in the community to restrain the exercise of his power.[17]

In arguing on the basis of representation and consent, Nicholas drops the elements of sacerdotalism which are present in his first argument. Even though composed of clerics, it is not because of any divine grant of sacramental power that the council is superior to the pope; it is because it represents the whole church, both the laity and ecclesiastics. The council as representative of the whole church can give its consent to church law and elect or depose the pope.

The greater representativeness of the council also makes it superior to the pope because it is more likely to possess the divine guarantee of infallibility. It had always been believed that Christ's words, "I will be with you all days even to the end of the world" (Matt, 28:20), had promised the church that it would be free from error on matters of faith. Otherwise, as Cusanus put it in a letter to the Hus-

---

[17] General discussions of the development of medieval conceptions of representation appear in E. M. Sait, *Political Institutions* (New York, 1938), chap. xx, pp. 467-499; H. J. Ford, *Representative Government* (New York, 1924), chap. i; and Helen M. Cam, "The Theory and Practice of Representation in Medieval England," *History*, 38:11-26 (1953). The development from impersonation to delegation parallels the change from a Christ-centered to a community-centered political theory, analyzed in Kantorowicz, *King's Two Bodies*, already mentioned.

sites, the faithful would be bound to the impossible. They would be required to observe doctrine which they could not know.

Yet in whom did the infallibility reside which everyone granted to the whole church? Occam had already discussed the possibility that the true faith might reside only in baptized infants. The predominant tradition, as expressed in the *Decretum*, granted the gift of infallibility to the Roman see, variously called the *sedes apostolica* and the *cathedra Petri*, and on this basis urged obedience to its decisions.

On the other hand, certain popes were believed to have been heretics, and Nicholas cites the case of Pope Liberius, who according to Augustine had "consented to error" in acceding to Arianism under imperial pressure.[18] Distinction 40, chapter 6, of the *Decretum*, already discussed, called for passing judgment on the pope in such cases.

Cusanus sought to find a way to harmonize these apparently contradictory statements, and at the same time establish the superiority of the council on matters of faith. Turning first to the question of the infallibility of the *sedes apostolica*, he distinguishes between the see and its incumbent, between the office and the person in the office. Although individual popes may have erred, he says, the *sedes* has remained free from error. How is this possible? Nicholas explains that the *sedes* is infallible by apostolic succession. All bishops may be considered as parts of that see which was founded by Christ. Individual popes and bishops may have been in error, but Christ has guaranteed infallibility to the church so that "the line of succession or sacred *cathedra* will remain free from error until the end

18 *DCC*, Book II, chap. v, p. 108. See also Book I, chap. xiv, p. 77, for a reference to the case of the heresy of Pope Honorius.

of time."[19] A majority of the church will always have the true faith, and the church consists of "the majority of the faithful united to their bishops and to Peter and his *cathedra*."

The *sedes apostolica* and the *cathedra Petri* are not, in this usage, identical with the papacy, but apply to the whole episcopate and even the whole church. This also seems to be the sense in which the terms are used in the letters to the Bohemians discussed earlier.

A few pages after this exposition, Cusanus makes another attempt to resolve the problem. This time he is discussing the *ecclesia Romana* and trying to determine in what sense it may be said to be infallible. Utilizing the argument of d'Ailly, he says that the term *ecclesia Romana* may be applied to many different institutions. It can stand for the pope alone, for his diocese, for his metropolitan province, for the patriarchate of the West, and finally "for the church composed of all the faithful united to the church of Rome as its head." Only in the last sense may it be said that it is and always will be infallible. In so far as the whole church is now practically coextensive with the Roman partiarchate (the Greek church was in schism, and the areas of the other patriarchates—Alexandria, Jerusalem, and Antioch—were under Moslem control), the Roman patriarchate is also infallible. In descending to the lower hierarchical orders, the archbishopric, the diocese, and so forth, there is less certainty, although in every case the Roman branch of the particular ecclesiastical subdivision—diocese, province, and so on—is less likely to err than any comparable unit elsewhere in the church. If the term *ecclesia Romana* is used

---

[19] *DCC*, Book I, chap. xv, p. 78. "Est enim ipsa linea sive cathedra sancta indefectibiliter duratura usque ad saeculi consummationem." For a later use of the distinction between the office and the occupant, *sedes* and *sedens*, see below, Chapter IX, n. 36.

to mean the whole church or the Roman patriarchate, then it may be said to be infallible.[20]

This infallibility does not rest in the pope alone but in the pope in the council of bishops. The *sedes Romana* cannot err, because the synod of the Roman patriarchate is as infallible as the universal council. "When it is said that the faith of the Roman church cannot be reviewed by any universal council, this means the faith of the whole church as expressed through its patriarchal synod."[21]

In this way, Nicholas has solved the problem posed by the contradictory statements in canon law concerning the infallibility of Rome. On the one hand, the pope as an individual has erred on doctrine in the past and in this sense he is subordinate to the infallible councils. On the other hand, the *sedes Romana*, understood as the patriarchal council of Rome, is infallible and hence its faith is not subject to review by the universal council.

However, when it is a question of the pope against the universal council, the universal council is superior to the pope. It is more likely to be infallible than the pope alone since it better represents the *major pars* of the priesthood which always maintains the true faith and law of Christ. If the council is more truly representative of the infallible priesthood, it is superior to the pope who is only "remotely" or "less certainly" representative.[22]

In Nicholas' writings the universal council is not in all cases absolutely infallible. When he ascribes greater repre-

20 *DCC,* Book I, chap. xvii, pp. 88-89, and Book II, chap. vii, pp. 120-121.

21 *DDC,* Book II, chap. v, p. 107. "Ex hoc etiam elici potest fidem Romanae ecclesiae in nulla synodo universali retractari posse, hoc verum de fide illius totius ecclesiae per suam synodum, sui scilicet patriarchatus, dictata." See also a similar statement in Book II, chap. vii, p. 123.

22 *DCC,* Book I, chap. viii, p. 63, chap. xiv, p. 78; Book II, chap. iv, p. 105, chap. xxvi, p. 254.

sentativeness to the council, in the argument summarized above, he draws a somewhat less than absolute conclusion concerning the council's gift of infallibility. "As that synod represents the church less uncertainly and with a greater tendency to the truth (than the pope), so its judgment tends more away from fallibility to infallibility."[23] Cusanus seems to be propounding some type of comparative infallibility. The council is more likely to be right than the pope.

One reason that he was reluctant to ascribe absolute infallibility to all church councils was that some councils were known to have made decisions which did not agree with orthodox Catholic doctrine. Nicholas quotes Augustine to prove that the earlier councils had been corrected by later ones, and he attempts to determine what distinguishes the recognized *concilium* from the heretical *conciliabulum*.[24]

For a genuine universal council, four characteristics are required. First, the council must be properly convoked. Here Cusanus faces one of the perennial problems of the conciliar theorists. It was clearly required by church law both that the pope convoke the council and that he be present in it. Nicholas accepts this as the normal procedure, and he notes that "universal councils cannot *regularly* be celebrated without his authority . . . the convocation of a universal council belongs to the universal patriarch."[25]

However, he notes that, as a matter of fact, the first eight councils were convoked by the emperor, although he adds that "the presiding authority of the Roman pontiff was in

23 *DCC*, Book II, chap. xviii, p. 194. ". . . quanto illa synodus minus confuse plus tendendo in veritatem repraesentat, tanto ejus judicium plus a fallibilitate versus infallibilitatem tendet."

24 *DCC*, Book II, chap. vi, pp. 110-111.

25 *DCC*, Book II, chap ii, pp. 96-97. ". . . universalia concilia sine eo rite eiusve auctoritate regulariter non celebrantur. . . Ad universalem enim patriarcham spectat universalis concilii convocatio."

those councils, without which there could not have been a council, at least provided that he was willing and able to participate."[26]

What about the situation in which the pope refuses to call a council? In this case, Nicholas says, the emperor should formally request him to do so. If he will not do so and there is an immediate danger to the welfare of the church, then necessity, "which has no law," will demand that the emperor call a council. Even though the clergy are normally exempt from civil law, they must obey the emperor in this case, "since the exemption was established for the conservation of the holy church, and we revert to the methods appropriate to the time to attain the same end."[27]

Once the meeting has been called, in order for it to be a true council all the principal officers of the church must participate either in person or through representatives. This applies especially to its *rector*, the pope. Cusanus cites the canonists' analysis of the relations of *rector* and *universitas* to demonstrate that the pope cannot legislate without the participation of the *universitas,* the church council, but he also notes that this seems to make it impossible for the *universitas* to legislate in the absence of the pope. He overcomes this difficulty by suggesting that even if the universal council cannot act, all the provincial councils can meet together simultaneously and take action for the needs of the church. In this case, there would be no need

26 *DCC*, Book II, chap. ii. p. 97. ". . . in conciliis fuit semper praesidentialis Romani pontificis auctoritas, sine qua universale concilium non fuisset, dummodo saltem interesse voluisset et potuisset." Representatives of the pope were present at all eight ecumenical councils.

27 *DCC*, Book III, chap. xv, p. 388. ". . . quoniam omnia propter conservationem ipsius sanctae ecclesiae ita constituta sunt, revertimur tunc ad habendum eundem finem ad aptos congruos modos tempori. . ." The influence of Occam and the earlier conciliarists can be seen in the appeal to "necessity," probably derived originally from Bartolus' fourteenth century commentary on Justianian's Code.

for the presence of the *rector* of the universal council (the pope). However, he ignores the fact that the pope by his own analysis is also *rector* of his provincial council, and if he refused to participate his provincial council could not take part. At another point, Cusanus recommends that the council continue to urge the pope to participate, and await his attendance for a considerable period (in the case of the eighth council, this period exceeded a year). If he still refuses to come or to send a legate, "the council can provide for its needs and the safety of the church."[28]

There is one case in which the pope or his representative must be involved—in decisions on matters of church dogma. "Even when the council has been properly convened, if the authority of the apostolic see is absent thus far, no decision can be taken on matters of faith without considering the opinion of the Roman church." This is necessary because a decision on matters of faith is only certain if it is taken unanimously, since "the greater the agreement *(concordantia)*, the more infallible the judgment."[29] The requirement that the pope participate in decisions on faith assumes, of course, that the pope is not a heretic. If he were, his consent would not be required, since, according to the canonists, he would then no longer be a part of the church. This exception, while necessary, makes it possible for a council at any time to accuse the pope of heresy when he refuses to subscribe to a conciliar decree, and, in fact, charges of heresy were utilized as part

28 *DCC*, Book II, chap. xiii, pp. 156-160, and chap. ii, pp. 98-99. Compare *DAP*, p. 32, where Cusanus states that, as judge of the universal church, the presence of the pope or his legates at the council is necessary to the council.

29 *DCC*, Book II, chap. ii. p. 99. "Et in his quae ad fidem spectant sine deliberatione de qua constet Romanae ecclesiae, etiam in concilio rite congregato, licet absens adhuc sit auctoritas apostolicae sedis, procedendum non est." Chap. iv, p. 105. ". . . de quanto maior concordantia, de tanto infallibilius iudicium." See also chap. xv, p. 170.

of the justification for the deposition of the Pisan pope at Constance, and for the deposition of Pope Eugene attempted later at Basel.

At any rate, the pope cannot use his right, *regulariter*, to call the council and to be present in it, to prevent the assembly of the council. The emperor can convoke it in cases of necessity, and if the pope refuses to participate it can continue without him, although it cannot take decisions on dogma without him so long as he is believed to be orthodox.

Another requirement for a universal council is free discussion and open meetings. There must be no pressure exerted from the outside by secular rulers or by any of those in the council. Otherwise, the free operation of the Holy Spirit in inspiring the council to take the right decision will not be able to work properly. The discussions must be carried on peacefully and decisions should be taken harmoniously.[30]

The final mark of a genuine council is that it is brought to a harmonious conclusion. This is a sure sign of the presence of the Holy Spirit, "the author of peace and concord." The more agreement there is at the conclusion of the discussion, the surer one may be of the infallibility of the decisions of the council. This is why, in decisions on faith where there is a need to be certain of infallible inspiration, the decision should be unanimous.[31]

If all these requirements are observed,

> if a council which has been properly and legitimately convoked and assembled and all called, freely celebrated, and concluded with the common consent of all, has issued a decree concerning the salvation of the faithful in any way—

[30] The partisan atmosphere of the Council of Basel in 1437 was one of the contributing factors to Nicholas of Cusa's change of position. See discussion in Chapter IX.

[31] *DCC*, Book II, chap. xv, p. 170.

since it proximately represents the whole Catholic church and has the consent of all their faithful through their representatives *(legati)* and rulers *(praesides)*—we read that it has never erred. . . The universal council coming to such a conclusion by consent and representation *(legatione)* of all the faithful necessarily, truly, and infallibly comes to that conclusion in the presence of Christ and by the inspiration of the Holy Spirit.[32]

In addition to the requirement that the pope participate in decisions on faith, another element in Cusanus' theory which favored the papacy was his doctrine of *libera potestas administrandi.* In opposition to the actions taken by the Council of Basel at the time of its first differences with the pope, Nicholas feels that the pope cannot be suspended, but only deposed. Suspension, he says, is a contradiction in terms. Either the pope's office should be taken from him by deposition, or he must be allowed the power to exercise its duties. The pope's office consists in a divine grant of the power to bind and loose. If these prerogatives are taken away from him, he ceases to be pope. Yet the pope was suspended at Constance. However, the decrees issued at Constance apply only to "external acts dependent on man." (Possibly Nicholas is thinking of taxes and the power over elections, both important issues at Basel.) The papal power of binding and loosing, in particular the power of absolution of sins, no council can touch as long as he is pope. If

[32] *DCC,* Book II, chap. xxxiv, p. 292. ". . . si rite et legitime convocatum et omnibus vocatis collectum, liberrime celebratum et iuste finitum communi omnium consensu sententiam in quomodolibet salutem fidelium concernentibus dictaverit, propter propinquam repraesentationem totius catholicae ecclesiae et propter omnium fidelium consensum qui per legatos et praesides concurrit, numquam legimus errasse . . . Universale vero concilium dictans talem conclusionem consensu et legatione omnium fidelium necessario ex Christi assistentia et sancto Spiritu inspirante vere et infallibiliter dictat eandem."

it wishes to take this away from the pope, the council must depose him.[33]

There is no doubt that the pope has an important place in Nicholas' conciliar theory. He is the captain, "the pilot of the ship of St. Peter," whose special task is to prevent division in the church. He is the ecclesiastical *princeps*, the ruler of the church and the symbol of unity.[34]

Yet, although the pope is greater than any individual member of the church (*distributive*), he is the minister of the whole church, *collective*.[35] The universal council once assembled is in every respect over the pope. It can depose him for reasons of negligence of duty (*quando inutiliter administraret*), as well as on the more traditional grounds of heresy. Moreover, it can review the decisions taken by the pope, and Nicholas cites here the Council of Chalcedon's review of Pope Leo's condemnation of Dioscorus as a heretic.[36]

While the universal council is over the pope, his patriarchal council is subject to him. As noted already, its decisions are infallible and are not subject to review by the universal council. However, it has no power to depose the pope who is its head, except on the universally accepted ground of heresy. This explains, says Nicholas, the contradictory statements in the *Decretum* which say that the pope cannot be judged by the council and then say that he can be judged. The former statements refer to the patriarchal council of Rome, sometimes called the general patriarchal

33 *DCC*, Book II, chap. xviii, p. 198.
34 *DCC*, Book I, chap. vi, p. 57, chap. xi, p. 68, chap. xvi, p. 80; Book II, chap. xxxiv, pp. 300-303.
35 *DCC*, Book II, chap. xxxiv, p. 302.
36 *DCC*, Book I, chap. xvi, p. 81; Book II, chap. viii, p. 130, chap. xvii, p. 182, chap. xviii, p. 197. See also *DAP*, p. 28, which says that the pope can be deposed for reasons of mere convenience (*propter utilitatem*).

council, which is often confused with the universal council because of the disappearance of the other patriarchates.

The fact that the patriarchal council can depose the pope on account of heresy is not an assertion of superiority over him, because in becoming a heretic he has ceased to be pope, and the council's action is simply declaratory. If the pope is guilty of malfeasance in office and oppresses or abuses his subordinates, there is nothing that the patriarchal council can do about it, aside from exhorting the pope to mend his ways. It is subject to the pope, and the only remedy is to endure papal oppression, since the pope is over the patriarchal council and cannot be deposed by it except for heresy.[37]

Parallel to the patriarchal council, but meeting continuously instead of only rarely, is the college of cardinals. As noted earlier, the cardinals are considered as representatives of the provinces, who remain in Rome to assist in church administration. As the representatives of the church provinces they elect the pope, but Cusanus, unlike John of Paris, does not say anything about the right of election implying any right of deposition. The cardinals comprise the pope's privy council, and they must consent to papal dispensations from laws adopted by the universal councils.[38]

Below the college of cardinals there is the hierarchical system of councils outlined in the last chapter. First come the provincial councils made up of the archbishop and his bishops. Rome has its own provincial council, which is first of all such councils. These councils should meet once or twice a year, following the example of the provincial councils of France and Spain.[39] Below them are the diocesan and parish synods which meet more often.

37 *DCC*, Book II, chap. xviii, pp. 173-178.
38 *DCC*, Book II, chap. xiii, p. 151, chap. xxi, pp. 235-236, chap. xxv, p. 245.
39 *DCC*, Book II, chap. xxii, pp. 237-239.

In each case the law for the ecclesiastical unit should be made by a synod meeting with its *rector,* because

> ecclesiastical laws cannot be adopted except by the ecclesiastical congregation which is called a synod or meeting *(coetus).* . . All binding church legislation must be contained in Holy Scripture or adopted by the bishops in council or through the custom of the whole church.[40]

It is true that by custom the church has tolerated the making of laws by the pope alone through the issuance of the papal decrees, but even this is permitted only because of the tacit consent of the church. Papal decrees formerly were issued with the consent of the pope's annual metropolitan council, and now they should at least have the consent of the cardinals standing for the whole church. When it comes to laws touching the general welfare *(status)* of the whole church, these may be made only in the universal council, where the pope is only one member with authority similar to, or even less than, that of a patriarch in the patriarchal council or an archbishop in the provincial council.[41]

The pope has made legislation in the past with the tacit acceptance of the church, but Nicholas wishes to consent of the church to canon law to be expressed through the council or the college of cardinals. The same is true, "according to their quality," of laws for kingdoms, provinces, dioceses, or other administrative subdivisions of the church. In each case legislation is to be carried out by the

40 *DCC,* Book II, chaps. ix-x, pp. 135 and 137. "Ecclesiastici enim canones non possunt nisi per ecclesiasticam congregationem, quae synodus vel coetus dicitur, statui." "Oportet enim, quod omnia talia, quae ligare debent, contineantur in auctoritatibus sacrarum scripturarum, statutis episcoporum in conciliis editis aut consuetudine universalis ecclesiae."

41 *DCC,* Book II, chaps. xi-xii, pp. 139-145. The prohibition on changes in laws affecting the *status ecclesiae* is derived from canon law doctrines concerning diocesan administration. Cf. Tierney, *Foundations, passim.*

rector of the *universitas*—and just as the pope should not legislate without the approval of the council or the college of cardinals, the patriarchs, archbishops, and bishops cannot make law without the approval of their councils or synods.[42]

To those who say that the pope as supreme judge of the whole church should be able to make law, Nicholas replies with an argument for the separation of the judicial and legislative powers. The judge, he says, must decide according to the law, and not be able to change it at will. If he could do so, no one would ever be able to appeal an unjust judicial decision, since every decision would be according to the law. The judge interprets the law, but some other organ should make it, or there would be no stability in the laws.[43]

When Nicholas uses verbs such as *statuere* or *canones condere* he is speaking in terms of the modern concept of deciding what the law should be—not merely discovering pre-existing law. He is fully aware that legislation is something different from the judicial power. The pope has jurisdiction, but only the council has legislative power.[44] It was natural for Cusanus to take this view, since he was writing for a council which was making a mass of reform legislation for the church, and however much the council appealed to the example of the primitive church and the old ways of doing things, it was conscious of the fact that it was changing the *status quo* and altering the present distribu-

42 See also *DAP*, p. 30, and the reference to the Archdeacon Guido de Baysio's statement that in order to legislate (*statuere canones*) in a church province the archbishop must have the consent of the bishops. This is the doctrine which Cusanus was applying to the whole church.

43 *DCC*, Book II, chap. xiv, p. 163, chap. xx, pp. 208-210, but note that the law is made by the emperor or pope in council—so that there is not a complete separation of powers.

44 *DCC*, Book II, chap. xiii, pp. 156-157.

tion of powers in the church by means of legislative decisions.

While the pope is subject to the laws of the universal church council, he can change the canons of all lower councils, including those of the Roman patriarchal council. He should not arbitrarily alter decrees to which he has consented, but if he does so the alteration or revocation is valid since all lower councils are subject to him. Once again, all statements that the pope is over the councils and laws are to be interpreted as applying to the Roman patriarchal council, sometimes called the general council—which is often confused with the universal council but is distinct from it.[45]

Since the reintroduction of Roman law in the twelfth century, it had been a commonplace of legal theory that the ruler had the power of *epieikeia* or equity, by virtue of which he could dispense with the law when the circumstances to which the law applied were altered.[46] Cusanus also believes that the pope possesses this power over all church legislation, even the conciliar decrees to which he is subject. This dispensation must take place "on account of necessity or utility" and must be for the general good (*ad aedificationem*) of the church. The grant of *epieikeia* could be used by the ruler to justify almost any action on the ground of necessity or utility, and it was this plea which Pope Eugene used to justify his attempted dissolution of the Council of Basel in 1431. Nicholas criticized this attempt, saying there were no true causes for the dissolution, and, if there had been, the council would have consented to its own dissolution.[47] At any rate, he wishes to put safe-

---

45 *DCC*, Book II, chap. xx, pp. 206, 215, and 233.
46 The classic discussion of equity appears in Aristotle, *Nicomachean Ethics*, Book V, chap. 10.
47 *DCC*, Book II, chap. xx, pp. 206 and 227-233.

guards around the use of *epieikeia* to disregard conciliar decrees, and so he writes that the consent of the cardinals is also necessary for dispensations. No matter how urgent the cases, the cardinals representing the whole church must give their consent. These dispensations only apply to an individual case, and the canons of the universal council still stand. They may not be changed or annulled except by the council which made them. To prove this, Cusanus uses what he calls the argument from analogy *(argumentum a simili)*. He compares the alteration of conciliar decrees to *alienatio,* the taking of church property by a bishop. It was generally accepted in canon law that church property could not be disposed of by the bishop without the consent of the priests of the diocese or of their representatives in the cathedral chapter. As the bishop is *dispensator* of church property and can only dispose of it with the consent of his priests, so the pope "cannot change or dispose of the goods of the church, among which I believe are the most holy canons, without the consent and agreement of his clergy."[48]

The entire section on the making and dispensation of church law is much influenced by earlier canonistic theory, and it is filled with references to the *Decretum* and its commentators. However, as in the above case, the original canonist discussions dealt with relations of the bishop and clergy within the diocese rather than with the pope and council or whole church. Like other conciliar theorists before him, Cusanus took what was said about the lower administrative subdivisions of the church and applied it to the church as a whole.[49]

---

[48] *DCC,* Book II, chap. xxi, pp. 234-235. ". . . tamen res ecclesiae, inter quas maxime sacros canones esse credo, iuxta superiora mutare vel alienare non potest sine sui cleri consensu et subscriptione."

[49] See for example the Archdeacon Guido de Baysio's comment on

Near the end of the second book of *De Concordantia Catholica,* Nicholas discusses the reforms which he proposes for the whole church. In addition to the introduction of government by a hierarchical system of councils consenting to law and electing the rulers, he also suggests reforms in the financial and legal systems. The financial centralization and corruption in Rome must be changed, and one way to do it, he suggests, is by an annual collection for the papacy (something akin to the present-day Peter's Pence collection), which would provide for administrative expenses in Rome and end the need for the taxes and petty charges of all sorts which were at that time the source of income for the papacy. The amount of this collection would be set by each universal council, to be in effect until the next council met. If the pope needed more money, he would be obliged to call a universal council to provide it.[50]

This short chapter suggests a parallel with the constitutional history of the contemporary kingdoms in Europe. In England, for instance, when the king needed more money, he was compelled to consult with his vassals and later with representatives of the shires and boroughs. Before the grant of financial relief, he would hear petitions from the representatives assembled, and in some cases these petitions became the basis of general legislation. Thus parliamentary participation in legislation and the financial needs of the monarchy were intimately related.[51] Possibly the introduction of Cusanus' suggestion would have had a similar effect on the future constitutional development of the church.

D. 19 c. 6 of the *Decretum* quoted in footnote to the Heidelberg edition of *DCC,* Book II, chap. xx, p. 208, and another statement by the same author quoted in footnote to p. 229 of the same chapter.

50 *DCC,* Book II, chap. xxx, pp. 268-270.

51 See G. O. Sayles, *The Medieval Foundations of England* (London, 1950), chap. xxvii; Sidney Knox Mitchell, *Taxation in Medieval England* (New Haven, 1951), chap. iv.

Nicholas also criticizes the excessive concern of the papacy with its temporal possessions. He quotes with approval the suggestion of Hugh of St. Victor ("our German, most learned in every type of knowledge"), in his work *De Sacramentis,* that lay administrators be appointed to carry out the administrative and judicial functions in the lands belonging to the church, and suggests that the church return to the earlier practice of recognizing the legal jurisdiction of the earthly prince over church lands and the *rectores* and *patricii* appointed by him "with the consent of the churches."[52]

Cusanus is especially strong in his condemnation of the holders of pluralities—those holding several church offices at the same time. He recommends that papal dispensations for this purpose be abolished, because "such a number of petty benefices and of many ignorant priests disgraces the church very much, and makes the laity detest the clergy whom they see living a life of ease and vice."[53] The fact that Nicholas himself was from the beginning of his career a notorious "pluralist" makes the bitterness of this attack all the more curious.

Nicholas also suggests a system of appeals in the church courts. When a bishop takes action against a priest or deacon, he says, the priest or deacon should be able to appeal his decision one step above in the hierarchy to the archbishop. Bishops judged by archbishops should be able to go to their patriarchs on appeal. Judgment by peers would not be advisable, he thinks, because neighboring bishops might be envious and hope to get some of the con-

52 *DCC,* Book II, chap. xxix, pp. 265-268.
53 *DCC,* Book II, chap. xxxiii, p. 288. "Unde tanta pluralitas parvorum beneficiorum et subsequenter multorum sacerdotum ignarorum multum decolorat ecclesiam et facit laicos clericis infestos esse, dum tot sacerdotes conspiciunt, quos vident otio et vitiis vacare." On Nicholas' numerous benefices, see Meuthen, "Die Pfründen," pp. 15-66.

demned man's territories. He therefore proposes a hierarchy of church courts in which appeals might be carried in each case to the next higher rank in the hierarchy, if one's immediate superior had not been just in his decisions. This would prevent the practice of excessive appeals to Rome and direct papal intervention to transfer a judicial procedure to Rome, since appeals would first be required to go up through the court system and would normally not be carried any further than two degrees above the rank of the appellant.[54] Thus, once again Nicholas' concern to preserve the natural hierarchical order in the church is demonstrated. Even when later developments induced him to modify his attitudes on the subject of papal centralization, he still maintained his concern for the rights of the lower ranks in the church hierarchy.

The discussion of the constitution of the church with which the second book of *De Concordantia Catholica* is concerned centers around the primary problem of interest to the Council of Basel—the relations of pope and council. In Cusanus' theory, the pope has a very important role as head of the church. Special powers are attached to that office by divine intention, and he is particularly charged with maintaining church unity. Yet *De Concordantia Catholica* is a theory of conciliar supremacy, not of coordinate powers between pope and council.[55] Nicholas assumes that in ordinary circumstances council and pope will cooperate, but in the event of conflict the council is supreme. It is not required that the council be called by the pope. In case of necessity the emperor can do so, or all the provincial councils can meet together. Papal adhesion is not necessary

---

[54] *DCC*, Book II, chap. xxxi, pp. 270-272.

[55] Sabine, *A History of Political Theory*, p. 324, accuses Cusanus of contradictions which in context are not contradictory, and attributes this to a theory of the sharing of power between pope and council which is not contained in the *Concordantia*.

for the council to act. In the face of the pope's persistent refusal to attend, it can proceed without him. Laws which apply to the whole church must receive its consent. The council is over the pope and it can depose him either for heresy or for maladministration.

The council is supreme, first, because it is made up of bishops, who are the highest sacramental rank in the church, and the pope is chosen as their head in order to carry out administrative and judicial duties. Although the pope can be said to represent the church in a vague way (*confuse*) the council is more representative of the consent of the whole church because it contains the heads of the lower ranks in the church, and hence can give the consent of the church to law and papal rule. Since it is more representative and is composed of all the bishops, it also embodies more certainly the gift of infallibility given to the church by Christ. However, in order to be absolutely certain of infallible inspiration, the pope must be consulted concerning any decree on matters of faith.

Below the universal council is the patriarchal council of Rome. The pope is over this council, except that it may declare him deposed if he is guilty of heresy. In continual attendance at Rome is the college of cardinals, made up of representatives of all the provinces in the church. Their functions are to elect the pope if the universal council is not in session and to express the consent of the church to such papal actions as dispensations from conciliar laws. Below the highest level, there are councils which make law and elect their *rectores* at every level in the church, each expressing the consent of those in the rank immediately below. The whole structure is strictly hierarchical, and yet, at the same time, Nicholas attempts to build it on a foundation of free consent and voluntary subjection. At some levels it corresponded to existing practice in the church. In others, it was radically revolutionary. Delicately balanced and imposing as it was, it could not last, and only four years after its completion it was abandoned.

CHAPTER VIII

. . .

THE CONSTITUTION
OF THE EMPIRE

W H I L E the occasion for the publication of *De Concordantia Catholica* was a crisis in the government of the church, Cusanus was also interested in reform of the empire. In keeping with the parallelism of his thought on the structure and legitimation of the spiritual and temporal hierarchies, he saw the church and the empire in a relationship of correspondence and parallelism so that what is true for one should also be true for the other, "always keeping in mind the difference of the two orders." The third book of the *Concordantia* is concerned with the temporal order, but it is much influenced by the general theory of both consent and hierarchy outlined in the discussion of pope and council in the first two books of the work. Moreover, Cusanus in his youthful idealism looked to the conciliar method as the best way to achieve reform in the empire as well as in the church, and Basel, at the time of the arrival of a vigorous emperor who had brought about the convocation of the successful Council of Constance, seemed to be the appropriate place to begin.

The third book appears to have been the most hastily written of the three parts. It varies in quality, containing the most interesting practical proposals of the work and its loftiest political theory, as well as its most irrelevant discussions and citations. References in the work indicate that Nicholas engaged in considerable research into original historical records as background for the book. He is proud of his knowledge of the sources, and boasts that he has examined at Cologne the complete correspondence between Charlemagne and Pope Adrian, that he has studied the records of the earlier imperial councils, and that he knows from both study and litigation the legal systems in use in Germany.[1] The result of his efforts is a book which is an only partly successful synthesis of medieval legal theory, the constitutional history of the Holy Roman Empire, and the hierarchical cosmology.

Written later than the first two books of the *Concordantia*, Book III differs from them in its omission of references to the canon law, and its heavy reliance on what from the text appears to be Aristotle but turns out on examination to be Marsilius. As already noted, Nicholas read Marsilius as he was completing the second book of the *Concordantia*. The preface is largely a paraphrase of passages in the *Defensor Pacis*, and the abundant references to Aristotle are all derived from that work, although sometimes inaccurately cited. From the citations it appears that Nicholas had not read the *Politics* itself at the time of the composition of the *Concordantia*, although William of Moerbeke's translation is now in the library at Kues. The argument of the preface is from Aristotle as he appears in the *Defensor Pacis*, not in the *Politics*.

Marsilius had been mentioned twice near the end of the second book, once in order to refute his theory that St. Peter had never been at Rome, and again to attack his assertion that the Bible is the only source of faith. In the preface to the third book, he is repeatedly paraphrased and his quotations from Aristotle are taken over directly, but it is a mark of both his bad reputation and his wide influence that he dominates the preface without ever being

---

1 *DCC*, Book III, chap. iii, p. 340, chap. xxv, pp. 422 and 423.

mentioned by name.[2] Nevertheless, both his ideas and those of Aristotle which he mediated are submitted to important modifications by Cusanus.

A distinctively Aristotelian note is struck at the beginning of the preface when Nicholas derives the political order from man's instinct of sociability (*consodalitas*) which leads him to form communities. This is an element which is not stressed by later consent theorists, such as Hobbes and Locke, for whom the entrance into civil society was an act of calculation of advantages and disadvantages by individuals who could decide to stay out of or enter into society. For Nicholas, as for Aristotle, an instinctive drive to society and political organization, not any utilitarian calculus of advantages and disadvantages, is the historical origin of life in the political community, for "man is by nature an animal destined for political and civil life."[3]

Man's natural drive to society must have an objective or final cause in Aristotelian teleological terms, and this end is political and civic life. However, many of the inhabitants of the community are ignorant or corrupt, and therefore laws are necessary "to preserve unity and concord." When Nicholas begins to describe the process of legislation, he departs from Marsilius, whom he has been paraphrasing, and the extent of his departure is a mark of the difference between the two writers. While Marsilius had insisted on the participation of all the citizens in lawmaking and had argued that they had special qualifications in addition to

2 Cf. the reference by Dietrich of Niem (referred to earlier), who ascribes Marsilius' ideas to a "great theologian," and discussion in my article, "The Influence of Marsilius."

3 *DCC*, preface, pp. 314-315. "Videmus enim hominem animal esse politicum et civile, et naturaliter ad civilitatem inclinari." Cusanus' version of Aristotle's *politikon zōon* differs from that of William of Moerbeke, the Latin translator of the *Politics* (*"animal civile"*) and that of St. Thomas (*"animal politicum et sociale"*). See A. P. d'Entreves, *The Medieval Contribution to Political Thought* (Oxford, 1939), p. 25.

those of the intellectually superior, Cusanus believes that the wise should make the laws on the basis of their natural superiority, and quotes a long passage from St. Ambrose on the inconstancy of the foolish (*stulti*). To add to the confusion, he quotes Marsilius' statement that the "weightier part" (*valentior pars*) of the community should be taken for the whole and, by a misreading of the text of the *Defensor Pacis*, attributes it to the first chapter of the *Politics*.[4]

Despite the heavy admixture of Platonic rationalism in his discussion of legislation, Nicholas does not abandon his basic doctrine of consent to law and government. As mentioned earlier, he assumes that the ignorant will naturally agree to the rule of their betters, and will consent to laws framed by the wise. Since Nicholas believes that he is living in a harmonious universe, governed by Divine Providence, he can resolve the tension between government by universal consent and control by a rational elite through his belief in the "natural instinct" or "natural servitude" of the intellectually inferior. If sometimes this intellectual inferiority becomes moral inferiority, as when he cites a quotation from Ambrose referring to the natural servitude of the sinner,[5] Cusanus once more demonstrates the influence of Platonism mediated to him through the Neo-Platonic philosophers and the church fathers.

When Cusanus discusses the role of consent to law and

4 *DCC*, preface, pp. 314-315. Nicholas' argument on the incompetence of the *stulti* is directly contrary to that of Marsilius in D. I, chap. xiii, 1. Marsilius refers to the *valentior pars* in two passages in the *Defensor Pacis*. In D. I, chap. xii, v. 3-5, he argues that the whole citizenry or "its weightier part as to quality and quantity" should legislate, and in D. I, chap. xiii, v. 2, he quotes Aristotle's dictum that those who desire the continuation of a polity should be stronger (*valentior* in William of Moerbeke's translation) than those who do not. Nicholas' error in the citation of Aristotle is based on a misreading of Marsilius' text in chap. xiii.

5 *DCC*, Book III, preface, p. 317.

government, he distorts Aristotle even more than he has Marsilius. Basing his citations of Aristotle entirely on those in the *Defensor Pacis*, he attempts to enlist Aristotle in support of the doctrine of consent. When he quotes Aristotle's statement in favor of government by an aristocracy of merit, he inserts the words, "with the consent of the others," which do not appear either in Marsilius or Aristotle.[6] Following this, he correctly summarizes Aristotle's belief in the superiority of the rule of law, but when he comes to distinguish good and bad forms of government, he is again guilty of attributing ideas of consent to Aristotle. He employs the classical sixfold division of Aristotle, dividing constitutions into three good forms—monarchy, aristocracy, and "polity"—and three perverted forms— tyranny, oligarchy, and democracy. As in Aristotle, the difference lies in whether the rulers aim at their own good or that of the whole. However, Nicholas adds that in the good forms rule is also exercised "with the consent of the subjects," while the "intemperate" forms are governed contrary to their will. In this case, the references to consent were inserted by Marsilius rather than Cusanus.[7]

The same procedure takes place in the next section, where Cusanus, reflecting the practice of the Holy Roman Empire, argues in favor of elective monarchy. At first, he seems to allow for different forms of government provided that they are ruled for the common good and by consent, but it soon becomes clear that his preference is strongly for elective monarchy. Noting that if there are several ruling the state, "confusion" will arise as to which has the final decision, Nicholas concludes, "A plurality of rulers is bad, because there ought to be one authority with the

6 *DCC*, Book III, preface, p. 318.
7 *DCC*, Book III, preface, p. 319, based on Marsilius, *Defensor Pacis*, D. I, chap. viii, v. 3.

final decision."[8] The monarchy should be elective in order to avoid the danger of degeneration in the heirs of a ruler who has been chosen *cum successoribus*. "Hence although there are also many good and strong reasons for hereditary monarchy, nevertheless there is no better way of ensuring that the community will have the best possible person ruling for the common good by the will of all, than by a new election by all the citizens or a majority or at least by those nobles who represent all the citizens with their consent."[9] To prove that Aristotle also favored elective monarchy, Nicholas mentions five references to the *Politics*, once again drawn from Marsilius (and once more with an error of transcription). In Aristotle, they are merely passing references to instances of elective monarchy or to the necessity of participation in government by the citizens. In Marsilius they are cited in the course of an argument for elective over hereditary monarchy, but in Cusanus they are used to support the assertion of elective monarchy as the ideal form of government, which is neither the position of Aristotle nor of Marsilius.[10]

8 *DCC*, Book III, preface, p. 321. "Pluralitas igitur principum mala, quoniam unum oportet principantem esse, ad quem ultimo secure recurratur." The argument again distorts Marsilius, who had argued (D. I, chap. xvii, v. 1), for a single government (*principatus*), not a single ruler (*princeps*). Cf. St. Thomas Aquinas, *De Regimine Prinicpum*, chap. ii, and discussion of the "argument from unity" in Otto von Gierke, *The Political Theories of the Middle Age* (Cambridge, 1900), pp. 9ff.

9 *DCC*, Book III, preface, pp. 321-322. "Unde etsi multae etiam rationes praegnantes et fortes pro successorio monarchatu existant, nihilominus ut optimus omnium voluntate ad commune conferens praesit rei publicae semper, non est melior quisquam statuendi modus, quam per novam electionem omnium aut maioris partis vel saltem eorum procerum, qui omnium vices ex consensu habent." This discussion and the references to Aristotle which accompany it, parallel similar statements in Marsilius, *Defensor Pacis*, Book I, chap. xvi, v. 17. The danger of degeneration in a hereditary monarchy had been noted by Plato (*Republic*, Book VIII), St. Thomas (*Summa Theologica*, Ia IIae, q. 105), and John of Paris (*De Potestate*, chap. xx, p. 137).

10 The citations are drawn from Marsilius, D. I, chap. xvi, v. 13. As

While manuscript evidence indicates that the preface was written after the body of the third book, it does not conflict with the argument of the rest of the work, although it is drawn from different sources. Despite the dependence on Marsilius, the principles developed in the introduction to the third book are those of Cusanus. He outlines a system of elective monarchy under law in which the rationally superior frame legislation to which all the citizens consent either tacitly or through representatives. Cusanus appeals to Aristotle in support of his doctrine of consent, but, like Marsilius whom he followed, reads theories of consent into passages where they are not present. He departs from Marsilius in the strong element of Platonic rationalism which he includes in his theory of legislation, and his assertion of the superiority of elective monarchy differs from Marsilius' complete subordination of the ruler (*pars principans*) to the legislator.

On the issue of relations between the spiritual and temporal powers, Cusanus takes a characteristically middle position between the extremes, represented respectively by Marsilius and by the papalist advocates of ecclesiastical supremacy. The civil authorities are neither inferior nor superior to the spiritual rulers; they are parallel to them. They too receive their authority directly from God, and they are ordered hierarchically in a structure which ideally will correspond exactly to the structure of the ecclesiastical hierarchy. They also must be elected or at least rule and make laws with the consent of the people.

Nicholas' concern in this section of the book is not to

---

cited in Marsilius and Cusanus, they are often several chapters removed from the present enumeration. The references to elective monarchy appear in most modern editions of Aristotle's *Politics* as chap. xiv of Book III and chap. xi of Book II. The other references are to Aristotle's definition of citizenship as ruling and being ruled (*Politics*, Book I, Chap. 12; III, 4; VII, 14).

discuss the civil authorities (in the plural). The temporal order in society, like the spiritual, is a single hierarchy—the Holy Empire, the body of the church. Although Europe was already as divided as it would ever be, and Nicholas' own writings give ample evidence of the spirit of nationalism, he was no more ready to see a pluralistic organization in the temporal order than he would have been to see the multiplicity of churches which were the result of the Reformation. The third book of the *Concordantia* is convincing evidence of the continuing attraction of the myth of the one Holy Roman Empire. To discuss the temporal order was to discuss the structure and functioning of the *sacrum imperium*.

Yet the focus changes in the third book. Where the earlier books had centered around the relations between the pope and the church council, the third book contains virtually no discussion of the imperial council in its relationship to the emperor. The position of the emperor in the constitutional framework of the empire is considered chiefly in order to reply to the claims of the defenders of the papacy to direct jurisdiction over the temporal order. Nicholas is concerned to establish the independent derivation of the imperial authority, as well as his special religious duties, because he sees in the emperor an important instrument of reform. It was Sigismund who, by his initiative at Constance, had assured the success of the efforts to end the schism which had divided the West. Now perhaps Sigismund could heal the rupture between council and pope and bring back the Bohemians to the unity of the church. It is primarily in his religious role that Nicholas discusses the position of the emperor, although he also devotes several chapters to a program for the reform of the institutions of the empire.

To derive the emperor's legitimacy from God and the

consent of his subjects, Nicholas exercises his considerable powers of historical criticism to challenge for the first time the historical validity of the Donation of Constantine, the supposed gift by Constantine to Pope Sylvester of the western part of the Roman Empire. Although Dante and Marsilius had questioned the legitimacy of Constantine's donation, they had accepted it as historical fact. Nicholas was the first to demonstrate by appeal to the historical sources that the Donation was apocryphal.[11]

He observes that there is no mention of the Donation in contemporary histories or the records of the church councils of the time, nor in the writings of Saints Jerome, Augustine, Ambrose, and Pope St. Damasus. The story is contained in the legend of St. Sylvester, which is said to have been written by an unknown author and flatly contradicts the account of the baptism of Constantine given by St. Jerome. Moreover, it is curious that no mention is made of the Donation in Gratian's *Decretum*, that great storehouse of early church authorities. It is only in a later addition that it appears, as a *palea* on Distinction 96. The conclusion is that the *palea* and the Donation are falsehoods (*confictam scripturam*), "as are many things taken from apocryphal books."[12]

The papal possessions in Italy come from a donation by Pepin, later repeated by Charlemagne, when he liberated parts of Italy from the Lombards. Nicholas quotes historical records to prove that until the time of Pepin in the

11 See Dante, *De Monarchia*, Book III, chap. x. and Marsilius, *Defensor Pacis*, D. II, chap. xxviii, v. 19. A disciple of Arnold of Brescia, writing to Frederick Barbarossa in 1152, had called the Donation a "fabula heretica" (quoted in Vansteenberghe, *Nicolas*, p. 27, n. 2).

12 *DCC*, Book III, chap. ii, p. 332. Carlyle, *History*, II, 210, indicates that it is surprising that the Donation was not included in the *Decretum*, since it was contained in earlier canon law collections (e.g., the Pseudo-Isidorean Decretals). It was added by Paucapalea, the first of the commentators on the *Decretum*.

eighth century the eastern emperors continued to be overlords of Rome, Ravenna, and the Marches, and the popes recognized them as such.

The disproof of the Donation by Cusanus was written seven years before the more famous effort by Lorenzo Valla. Valla's attack, entitled "De Falso Credita et Ementita Constantini Donatione," also noted the absence of references in contemporary writings, but as a humanist he argued principally from style and vocabulary, noting the German expressions and the anachronistic references in the work, to establish its unhistorical character.

While he is involved in apocryphal insertions in Gratian's *Decretum,* Nicholas devotes some pages to proving that certain supposed letters of Pope Clement to St. James are also not genuine. He observes that, since James died before St. Peter, Clement could not have written to him. Moreover, the letters differentiate bishops from priests, a development which Nicholas rightly believes did not take place until some time after the apostolic period, when these letters were supposed to have been written.

Nicholas' purpose in these exposures is not to discredit the papacy, but only to show that the emperor is not dependent for his authority upon the pope. As he says in concluding the chapter, "Even if all these writings are removed from our midst, any Catholic would confess that the holy Roman church holds the primacy of highest power and excellence in relation to all other diocesan seats."[13]

Nicholas also attempts to refute a second argument for papal power over the empire, the Translation of the Empire—the theory that, having received it from Constantine,

---

13 *DCC,* Book III, chap. ii, p. 337. "Quia etiam illis omnibus scripturis e medio sublatis, sanctam Romanam ecclesiam primam summae potestatis et excellentiae inter cunctas sedes, quisque catholicus fateretur." This is another indication, if any is needed, that Nicholas could never be described as an antipapal writer.

the pope transferred the rulership over the Western Empire to Charlemagne and through him to his successors, the present Holy Roman Emperors. What actually happened, he says, was something quite the reverse of the transfer of the empire to the Franks. The King of the Lombards invaded the Exarchate of Ravenna, and when the pope asked him to return this territory to the Byzantine emperrors he refused. Whereupon the pope asked Pepin to recover the territory, and, when this was done, Pepin *gave the pope* certain territories in central Italy (Rome, Ravenna, and the Marches). When it was difficult for these areas to defend themselves from external enemies, they took on Charlemagne, Pepin's successor, as their feudal overlord and protector, and hence he was called *patricius Romanus*. Cusanus claims (erroneously) that the term *imperator* was not used by Charlemagne. He was called "King of the Romans" and *patricius Romanus*. No mention was ever made of the transfer of the empire in the entire correspondence between Charlemagne and the pope, copies of which Nicholas claims to have been in a *volumen ingens* in Cologne (probably the *Codex Carolinus,* now in the Vienna library).[14]

When Conrad, the last descendant in Germany of Charlemagne, died, he asked that Henry, Duke of Saxony, be elected as his successor. Italy at this time was under many warring kings, but "from the time of Henry I, and especially under Otto I, the Germans by force of arms gained control of the kingdom of Italy, the city of Rome, the kingdom of Arles, and of Germany itself."[15]

14 *DCC,* Book III, chap. iii, p. 340.
15 *DCC,* Book III, chap. iii, p. 342. "Unde si cuncta resolvis, tunc ab Henrico primo, Alemanni per virtutes armorum et maxime per primum Ottonem, regni Ytaliae et urbis Romae, regni Arelatensis, ac ipsius Germaniae dominia acquisiverunt." Nicholas mentions his source for the constitutional history of Italy at this period—Liutprand, bishop of Cremona

Because Otto had liberated them from the petty tyrants who had controlled Rome, and because the eastern emperors were no longer protecting them, the *clerus et populus Romanus* declared him "with his successors" their king and emperor. He derived this title from the fact that he ruled over Italy and Rome, and from his election by the clergy and people of Rome who had always retained the right to name and depose their rulers.[16] In turn, he gave back to the popes the lands which had been given to them by Pepin and Charlemagne, although he retained the right of feudal overlordship and a corresponding duty to enforce the papal decrees. Thus the papal states are subject to the empire, and the emperor derives his position not from a papal transfer of power, but from election by the Roman people. "Who gave, I ask, the Roman people the power to elect the emperor if it was not natural and divine right, by way of voluntary subjection?"[17]

The empire passed by hereditary succession from Otto I to Otto II and III, and was later enlarged to include Burgundy, Hungary, Bohemia, Denmark, Norway, Poland, and Prussia.[18] In the time of Henry II, Otto III's successor, electors were established "by consent of the nobles and of the estates of the clergy and people," who would in the

---

under Otto I. His two histories are entitled *Historia Ottonis* and *Anta-podosis*. In fact, Conrad was not a Carolingian at all, the last one being Louis (899-911). Conrad was duke of Franconia. Italy was invaded first not by Henry but by Otto.

16 Nicholas quotes Cardinal Zabarella, the fifteenth century canonist, and Hostiensis, who wrote in the thirteenth century, in favor of the so-called concession theory, i.e., the belief that the Roman people did not surrender all their power in establishing the emperor. Zabarella claimed to have seen a bronze tablet in the church of St. John Lateran in Rome describing the transfer of power to the emperor Vespasian in this way.

17 *DCC*, Book III, chap. iv, p. 346. "Quis dedit rogo populo Romano potestatem eligendi imperatorem, nisi ipsum ius divinum et naturale per viam enim voluntariae subiectionis."

18 *DCC*, Book III, chap. xxvi, p. 427.

future elect the emperor in place of all. Their power to elect the emperor and his power to rule were derived not from any special power of the pope to distribute earthly rulership, but from the natural right of the people to choose their rulers, "based on the common equal birth of all men."[19]

In the previous book, consent had been used to demonstrate the necessary part which the council must play in the government of the church, since, as the most representative body, it expressed the infallible will of the *congregatio fidelium* on church doctrine and law. Now it is used to prove the independence of the empire from the papacy. The emperor's power is derived not from the pope but from the consent of the people and election by those who represent them.

Cusanus admits that the pope also consented to the establishment of the electors, but this was because the temporal possessions of the church were subject to the emperor, not because of any intrinsic dependence of the emperor upon the pope. Papal consent to the establishment of the electors was given along with the consent of all the others who were subject to the empire.

The fact that the emperor is crowned and anointed by the pope does not signify any more dependence on him than does the crowning of the King of France by the Archbishop of Rheims.[20] Although the emperor gets his title at the time of the coronation (where previously he had been called "King of the Romans"), there is no increase in his power or rights. He acquires the rights of office by election of those who act for all the people. "And so in

19 *DCC*, Book III, chap. iv, p. 348.
20 *DCC*, Book III, chap. iv, p. 350. Cusanus is arguing against the papalist argument (e.g., in the writings of Ptolemy of Lucca, Augustinus Triumphus, and Alvarus Pelagius) that papal anointing and coronation establishes the emperor in office.

fact, he was emperor (*imperator*) since he had full power to command (*imperare*), although he was not generally called this but this title was kept for his solemn coronation, so that the king would desire this ceremony."[21]

The pope has no power to depose the emperor. This, like his election, can only be done by consent of all. It is true that, if the emperor is a heretic, the pope can make a declaratory judgment by virtue of which he ceases to be emperor, but this is not due to any special dependence of the empire upon the church, but "the intention of the Roman people was to transfer the empire to the ruler only on condition of his orthodoxy, so that then a heretic would not gain power in the empire by election."[22]

In support of his theory of dualism, Nicholas could cite innumerable texts from the *Decretum,* including the Gelasian formula of dual administration of Christendom. This is why he could attack the opinions of the papalists as "doubtful and novel" when they argued for the direct power of the papacy. While Nicholas accepts the analogies of the sun and moon, and body and soul, used by Boniface VIII, the lesson he draws is that the emperor should receive guidance from the priesthood, not that he is dependent upon it for his power.[23]

Once he is elected, the emperor becomes much more than a mere minister of the people or of the electors. He acquires a special religious legitimation, deriving his power from God, the source of all ruling authority. His office is dis-

21 *DCC,* Book III, chap. iv. p. 351. "Fuit itaque in veritate imperator dum in libera potestate habuit imperare, etiam si vulgo non ita nominaretur sed ut ad ipsam coronationem anhelet rex servatur huic solempnitati hoc nomen."
22 *DCC,* Book III, chap. vii, p. 362. ". . . populi intentio non est nisi secundum suam qualitatem fidei imperium transfundere in rectorem, quod tunc hereticus non sortiatur potestatem imperii ex electione." For a similar argument see chap. xlii, p. 464.
23 *DCC,* Book III, chap. xlii, pp. 461-66.

tinct from the spiritual authority and he is the "minister of God" and the "vicar of Christ on earth" (the identity of these terms with current titles applied to the papacy indicates the extent of the "sanctification" of the empire). All kings have something of the divine in their rule, but the Christian emperor is king of kings and highest of all by virtue of his religious role. He is closest to God of all rulers, and below him are the Christian rulers whose laws also are based on the laws of nature and of Christian orthodoxy. Below them are the rulers in Islam who accept the Old Testament and parts of the New Testament, and further down in the hierarchy are the pagan rulers. This ranking is justified along lines which mark the influence of Augustine and Aristotle. "Every king and emperor holds public office for the public benefit. But the public benefit consists in peace. The foundation of peace is to direct one's subjects to their eternal end."[24]

The emperor has a special role as *advocatus ecclesias,* and hence he must be a Christian. When, like Justinian, he gives civil effect to church laws, they apply not only to his own domain but to all Christian kings, even those who do not normally recognize him as their overlord. This special role of enforcing conciliar definitions and "conserving" its decrees gives him a special ecclesiastical position —in addition to the mystical aura which surrounds his office as such. Lower kings also have a duty to protect the faith since "it is the office of the king to spread the Catholic faith among his subjects,"[25] but the enforcement of the

24 *DCC,* Book III, chap. vii, p. 360. "Omnis enim rex et imperator habet officium ad publicam utilitatem ordinatum; Publica vero utilitas est pax. Principium pacis est ad finem aeternum dirigere subditos . . ." Cf. also chap. v, pp. 354-55
25 *DCC,* Book III, chap. xi, p. 374. "Ecce officium regis est fidem catholicam dilatare in subiectis."

decrees of the universal council are the emperor's special responsibility.

The emperor also derives universal jurisdiction from succession to the universal Roman empire. The canon law, borrowing from the test of the *Digest*, calls him *dominus mundi*. Yet, the Roman empire did not include the whole world. The areas around the Caspian Sea, Scythia, Norway, Persia, India, Sumatra, Arabia, Ethiopia, Libya, and Mauritania were never part of it, "which regions, as is evident to me from the Cosmography of Claudius Ptolemy, include not a little part of the world, including half of the inhabitable land. For India alone is said to have nine thousand walled villages . . . The Ethiopian region contains the empire of the Negus John, whom we call Prester John, who is said to be a deacon and a most faithful Christian along with seventy subject kings. But I believe that they are not populous or large kingdoms."[26]

Yet the Roman empire included the majority of the population of the world, although Europe is only one

[26] *DCC*, Book III, chap. vi, pp. 357-58. "Quae quidem regiones, ut mihi ex Cosmographia Ptolemaei Claudii constat, non parvam mundi partem, immo paene medietatem terrae habitabilis occupant. Sola India enim muratas villas novem milia dicitur continere . . . Nam Troglodytica regio continet imperium Noges Johan, quem nos presbyterum Ioannem nominamus, qui Christianus et diaconus esse fidelissimus cum septuaginta subiectis regibus dicitur. Credo tamen non esse populosa et magna regna." As Nicholas indicates, the chapter relies on the Latin translation of Ptolemy's Geography, made in 1406 by Jacobus Angelus, although it also adds Norway not mentioned by Ptolemy. The discussion of Prester John is especially interesting as an indication of the status of the legend in the fifteenth century. Prester John was a mythical Christian ruler who was believed to have lands of immense wealth and magical powers. Variously located in India, the Near East, and Ethiopia, he was the supposed author of a letter to the Byzantine emperor which circulated in Europe from the beginning of the twelfth century. The various theories as to the origin of the legend and the letter are reviewed in K. Halleiner, "Prester John's Letter," *Phoenix*, 13:47-58 (1959), and in Vesevolod Slessarev, *Prester John* (Minneapolis, 1959).

fourth the size of Asia and one half that of Africa. The emperor could be called the lord of the world in the sense of ruling over the majority of the people in it, and if the Roman emperor had this dominion legally, the medieval emperor who succeeded to it legally could also be said to be *dominus mundi*.

In addition to the legal and theological bases for the emperor's universal jurisdiction, there is also the fundamental justification of government on which Nicholas has built his entire system—consent. At the end of his lengthy discussion of the geography of the empire, it suddenly occurs to him that if the standard of consent is used to determine the jurisdiction of the emperor, he can only be called lord or emperor of those areas over which he actually has the consent of the subjects. This recognition that, if the standard of consent is used, there are regions not subject to the emperor, even within the confines of the old Roman empire, is confirmed in Nicholas' later statement that, except for the laws enforcing conciliar decrees, imperial legislation does not extend to kings and princes "who *de facto* or because of exemption do not recognize the overlordship of the empire."[27]

The discussion of the constitutional history of the empire and its relation to the other kingdoms may be compared with an earlier work which Nicholas probably had read, the *Tractatus de Juribus Regni et Imperii Romanii* of Lupold of Bebenburg, written in 1340.[28] There are some

27 *DCC*, Book III, chap. vii, p. 363. ". . . qui de facto aut privilegio superioritatem imperii non recognoscunt." Papal recognition of the *de facto* independence of France had come as early as the beginning of the thirteenth century when Innocent III in his decree *Per Venerabilem* noted that "the king of France recognizes no superior in temporals."

28 Printed in Schard, *De Jurisdictione*, pp. 328-409. It is summarized in McIlwain, *Growth*, pp. 88-93, and excerpts are printed in Lewis, *Medieval Political Ideas*, I, 310-312, and II, 500-562.

striking similarities and differences in the two books. Lupold and Nicholas, both Germans, derive the juridical rights of the empire from the succession of the German emperors to Charlemagne's conquest of Italy. Both assert that the electors act in place of the whole people in electing the emperor. (Lupold gives greater emphasis to their legal character as a *collegium* acting *vice omnium* for the *universitas* of the whole people.) Both allow for the deposition of the emperor by the people, and both emphasize the German character of the empire since the time of Otto I.

However, Lupold seems to accept the Donation of Constantine and the transfer of the empire to Charlemagne as genuine. (There is no mention of Pepin.) Moreover, he maintains explicitly that by virtue of his coronation the emperor receives, in addition to his title, a new role—that of protector of the church throughout Christendom, giving him a vague type of overlordship in relation to the kings and princes of other lands. For Nicholas, *imperator* was a mere title (*nomen*), and by receiving this title the emperor did not acquire anything new. However, the similarities in their views are greater than the differences, leading to the conclusion that Nicholas either had read Lupold or was influenced by the same sources.

While his conception of a dual hierarchy under pope and emperor governing the world caused him to assert an ideal of a single head of the body politic, two considerations led Nicholas of Cusa to modify this ideal conception. First, he recognized that at his time, and even in the days of the old Roman empire, large sections of the world were not under the political control of the emperor. Secondly, Nicholas returned to his justification of rulership by consent. If it is consent and not legal succession which justifies government, then the emperor can be said to be *dominus* only of those sections of the world which habitually obey him. His overlordship of the rest of the known world is restricted to his religious role in enforcing church law, to which the consent of the other kings is assumed.

Nicholas is a firm believer in the use of force to back up ecclesiastical decrees. Every ruler's first duty is the protection and encouragement of the Catholic religion in his domain. He should accomplish this by laws which treat religious as well as secular matters, as did such great rulers as Charlemagne and Justinian. As Cusanus says at one point, "the strength of law lies in coercion. Power keeps and exercises coercion. Since we are inclined to forbidden things, and prone to evil from youth, if the punishment attached to law is removed, then peace and justice do not last long."[29]

This necessity for enforcement of religious laws is the basis of the universal role of the emperor. He has a special religious duty to enforce ecclesiastical legislation, especially the decrees of the church councils. In addition to his duty to enforce church law by civil penalties, the spiritual role of the emperor is also very considerable in the convocation of universal councils. The pope is the person charged with prime responsibility for calling the council, while "the emperor exhorts and persuades the bishops and commands the laity."[30] However, if there is an urgent need for a council and the pope refuses to call it, the emperor should do so.

Once the council has met, the question arises as to exactly

[29] *DCC*, Book III, chap. xxxix, p. 454. "Vigor legis in coerctione est; coerctionem potentia custodit et exequitur; qua sublata (quia nitimur in vetitum et sumus ab adolescentia proni ad malum) legalis censura et per consequens pax et iustitia non diu persistent." For examples of Nicholas' appeals to the secular arm to enforce spiritual decisions, see discussion in a succeeding chapter.

[30] *DCC*, Book III, chap. xv, p. 387. "Imperator vero exhortatur et persuadet episcopis ac praecipit laicis." Note the belief that the clergy are exempted from secular control.

what role the emperor should play in it. The records of early church councils made it clear that the emperors had been active in convoking and in chairing the councils. However, Nicholas maintains that the emperor did not act as chairman of any councils, but only of a *conciliabulum* against the adherents of the Nestorian heresy at which the papal legates had not yet arrived. The emperor and his retinue can take on special assignments for the council, as the emperor did at Chalcedon in deciding the conflict between the patriarchs of Rome and Constantinople, but this is done only with the consent of the council.[31]

Although, as noted earlier, the church council may be considered in some sense to represent the laity, participation is restricted to the clergy, principally the bishops. The emperor, however, has a special religious position and therefore, is entitled to participate in the council. With him are "the parts of his body"—the high nobles, imperial officials, and Roman senators. In addition, the imperial electors, representing the Roman people, have a right to participate. However, all these lay people, with the exception of the emperor, have the right only to listen and not to speak. In the case of the treatment of strictly ecclesiastical questions, they need the council's permission even to listen. The easiest solution, says Nicholas, is to have the secular princes send bishops to represent them. They, of course, will have full rights of participation. Otherwise, if the rulers wish to address the council, they can be granted special permission to do so, but "to debate and define church matters is the function of the priests."[32]

Following the example of the Council of Constance,

---

[31] *DCC*, Book III, chap. xviii, pp. 395-396.
[32] *DCC*, Book III, chap. xvii, p. 393. "Deliberare vero et res ecclesiasticas diffinire sacerdotum est." The reference to the senators and imperial advisors as parts of the emperor's body is drawn from Justinian's Code (*Lex Julia Majestatis*).

considerable care must be taken to get the agreement of the other kings besides the emperor, since the emperor does not have the power he once had. In attempting to secure this agreement Nicholas is willing to admit other kings to the meeting, and thus to compromise his principle that church councils are to be composed only of churchmen and (because of his special function as protector of the church) of the emperor and his retinue. To solve problems of precedence in conciliar processions and meetings, the kings of France and Spain, if they are present, should walk and sit on each side of the emperor, with the elder on his right and the younger on his left.[33]

In Cusanus' theory of the relations of the spiritual and temporal orders, there is a duality of administration, but no separation of over-all purpose and certainly nothing approaching a naturalistic view of the function of the state. Both the ecclesiastical and the civil rulers are subordinated to a single religious ideal, that of leading men to heaven. There is not a difference of spheres so much as a difference of method. Both are aimed ultimately at the salvation of souls, and, if force is necessary for this, Nicholas does not hesitate to recommend its application—provided it is used according to law by a ruler who has received his office by consent of the people or their representatives.

When Nicholas turns from the justification of the empire to its improved operation, he devotes the last part of the *Concordantia* to various proposals for the reform of the empire. To begin with, he sets up as the ideal the vigorous and harmonious state of the early days of the empire. Otto I received the empire from the Roman people and Otto II expanded it. Otto II was also the one who granted temporal power to the ecclesiastics in the empire, always accompany-

33 *DCC*, Book III, chap. xvii, p. 394.

ing the grant with feudal duties proportionate to the temporal holdings.[34]

At the time of Otto II, dukes and counts were directly responsible to the emperor, and removable at his pleasure. Their children could succeed them if they performed their duties properly, but succession was not automatic. This practice was combined with the feudal oath of loyalty to the emperor, and he took care to supervise the activities of his vassals and listen to all appeals, taking away feudal offices if there were abuses. Even representatives of the people were made judges so that the nobility would not oppress the people through fear of judicial retribution.

> And everything tended toward the public good. There was then an emperor with authority to defend the peace and possessing for this purpose a paid professional army. Everywhere the emperor was feared by the princes and leaders, and adored, venerated, and cherished by the people as the defender of the fatherland, the protector of liberty, the help of the oppressed, and the severest punishment of the disturbers of the commonwealth.[35]

These were the good old days to which Nicholas wishes to return, the days of Otto II, when the empire was in its glory and before feudalism had begun to undermine its unity.

All this contrasts with the present state of the church and empire. Rebellion and oppression are rife. Anticipating the complaints voiced at the Reformation, Nicholas attacks

---

[34] *DCC*, Book III, chap. xxvii, pp. 428-430. The more important bishops had their own courts, tax systems, and customs, making them virtually independent of the emperor.

[35] *DCC*, Book III, chap. xxviii, p. 432. "Et cuncta tendebant ad publicam utilitatem. Erat tunc imperator habens publicam defendendae pacis personam, ad hoc habens de publico exercitum stipendiatum; Undique per principes et rectores timebatur, undique per populum defensor patriae, conservator libertatis, relevator oppressorum, rigidissimus exsecutor in rei publicae turbatores, adorabatur, venerabatur, et colebatur."

the greed of the Roman curia and complains that ecclesiastical offices are bought at Rome, and at such a price that "throughout Germany all are overwhelmed not only to the point of being burdened but of being destroyed."[36] Cusanus adds (reflecting his case involving the disputed bishopric of Trier) that when there is an episcopal election the votes are divided, and when the bishop is appointed by the papal curia the office goes to the one who offers the most. The smallest matter is appealed to Rome, which should be reserved for only the important appeals. People come there from all of Christendom in the hope of securing benefices. "They bring gold and silver and return with charters."[37]

The evils of excessive centralization in the church are matched by the centrifugal tendencies in the empire. The electors force promises from the imperial candidates, and they are steadily increasing in power so that now they are stronger than the emperor. "The hierarchical order ceases to function. There is no head to whom one can go. And where there is no order, there is confusion. And when there is confusion no one is safe . . . because as the princes devour the empire, so the people will devour the princes."[38]

The remedy for these evils is the re-establishment of the proper hierarchy of rule by making the central government strong and effective in the empire, and using the emperor's power to reform the church as well. Recalling the supposed situation under Otto II, Nicholas proposes the "revival" of the professional standing army under the control of the

---

36 *DCC*, Book III, chap. xxix, pp. 433-434. "Ut per Alemanniam omnes se non gravatos tantum, sed destructos conquerantur."

37 *DCC*, Book III, chap. xl, p. 457. "Deferunt aurum et argentum, reportant cartas."

38 *DCC*, Book III, chap. xxx, p. 436. ". . . desinet hierarchus ordo. Non est primus ad quem concurratur. Et ubi non est ordo, est confusio. Et ubi confusio, ibi nullus tutus . . . Quoniam sicut principes imperium devorant, ita populares principes."

emperor. A central treasury in Frankfurt would be established, financed by annual taxes proportionate to feudal holdings, as well as by a given proportion of the salt tax (*gabella*) and customs duties (*theolonia*). This money would go to the support of an imperial army to replace the present wasteful system of local armed forces controlled by every petty prince, town, and community. This would enable the church rulers to carry out their spiritual duties, and there should be no exemption of church lands from the duty to pay taxes in return for protection received.[39]

The proposal for a central army is a logical conclusion of Cusanus' fear of the power of local rulers, and his belief in the value of force to back up law. "Law without force loses its binding power, and its life. It does not merit to be called law, any more than a corpse should be called a man."[40]

The army will abolish the practice of *diffidatio* or private war, whereby, after a ceremony of breaking of allegiance, the territories of feudal lords are invaded by their vassals and seized by force. What is needed in the way of reform, says Nicholas, is a strict law forbidding any act of occupation or seizure of another's land on one's own initiative. Only by a court judgment will it be permissible to take anyone else's property. This is a law which should be signed and sealed by all the princes of the empire; if it is violated, all the goods of the evildoer should be confiscated, and, if he is a clergyman, he should be degraded.[41]

To prevent agreements between the candidates and the electors, the secret ballot must be introduced. Here Nicho-

---

39 *DCC*, Book III, chap. xxxix, pp. 454-456. Nicholas quotes Hugh of St. Victor ("our most excellent Saxon"), probably deriving the quotation from Marsilius, D. II, chap. xvii, v. 19.
40 *DCC*, Book III, chap. xxvi, pp. 427-28. "Lex sine coerctione censuram non habens vitam perdidit, nec lex dici meretur; sicut nec mortuus homo."
41 *DCC*, Book III, chap. xxxi, pp. 436-37, and chap. xxxiv, pp. 440-42.

las puts forward a proposal for a preferential voting system, whereby each of the electors gets a ballot with the name of each candidate upon it (except his own, if he is running). He puts after each name on the paper a number ranging between one and the total number of candidates, in the order of ascending merit. Thus if there are ten candidates, the best would have the number 10 after his name, and the worst would be number 1. Then all the ballots are put into a sack, and a priest, having said Mass, takes them out one by one, recording the number next to each name. The candidate who gets the highest number of votes, when all are totaled, is elected. In a personal note, Nicholas modestly adds, "With much study, I have not been able to find a safer system, and believe me, no more perfect system can be found."[42]

Another way to strengthen the empire is to improve and centralize the legal and judicial system. Nicholas proposes that this be done by dividing the empire into twelve or more judicial districts. Each one would have a single court comprising three judges—one member of the nobility, one clergyman, and one commoner. All cases, both ecclesiastical and civil, could be appealed from the local courts to this court, where it would finally be decided by decision of at least two of the three judges. The final decision would be announced by the member of the panel of judges who is of the same social status as those involved in the case. The judges should be paid from the public treasury and the courts are to have final jurisdiction, except that when

42 *DCC*, Book III, chap. xxxvii, p. 450. "Quem securiorem ego non absque magno studio etiam non potui invenire. Et credas quod perfectior inveniri nequit." For an inconclusive attempt to demonstrate a link between this system of preferential voting and another electoral system proposed by Raymond Lull in a manuscript in the library at Kues, see Honecker, "Ramon Lulls Wahlvorschlag."

the parties are important personages, or the subject matter is serious, an appeal can be taken to the next imperial council.[43] Judicial and legal reforms are to be carried out by the imperial council. The exact composition of the council is difficult to determine, since Nicholas describes a number of different conciliar groups in the last book of the *Concordantia*.

First there is the universal imperial council, which is the secular counterpart of the universal council in the church. It is graded hierarchically with the kings and imperial electors in the first rank below the emperor. In the next rank come the dukes, the governors of the various provinces, and the prefects, and following them the marquesses and landgraves. In addition, the council should also include the heads of the great corporate groups in the empire (*universitates*), the professors (*magistri*), and those of senatorial rank (the last group subdivided into three ranks). This council examines, coordinates, and amends the laws for the whole empire.[44]

Another group is described, which has met once or twice a year in the past and which Nicholas feels should be revived—the *conventus*. Composed of the immediate vassals of the emperor, it met to decide judicial matters and to receive ambassadors and legates. Apparently Nicholas is thinking of this group when he later proposes the establishment of a *conventus annuus* of the seven electors and the thirty-six judges who should meet at the time of the feast of Pentecost in Frankfurt.[45] Its work would consist in deciding cases involving the princes of the empire, the emperor's immediate vassals. In particularly difficult cases

43 *DCC*, Book III, chap. xxxiii, pp. 439-440.
44 *DCC*, Book III, chap. xxv, pp. 421-425. Cf. also chap. xii, p. 375, for mention of participation by church leaders.
45 *DCC*, Book III, chap. xxxv, p. 442.

a larger meeting could be held, with the participation of all the princes.

In another description it is proposed that the council meet in Frankfurt for a month each May or September. It would include the representatives of all the cities and towns, as well as the princes, counselors, and nobles, and would be charged with working out a common law for the whole empire. Provincial legislation would be examined and harmonized and judicial formulae simplified so that simple peasants would not lose cases merely by failing to pronounce the proper legal formula *("qui cadit a syllaba, cadit a causa,* as I have often seen happen in the diocese of Trier").[46]

In addition every *princeps* should have a daily council of advisors, made up of *viri perfecti,* chosen to represent various parts of the kingdom. They should act as royal counselors in the same way that the cardinals advise and assist the pope.[47] The constitution of the empire which appears to emerge from these references consists, in addition to the emperor and his seven electors, of a great council largely legislative in character, a smaller annual representative council of electors, judges, and possibly other representatives, the business of which would be legal and judicial, and a privy council of advisors.[48]

Specific recommendations are made for the conduct of discussions in the councils. Two spokesmen are to be appointed to summarize the arguments for each side of the question under discussion. (The use of the adversary system in this way to polarize discussion contrasts with Nicholas' usual emphasis on harmony and finding "the

46 *DCC,* Book III, chap. xxxv, p. 446.
47 *DCC,* Book III, chap. xii, p. 376. The chapter talks about kings and the *respublica,* but the context indicates that Cusanus is also thinking of the empire.
48 *DCC,* Book III, chap. xli, p. 473.

concordant mean.") After their speeches, ballots listing various alternatives should be given to those voting, and they should cross out all but the alternative which they prefer. The ballots should then be placed in a sack and publicly counted. Drawing on his experience in Italy, Nicholas also mentions another method, used in Venice, in which woolen balls are dropped into two wooden containers shaped like hollow chalices.[49] This method would also have the advantage of secrecy and freedom from outside pressure.

The idea of reform of the empire through common courts, taxation, and an imperial army was not a new one when Nicholas put it forward. At the time of the Council of Constance, Sigismund himself had suggested a subdivision of the empire into four districts, each with its own court on which the various estates would be represented. At the Reichstag of Frankfurt in 1427, the Elector of Brandenburg had proposed a common army based on a tax levied on the whole empire, and very shortly before the composition of the *Concordantia* the proposal had been repeated at the Nuremberg Reichstag of 1431. It is not certain how much subsequent influence Nicholas' proposals actually exercised, although reform of the judicial system was discussed at the Reichstag in 1434. Only at the Reichstag of Worms in 1495 was a common tax decreed and a central court *(Reichskammergericht)* established, which continued in existence until 1806.[50]

The conciliar method is Nicholas' great solution for the ills of church or empire.

A mortal fever has attacked the German empire, and unless a cure is found immediately, death will certainly follow. You

---

49 *DCC*, Book III, chap. xxxviii, p. 453.
50 Theodor Stumpf, *Die politischen Ideen des Nicolaus von Cues* (Cologne, 1865), pp. 87-96.

will look for the empire in Germany and you will not find it there. Foreigners will take our lands, and we will be divided among ourselves and subjected to another nation. No better method can be suggested than to go back to the trodden and tried ways of the past to which we must resort if we wish to reform the empire. And the basic reform is the institution of annual general councils, which should start in this holy council of Basel, and be established as a rule for the future.[51]

No better summary could be given of Nicholas' conservatism, his nationalism, and his reform program for the future. The passage helps to explain the extraordinary interest in, and enthusiasm for Nicholas of Cusa in Germany down to the present day.

De Concordantia Catholica concludes with a return to the vision outlined at the start—a harmonious, freely cooperating *respublica Christiana,* in which body and soul, higher and lower organs, work together in concordance, freely consenting to a hierarchical order intended by God, and guided and inspired by the Holy Spirit. After an appeal to the emperor to bring about reform in church and empire, Nicholas of Cusa closes with a postscript which shows him to be a faithful Catholic and a loyal conciliarist.

This is the end of the collection *De Concordantia Catholica* made from various approved writings of the ancients for the glory of God almighty, which I, Nicholas of Cusa, dean of the church of St. Florin in Koblenz, and lowly doctor of the decrees, offer in all humility to this holy Council of Basel,

---

[51] *DCC,* Book III, chap. xxxii, p. 438. ". . . mortalis morbus imperium Germanicum invasit cui nisi subito salutari antidoto subveniatur mors indubio sequetur; et quaretur imperium in Germania, et non invenietur ibi. Et per consequens alieni capient loca nostra et dividemur inter nos et sic alteri nationi subiciemur. Non potest autem melius provideri quam per iam tritas et expertas antiquas vias, ad quas per reformationem accedere necesse habemus. Quare primus radix est instituere annuos conventus generales et in hoc sacro Basiliensi concilio incipere et futuris regulam dare."

judging and asserting nothing in all this to be true or to be defended as true, except what that sacred synod will hold to be true and Catholic, and ready to be corrected in all respects by orthodox doctrine.[52]

[52] *DCC*, Book III, chap. xl, p. 474. "Finit collectio de concordantia catholica ex variis veterum approbatis scripturis ad laudem Dei omnipotentis quam ego Nicholaus de Cusa, decanus sancti Florini Confluentiae, decretorum doctor minimus sacro huic Basiliensi concilio cum omni humilitate offero, nichil in omnibus verum aut defendendum pro vero iudicans seu asserens nisi quod ipsa sacra synodus catholicum et verum iudicaverit in omnibus ab omnibus orthodoxis corrigi paratus."

CHAPTER IX

. . .

FROM COUNCIL TO POPE

From the beginning of the Council of Basel, relations between the pope and the council had been bad, but in the period under consideration they deteriorated to the point of open rupture. Partly because the pope was in Italy and the council was in Basel in northern Switzerland, each side was ready to attribute evil motives to the other and to use whatever ecclesiastical or political weapons were available to force a settlement on its own terms.

The pope was represented at the council by his legate, Giuliano Cesarini, who presided over it and attempted to act as a moderating influence. In his first years as legate, he continued to urge the pope to submit to the council, but as its demands became more extreme, and as his own prestige in the meeting began to decline and that of the Cardinal of Arles to increase, he became more and more disturbed with the trend of the council's decisions. The fact that Cesarini, Nicholas' former teacher at Padua, also altered his views in the same period seems to indicate that the change from council to pope was not a matter of personal advantage in Cusanus' case, but that the conduct of the meeting might well have led him to be less enthusiastic about the conciliar ideal than in the earlier period.

The pope sent three representatives to the council with instructions to preside over it in their capacity as papal legates. When the council took up the question of whether they should be admitted and, if so, with what authority, Nicholas wrote his advisory opinion, *De Auctoritate Presi-*

dendi in Concilio Generali.[1] He attempted to reconcile the propapal and antipapal positions by maintaining that the council was obliged to take them in as representatives of the pope and should make them chairmen but without decision-making authority. The ultimate decision of the council, made at the suggestion of Emperor Sigismund, was very close to Cusanus' proposal. The legates were admitted (April 1434) provided they swore to adhere to the doctrine of conciliar supremacy (which they did "in their own names"), and it was agreed that they were to alternate as chairmen, but without jurisdictional power.

In the controversy over the seating of the two papal legates in 1434, it became clear that there was a group in the council that was intent on asserting conciliar supremacy at every possible juncture. Nicholas' views in his treatise on seating the legates already showed that he was more moderate. For him, the pope or his representatives had a special position, although decision making was vested in the council as a whole (including the pope).

At this point, Nicholas was taking a very active part in the debates on the relations of pope and council, but his original purpose in coming to Basel had not been forgotten. On March 15, 1434, the council, with the two claimants present, finally took up the question of the disputed bishopric of Trier. Linking his defense of the rights of Ulrich von Manderscheid to the general thesis propounded in his *De Concordantia Catholica,* he declared that every governmental authority depends on the consent of the governed, by natural law. As a result the papal transfers, reservations, and provisions were illegitimate.[2] The council

1 *DAP,* ed. Kallen.
2 John of Segovia in *Monumenta Conciliorum Generalium Saeculi XV,* II (Vienna, 1857), 323-324. The record of the debates and decisions of the council appears in Haller, *Concilium Basiliense,* III, 46-47, 56-57, 75, 99.

heard the representatives of the papal appointee, and examined the papal documents relevant to the case, and decided that, since it involved a disputed election, the intervention of the pope was justified (the case involved the predecessor of the present pope, which may have favorably influenced the council). Moreover, there was evidence that the election was held under duress. Hence on May 15, 1434, the decision of the council went to Raban, Bishop of Speyer, and Nicholas lost his case.

Nicholas, however, stayed at Basel and continued to participate in the meetings of the Committee on Faith. In the following year (1435) he was back in Koblenz, securing a final settlement for his client, whereby Ulrich received a financial indemnity for giving up his claims to the archbishopric. In 1435 Nicholas received the profitable post of provost of Münster-Maifeld, northwest of Koblenz, and it is an indication of his ambivalent attitude that he took pains to have his appointment confirmed both by the pope and by the council. On November 26, 1435, the Council of Basel gave him the desired confirmation, and a letter from Ambrogio Traversari, the papal representative at Basel, written in October to an Italian bishop, indicated that Nicholas had written him to get his support for papal confirmation. Traversari had been lobbying in Basel to prevent the council from taking away the papal right to the annates of benefices. He describes Nicholas as "most zealous and distinguished for the number of books he possesses" and "most learned," and notes that his case should be supported "since his friendship which I have been developing here by letter can be most useful to our efforts."[3]

On the politics behind the contest (the effort of the nobility to secure control of the electorship of Trier), see Meuthen, "Obedienz und Absolutionslisten," and "Nikolaus von Kues und der Laie."

3 ". . . quia multum studiis nostris conferre potest eius, quam hic mihi

Traversari was in Basel to work against the radically anti-papal financial decree of June 9, 1435, which had struck at the heart of the papal financial system at the moment when Eugene was in greatest need of money for reasons of domestic Italian politics. Between 1427 and 1436 papal revenues had declined from 170,000 florins to 60,000 florins.[4] Now the council attempted to abolish all papal charges for ecclesiastical appointments, including the annates or first year's income. The papacy was to be supported by grants from the bishops, to be decided on later by the council. In August the council further attempted to assert its financial independence by ordering papal tax collectors to send all money to Basel, and demanded that all taxes in arrears be paid to Basel rather than to Rome.

By the time Nicholas returned to Basel in March 1436, the council had been granting indulgences, dispensations from inpediments to marriage, and had even asserted the right to forgive certain sins that was reserved to the pope. Cesarini was no longer the dominant figure. The council looked to Louis Aleman, Cardinal of Arles and an avowed enemy of the pope, who had resolved to take revenge on the pope for an earlier slight in Rome.[5] Traversari wrote to the emperor complaining that in the council "the voice of the cook has as much value as that of a bishop or archbishop," and "whatsoever this raging mob decrees is attributed to the Holy Spirit."[6] After a last attempt at com-

literis comparavi, familiaritas. *Ambrosii Traversari Epistolae*, ed. Petrus Cannetus (Florence, 1759), vol. II, letter 48, col. 174. An earlier letter to the pope, written September 23, 1435, describes the confused political situation at Basel, indicating which bishops are favorable to the people (vol. II, letter 15, col. 33). On Nicholas' appearances in Basel, cf. Haller, *Concilium Basiliense*, III, 319, 576.

4 Peter Partner, "The Budget of the Roman Church in the Renaissance Period," in E. F. Jacob, ed., *Italian Renaissance Studies* (London, 1960), p. 260.

5 Gabriel Pérouse, *Le cardinal Louis Aleman*, (Paris, 1904), chap. iii.

6 Letter no. 176, quoted in Gill, *Council of Florence*, p. 67, n. 3

promise in the spring of 1436, the pope decided that no further accommodation was possible. Henceforth his principal concern was to destroy the meeting at Basel.

One of Cusanus' first acts after being reincorporated into the Committee on Faith *(deputatio de fide)* was to refuse to act as a judge for the committee. However, he continued to take an active role in the work of the committee and of the council, so that this refusal does not seem to prove that he was already on the point of defection.[7] He served on a peace mission to Bavaria in the spring and summer of 1436, and he was appointed *conservator decretorum* of the the council in October. As usual, he also was collecting benefices, in this case the parish church of Bernkastel, across the Moselle from his native village of Kues. Significantly, he again attempted to have this appointment confirmed by both pope and council.[8]

The issue which led to his departure from the council was the controversy over the site of the proposed union council with the emissaries of the Greek church. Negotiations on the council had been going on for a number of years, and it is important to note that an agreement on the subject had been concluded as early as 1430 between the emperor in Constantinople and Pope Eugene's predecessor. It specified that the emperor and the patriarch should come to Italy to a city on the Adriatic coast between Calabria and Ancona for a council of union.[9] In 1434 after the submission of the pope, when the council's power was at its height, a delegation from Constantinople had come

---

[7] Haller, *Concilium Basiliense*, IV (Basel, 1903), 74. Vansteenberghe, *Nicolas*, pp. 59-60, interprets this as a sign of Cusanus' reluctance to associate himself with new measures which the council was undertaking against the pope.

[8] Haller, *Concilium Basiliense*, IV, 149, 240, 291 and Meuthen, "Die Pfründen," pp. 35-39.

[9] The text appears in Gill, *Council of Florence*, p. 43.

to Basel. The Greeks were told that they should come to Basel for the union meeting, since if it were held in Italy the Basel meeting would have to be dissolved. However, the Greek emissaries indicated that their instructions did not allow this, and further negotiations in Constantinople in 1435 indicated that the emperor was insistent on the Italian seaboard site and on the participation of the pope.[10] When the council turned its attentions once again in the fall of 1436 to the question of the site of the union council, there appeared a clear division of opinion. On the one side were those who favored Basel, or, if the Greeks insisted on a place accessible by sea, Avignon. On the other side were those who argued for an Italian city, both because it was favored by the Greeks and because this would assure the participation of the pope. Louis Aleman headed the anti-papal group, while Cesarini (and following him, Nicholas of Cusa) adopted a more conciliatory attitude.

Cesarini and Cusanus worked for postponement of the final decision, so that a compromise could be worked out with the pope and with the Greeks, but the antipapal party pushed ahead. In early December 1436 the vote was taken. Basel and Avignon received 242 votes out of 355 voting, more than the required two-thirds majority. The other votes were divided about evenly among Florence, Vienna, Udine, and Parma. Nicholas of Cusa voted for "any place suitable to the pope and to the Greeks."[11] When Cesarini refused to announce the vote, Cardinal Aleman did so.

In February the emissary of the Greek church, John Dishypatus, protested that neither Basel nor Avignon would be satisfactory to the Greeks, and that the presence of the

10 *Ibid.,* pp. 55 and 64.
11 Haller, *Concilium Basiliense,* IV, 358ff, gives the vote and lists those voting individually, from the original records of the Council. The list includes only three cardinals and twenty bishops and archbishops. Nicholas of Cusa's votes are listed on pp. 338 and 351.

pope was indispensable to a union council. In February 1437 the party of reconciliation with the papacy succeeded in attaching a time limit to the negotiations with the citizens of Avignon, who were very wary about getting involved in a council without financial guarantees. When this time expired, the whole question came up for discussion once more. In the meantime, considerable lobbying with the upper clergy had been going on, and although the original decision in favor of Basel and Avignon had been taken with the support of 44 of the 52 prelates present, in the interim additional converts had been made to the papal position, although nothing like a majority. When the matter was again discussed in the committees in April 1437, three of the four chairmen supported the minority position and the council split into two factions. The larger Avignon faction claimed to be the true council because it was the majority, while the other group, which included three cardinals and twelve bishops, maintained that it was the *sanior pars* acting in conformity with the past agreements with Constantinople.[12]

Tempers grew heated in the controversy. At the end of April the partisans of the Italian site came to the cathedral early one morning and occupied the main altar. When the others heard this they tried to storm the altar, and only the intervention of the Basel citizenry prevented violence. Negotiations were carried on between the two parties in an atmosphere which Aeneas Sylvius, one of the chroniclers of the council, compared unfavorably to the conduct of drunkards in a tavern.[13]

The final rupture took place on May 7. Both groups came to the cathedral intent on the formal adoption of their decrees convoking a union council with the Greeks.

[12] Gill, *Council of Florence*, pp. 72-73.
[13] Valois, *Le Pape*, II, 54.

When last-minute negotiations broke down, the two groups each read their decrees. Since the minority decree was shorter, that group finished first and intoned a *Te Deum*, which was followed by the *Te Deum* of the majority. On May 20 the bishops of Digne and Oporto, and Nicholas of Cusa in the company of the two Greek representatives, left Basel with the minority decree, signed by the council notaries but without the council's seal.[14] They directed themselves to Bologna to get papal confirmation before going to Constantinople to make arrangements for the Greeks to come to an Italian city for the union council. In September the pope formally transferred the council to Italy, this time succeeding where he had failed in 1431. The council in reply voted to suspend the pope and to confiscate the ecclesiastical offices of his adherents, including Nicholas of Cusa.[15]

How did it happen that the partisan of conciliar supremacy, the one who saw in the *concilium universale* the fullest representation of the consent of the church endowed with power to control all church offices and legislation, even to the extent of deposing the pope, should have become, in such a short time, one of the strongest and most effective opponents of the gathering of Basel?

Some of Cusanus' immediate contemporaries were harsh in their criticism of what they viewed as treason to the conciliar cause. Gregory of Heimburg, one of the most vehement opponents of the papacy throughout the period in which Nicholas lived, attributed the change to the

14 Cesarini had given up the chairmanship, and Aleman was presiding over the meeting. However, Cesarini still had the council seal, which was broken into after Nicholas' departure and affixed to the minority decree.

15 G. Hofmann et al., *Concilium Florentinum*, vol. I, part II (Rome, 1944), p. 58, reproduces the papal letter of December 21, 1438, to the bishops of Cologne and Liege, annulling the council's confiscation of the numerous benefices which Nicholas then possessed.

council's adverse decision on his lawsuit involving the archbishopric of Trier. His best biographer, Vansteenberghe, also tends to view the loss of the case as the "initiating cause" of his change of position. The other biographers, particularly if they are Protestants, are often unsympathetic to his action. One nineteenth century author maintains that it was ambition, if not financial greed, which dictated the move.[16] Others try to relate the change to Cusanus' philosophical and political ideas, particularly as expressed in the *De Concordantia Catholica*. For these commentators, the change in position was an application of ideas which he had expressed in his principal conciliar work.[17]

For the "opportunist" hypothesis, we have the evidence of Traversari's letter, which shows that Cusanus was very much concerned with securing papal confirmation for his provostship in Germany. On the other hand, his friend and former teacher, Cesarini, also altered his opinions during the period in question, and in his case, as a cardinal and one of the most influential members of the council, it only led to hardship and opposition. There must have been something about the conduct of the council which would lead a man like Cusanus to pass from conciliarism to papalism in the three or four years before 1437.

One evident factor was the council's increasingly antipapal attitude. While there had been friction and even outright opposition between pope and council earlier, the

---

[16] Gregory of Heimburg's attack is printed in Goldast, *Monarchiae*, vol. II, col. 1626-31. It is summarized in Andreas Posch, *Die "Concordantia catholica" des Nikolaus von Cues* (Paderborn, 1930), p. 18, and in Peter Mennicken, *Nikolaus von Kues* (Trier, 1950), p. 52. The reference in Vansteenberghe occurs on page 58, and "Ehrgeiz von edelm Metalle" is the motive attributed by Theodor Stumpf in *Die politischen Ideen*, p. 101.

[17] See for instance, Birck, "Hat Nikolaus von Kues seine Ansicht über den Primat geändert?" in *Tübinger Theologische Quartalschrift*, vol. 74 (1892) and F. A. Scharpff, *Der Kardinal und Bischof Nikolaus von Cusa* (Mainz, 1843), p. 110.

council had not taken such drastic steps as cutting off papal revenues and directing that all church taxes be paid to Basel rather than to Rome. By 1436, however, the council was arrogating to itself the granting of indulgences and canonizations, in fact, acting as if Basel were Rome. This uncompromising attitude came out most clearly in the question of the site of the union council. Papal wishes, or even those of the Greeks, were ignored in favor of a site which only made church union difficult if not impossible. The controversy in turn led to violent disagreements within the council which did not stop short of resort to arms.

Nicholas of Cusa's ideal in church and state was one of concord—harmony among the varying interrelated parts of a hierarchical organism. The council seemed at first to be the instrument to achieve this unity. In it a divinely inspired consent would bring about harmony and even unanimity among the various members. *De Concordantia Catholica* had held that only when a council concludes in agreement can it be considered to be a *concilium* and not a *conciliabulum*. "Where there is disagreement, there is no council," Cusanus had written. "God is where there is consent," and "on account of the unanimity on which the authority of the acts of a council depends, we know that the Holy Spirit, who is the spirit of union and harmony *(concordantiae)* has inspired the council's decision."[18]

The actions and the atmosphere of Basel in the period preceding Nicholas' departure were anything but harmonious. The personal rivalries, quarrels, and even physical violence which characterized the meeting were far from the consensus which was the sign of the presence of divine inspiration. His conclusion, then, was that the Holy Spirit was no longer present, that even if the council had been

18 *DAP*, p. 24, and *DCC*, Book II, chap. i, p. 93, and chap. x, p. 138.

rightly convoked it did not embody the other requirements of free discussion and a harmonious conclusion which were the prerequisites for a true church council.[19]

Another consideration which must have been in his mind, and his subsequent writings and speeches bear this out, was the question of reunion with the Greeks. The Greeks were a part of the church in schism, and in *De Concordantia,* which relies heavily on records of councils held in the Eastern church before the division, Cusanus had shown himself acutely aware of the problem of reunion. Now the conciliar majority opposed the repeated wishes of the Greeks that the meeting be held in an Italian seaport. How could the Catholic concord be attained if the council let partisan considerations prevent achievement of union with the East? The council said that it represented the entire Church, but at the moment when it appeared that the centuries-old split with the Byzantine church could be healed, the fathers at Basel saw the problem of reunion with the Greeks only in terms of their conflict with the pope.

The Council of Basel also ignored the wishes of the pope. Although, in his earlier writings, Nicholas had allowed the council to be called and to proceed without the pope if there was an urgent need and if the pope refused to do anything about it, nevertheless he believed that the pope must participate in any decisions on articles of faith. On the basis of his legal training he felt that, as long as the pope remained pope and had not been deposed, he should be allowed freedom to administer the church as he saw fit. Moreover, the *Decretum* of Gratian was very

---

19 The case of the council shows how far Cusanus' conception of consent was from modern parliamentarism. Clearly the existence of an organized opposition and competition among various parties would be regarded by him as the work of the devil, preventing the attainment of unanimity.

specific on the primacy of the pope and the divine institution of the office. At the point when Cusanus left the council, it had asserted for itself more and more of the administrative prerogatives of the papacy, in spite of the fact that the pope had not been deposed. Several of the papal legates had left the council, and although Cesarini remained he was no longer presiding over the meetings as chairman. The council had taken over the functions of the pope, not because of an emergency situation as at Constance, but because of a desire to assert itself as the supreme governing body of the church on a permanent basis.

It is true that Nicholas' change in position violated certain other tenets expounded in *De Concordantia Catholica*. The decision of the majority clearly was in favor of the choice of Avignon. However, there was some question as to the representative quality of those voting, a standard criticism of the council being that anyone present was allowed to vote. Nicholas' consent theory always had contained an admixture of hierarchical elements. He had restricted the vote in the council to priests, and sometimes viewed it only as a meeting of bishops and prelates. From the records of the council it seems that the lower clergy dominated the meeting at the time Cusanus left, although there is no evidence that if they had been excluded the vote would have gone in favor of the pope.

These arguments over the legal character of the council and its voting procedure miss the real heart of the decision to change. Nicholas was a man who passionately desired unity and harmony throughout his life, and the council rent by divisions seemed to him to be "not the church of God, but the synagogue of Satan." The consent of the church in the council was not to be given by counting heads or balancing off factions. The Holy Spirit should inspire *consensus* on what was to be done. Cusanus was undoubtedly one of those quoted by John of Segovia as replying to the reading of the rival decrees on May 7 with neither "Placet" nor "Non placet," but with "Non placet contrarietas et divisio Spiritui Sancto."[20]

In a sense, it was inevitable that Nicholas should opt for the pope in the case of a clear split between pope and council. In the last book of *De Concordantia Catholica*, when Nicholas discussed the empire, he never discussed the power of the *Reichstag* to depose and limit the emperor. His great fear in the empire was the fragmentation and strife which resulted from the weakness of the central power and the strength of the emperor's feudal subordinates, particularly the imperial electors. When he saw danger of a similar dissolution of the church in a schism between pope and council, and when he became aware that the council was asserting for itself prerogatives which, in his theory, belonged to the pope, his own ideas on concord and harmony demanded that he work to restore the unity of the church and strengthen the power of the pope, the head of the church hierarchy whose function he had described as the prevention of schism.

Nicholas conceived of church government as normally consisting of a harmonious relationship *(concordantia)* among a representative council, meeting periodically to adopt legislation, a more or less permanent college of cardinals, and a strong papacy. In justifying the church council, he had utilized legal categories of consent and representation which in the event of a division between pope and council seemed to imply conciliar supremacy. Yet when the division took place, he reverted to an older integralist view also present in his thought which saw society and government as a harmonious organism of interrelated, functionally differentiated, and hierarchically

20 John of Segovia, quoted in Valois, *Le Pape*, II, 59.

graded parts. This harmonious cooperation was guaranteed by the operation of the Holy Spirit, and its structure reflected the hierarchical structure of the universe outlined by the Neo-Platonic writers. Consent was unanimous and representation was personal. The council was not a *universitas* of all the faithful but a gathering of the various orders of the church hierarchy under the pope and guided by the Holy Spirit.

When Nicholas and the two bishops arrived in Italy at the end of May 1437, the pope confirmed the minority decree. In July they continued to Constantinople, accompanied by two papal emissaries. The delegation arrived in September, some time before the representatives of the Council of Basel, who first had to make financial arrangements with the citizens of Avignon to assure that the city would receive the Greeks. As the Greek emissary at Basel had indicated, the Greeks preferred an Italian city and a council in which the pope would be present. Nicholas' principal assignment seems to have been to gather the records of early councils and other manuscripts which would be useful at the union meeting.[21] After some negotiation, the Eastern emperor and the Patriarch of Constantinople set sail for Italy on November 27, 1437, arriving in Venice in February 1438.

At this point there was some hope that the council in Basel might still come to agreement, in view of the appearance of the Greeks in Italy. However, when Cardinal Cesarini left in January 1438, the last moderating influence had disappeared, and the council began formal proceedings

---

21 Nicholas' renown as a collector of manuscripts and his knowledge of canon law seem to have been the reasons for his inclusion in the mission. Cf. Cesarini's letter to Traversari asking about a Greek collection of records of the sixth, seventh, and eighth councils which "lord Nicholas of Cusa" brought back from Constantinople, in G. Hofmann, *Concilium Florentinum*, V (Rome, 1953), 297.

against the pope which were to culminate in his deposition and the election of an antipope during the following year. In the same month the princes of Germany made a declaration of their neutrality in the conflict between the pope and the council. The principal effect of the declaration was that the German princes ceased to pay tithes and other church taxes to either side. Most of Cusanus' efforts during the ensuing ten years were devoted to bringing Germany into obedience to the Holy See.

The Council of Ferrara (later transferred to Florence) opened in April 1438, but Nicholas did not remain in Italy to observe the proceedings which were to lead to the declaration of union of the Greek and Roman churches in July 1439. In June 1438 he returned to Germany to commence his long struggle for the papacy at the meetings of the German *Reichstag*.[22]

The speeches and actions of the German *Reichstag* in the fifteenth century have been collected in the *Reichstagsakten,* and it is possible to learn from them, with varying degrees of accuracy, the content of the defense of the pope which Nicholas of Cusa made there. Since they cover a period of a number of years, it is possible to follow the evolution of his thought after the break with the council, and to see what modifications, if any, were introduced into his political theory as a result of his action.

Nicholas was sent by the pope to represent him in the *Reichstag* held at Nürnberg in October 1438. No direct

---

[22] Koch, *Nikolaus von Cues und seine Umwelt,* p. 12. It is interesting to note that the voting system established at the council was quite different from that at Basel. In Florence there were three estates, one comprising cardinals, archbishops, and bishops; a second which included abbots and prelates; and a third made up of doctors of canon law. Each group had to adopt decisions by a two-thirds majority (the proportion deemed sufficient to assure that the *major pars* was also *sanior*). The Council of Ferrara had 170 bishops at its opening session, far more than Basel. See Hefele-Leclercq, *Histoire,* vol. VII, part 2, pp. 956, 974.

transcript of his speeches survives, but the general content of his presentation can be deduced from the rather fully reported reply of Thomas of Courcelles, the representative of the conciliar majority, who came to win the emperor and princes over to the council's side.

Two principal points are answered by Thomas. One of them is of no political interest, but it demonstrates the way Cusanus used concepts drawn from other fields to support his political point of view. He seems to have attacked the council on the ground that Basel at that time lay under the adverse influence of the stars, so that division and discord were produced there. With a transfer to Italy, of course, this astrological obstacle would be overcome. His adversary apparently felt it necessary to spend some time in his speech refuting this view.[23]

A more important point to which Courcelles refers is Cusanus' argument that the council, being divided, was no longer a true council, since true councils require unanimity for their decisions to be divinely inspired. Here the theory of *De Concordantia* was used directly to justify the change of position to the papal side. There Nicholas had said that the mark of the council was that it was concluded in harmony, by which he seems to have meant by unanimous agreement. He had also said that any definition on matters of faith should be adopted unanimously to guarantee infallibility. This was a specific application of his general consent theory in its theological rather than its legal or canonistic form. Consent in theological matters meant unanimity. The council was deeply divided, and hence had ceased to be a council.

23 Courcelles' answer to the astrological argument is contained in the transcript of his remarks printed in *Deutsche Reichstagsakten* (*RTA*), vol. XIII, part 2, ed. Gustav Beckmann (Stuttgart-Gotha, 1925), p. 806. It is also referred to in John of Segovia's history of the Council of Basel, quoted at p. 833, n. 3.

This, of course, would mean that the meeting in Florence could not be called a council either. The argument could be used destructively against the Council of Basel, but to establish the theological validity of the Council of Ferrara-Florence would take further argumentation. Unfortunately, it is impossible to reconstruct this argument from the records of the 1438 Nürnberg *Reichstag*.

The records of the March 1439 meeting of the imperial electors in Mainz are not much more helpful on this score. Nicholas was present at the meeting, at which the delegates of the council called for support against the pope. Since he was not officially sent by the pope to the meeting, he was at first refused a hearing but was subsequently permitted to participate. The princes adopted the *instrumentum acceptationis*, agreeing to the principle of the superiority of the council to the pope, but reaffirming their neutrality in the current conflict between Basel and Eugene. In reply to Nicholas' report on the meeting, one of the cardinals at Rome stressed the importance of getting the support of the German princes, since "the madness of the conciliarists must be repressed not by laws or letters, but by the power of the princes."[24]

On June 25, 1439, the Council of Basel finally deposed Pope Eugene, an action which was met on the papal side by the formal decree at Florence of union with the Greeks (July 5, 1439). A number of bishops and higher clergy refused to participate in the deposition at Basel. The final act was approved by only seven bishops, but over three hundred priests and doctors of theology participated. The deposition of the single universally acknowledged pope (in contrast to the deposition of the disputed popes at

[24] *RTA*, vol. XIV, part 1, ed. Helmut Weigel (Stuttgart, 1933), pp. 142-144. Cardinal Condulmari's advice, "sed comprimendus esset illorum furor non juribus aut litteris, vero potencia principum," appears at p. 159.

Constance) came as a shock to those who feared a new schism like the one which had divided the church for forty years between 1378 and 1417. The fact that it had been carried out by so few members of the higher clergy laid the council open to the charge which had already been made some years before, that the council was dominated by an irresponsible mob of lower clergy. John of Segovia, defending the council's action at a provincial council in Mainz, had to answer Nicholas of Cusa's charge that there were few bishops and no archbishops present at the deposition, except for Louis Aleman, the Cardinal of Arles, who presided.[25]

The first fairly complete statement of Cusanus' theories after the change of position comes in two letters written toward the end of 1439, after the deposition of the pope but probably before it was known that the council had elected Count Amadeus of Savoy as antipope (November 17, 1439).[26] The theories set forth in these letters are important for the history of the development of Cusanus' political philosophy, since they express his views before the publication of the *Docta Ignorantia,* which profoundly influenced his later political theory.

The first letter was addressed to a Carthusian monastery, which had written to ask his opinion on the division between the pope and the council. He replied in a long letter in the form of ten questions and answers. The letter illustrates Nicholas' use of his consent theory for the benefit of the papacy, where previously it had been used for the benefit of the council.

25 Hefele-Leclercq, *Histoire,* vol. VII, part 2, p. 1069, gives the numbers of clergy of various ranks present at the deposition. Segovia's defense against Nicholas' charge appears in *RTA,* vol. XIV, part 2, ed. Helmut Weigel (Stuttgart, 1936), p. 348.
26 The letters to be discussed are contained as no. 4 and no. 5 in the collection by Koch, *Briefwechsel des Nikolaus von Kues,* pp. 36-50.

The council is not the universal church "spread out through the world." It is a gathering, drawn *from* the universal church. There are many different kinds of councils, and their "strength *(vigor)* depends on consent" (a sentence used often in the *Concordantia*). Where the universal church accepts the decisions of a council, it may be said to be a universal council. "Without this, it cannot be said to be a council, especially when a notable part of the church does not consent."[27]

The same theory is spelled out in greater detail in another letter, written about the same time to a representative of the emperor (since the new emperor had not been crowned, he is called in the letter "the king of the Romans"), and sent to the Frankfurt *Reichstag*. The Basel council cannot represent the church because "representative character *(representacio)* comes from express or tacit consent, on which the strength *(vigor)* of councils is based." In the case of Basel, the actions of these few *(pauci)* against Pope Eugene IV had aroused protests from "the Italian nation," kings and princes, and the church throughout the world.[28]

This argument is a variation on the argument from unanimity, referred to above. If a section *(notabilis pars)* of the church does not agree with the council's decision, it can no longer be considered a true council. Nicholas has added, however, an additional requirement beyond that of unanimity in the council. The council does not represent the whole church but is drawn *from* the church, and its decisions must be approved by the church, *per orbem diffusa* ("spread throughout the world").

If the council at Basel cannot be considered to be repre-

[27] Koch, *Briefwechsel*, p. 39. "Sine quo non potest dici concilium, maxime ubi notabilis pars non consentit."
[28] Koch, *Briefwechsel*, pp. 46-47.

· 236 ·

sentative of the church, because of the opposition of a notable part, it might appear that the course which the German princes took the year before, that of neutrality between pope and council, was the correct one, since neither side seemed to have the support of the whole church. However, Nicholas' prime objective in his work in Germany was to end German neutrality, so that he could not accept this conclusion.

At the same time, he was unwilling to come out in favor of the absolute superiority of the pope to the council. This would be too much of a change from his previous position. Therefore, he develops a new theory, which Koch has entitled the *Gleichgewicht* theory, the principle of equal balance between the pope and the other members of the council.[29] "Dismissing for the present as doubtful the question whether the pope is over the council or vice versa. . . I answer that where any part of the council adheres to the Roman pontiff, even if a much greater part opposes him, that part united to the pope makes up the church, and hence the council."[30]

To call this theory a doctrine of equal balance between pope and council is not quite an accurate description because the whole council is *superior* to the pope. Cusanus, in speaking of the Council of Constance, distinguishes it from that of Basel by showing that at Constance the whole church was against the pope. When a truly representative council, in which "the consent of the whole church

29 Koch, *Nikolaus von Cues und seine Umwelt,* pp. 18-20.

30 Koch, *Briefwechsel,* p. 42. "Hinc dimittendo hoc tamquam dubium, an papa sit supra concilium vel e converso . . . respondeo quod ubi Romano pontifici aliqua pars concilii adheret, eciam si multo maior pars ab ipso recederet, illa pars pontifici unita ecclesiam facit et sic consequens concilium." For the anticipation of this theory in the canonist discussion of the relations of bishop and chapter, see Tierney, *Foundations,* p. 115, n. 1, where he quotes Hostiensis: ". . . in hoc casu dummodo habeat de capitulo secum duos vel unum saltem majorem partem habet."

concurs, as expressed by its ruling bishops and their representatives," takes action, the pope should submit, since the unanimous consent of the whole church shows that the meeting is divinely inspired. But, Cusanus adds in the second letter, no pope has ever opposed such a council.[31]

Nicholas also alters his theory concerning the calling of the council. In *De Concordantia Catholica,* while the pope was the one who normally convoked the council, in cases of emergency the emperor could do so if the pope refused to act. Now he says that the first requirement of a council is that it be called by its *caput* or head. A parochial council should be called by the pastor of the parish, a diocesan council by the bishop, a provincial council by the archbishop or metropolitan, and the universal council by the "pastor of the universal church, the Roman pontiff."[32]

The pope is now more than simply an administrator established by the bishops and the church, as he sometimes appeared to be in *De Concordantia Catholica.* He is the *caput* of the ecclesiastical corporation, which is the universal church. Where the *Concordantia* had said that the *heads (capita)* of the church had to be present in order for there to be a true council, the letter to the Carthusians requires the presence of "the *head* of the church and the bishops to whom Christ has committed the church."[33]

Cusanus' doctrine of infallibility is modified as well. In *De Concordantia Catholica* he tended to speak in comparative terms when he discussed infallibility. The council was more infallible than the pope and less subject to error *(minus deviabile).* When he came to discuss canon law

---

31 Koch, *Briefwechsel,* pp. 43, 49.
32 Koch, *Briefwechsel,* p. 40.
33 *Ibid.* ". . . quod per illos celebretur quibus per Christum ecclesia commissa est, scilicet per caput ecclesie et per pontifices." Cf. *DCC,* Book I, chap. iv, pp. 74-79, and Book II, chap. iii, p. 100.

statements attributing infallibility to the *sedes Romana,* he interpreted this not as the papacy but as the synod or patriarchal council of Rome, which had come in the course of time to be identical with the universal council. The *cathedra Petri* or *sedes apostolica* was also said to be infallible, but in the *Concordantia* Cusanus had stated that all the bishops and not just the pope had succeeded to this *cathedra,* so that it could remain free of error even though individual popes might fall into heresy.[34]

In the letters, the *sedes apostolica* is again infallible. But now it is redefined as the pope and the college of cardinals. "This is what we have always told the Bohemians and the Greeks and all schismatics, the Apostolic see made up of the pope and the college of cardinals never has erred and never will err, since it is 'upon this rock' that we believe the church was founded."[35]

It is true that in the *Concordantia* the cardinals had played a special role as representatives of the church provinces and in approving papal legislation and dispensation, but it is something quite different to attribute to the pope and cardinals the absolute infallibility which previously had only been granted to the church councils. Gone, too, is the notion of comparative infallibility. The letters are quite explicit. The pope and cardinals together constitute the infallible *sedes apostolica.*

Why not the pope alone? One reason that Cusanus was

34 *DCC,* Book II, chap. vii, p. 123.
35 Koch, *Briefwechsel,* letter no. 5, p. 49. "Ista solebamus Bohemis aliquando et Grecis et omnibus Scismaticis allegare, dicentes Apostolicam sedem in papa et collegio cardinalium constitutam nunquam errasse neque errare posse, quoniam 'super hanc petram' ecclesiam credimus fundatum." Note that the interpretation of the rock spoken of in Matthew 16:18 differs from that given in the *Concordantia,* where the rock was the church as a whole, which Peter "figured" (*DDC,* Book I, chap. xi ff). The *sedes Apostolica* is also defined as the pope and cardinals in the first of the two letters being discussed; cf. Koch, *Briefwechsel,* letter no. 4, p. 44.

reluctant to grant infallibility to the pope by himself was the established church tradition that individual popes had erred, although the *sedes* remained free of error. "Truth is promised to the *cathedra,* even if the one sitting in it *(sedens)* departs from the path of righteousness." If he also included the cardinals this point would be covered, and, in addition, there was some means provided for the corporate expression of the consent of the church, which still remained basic to his political theory even after the change to the papal side. When the college of cardinals consents, the church consents, because the cardinals represent (in the canonistic sense of "take the place of," *vices gerere)* the provinces of the church. Therefore the decisions can be considered to be divinely protected from error.[36]

Nicholas had one more argument for the superiority of the papacy in the dispute, and the great emphasis he placed upon it, particularly in the second of the two letters we are discussing, is an indication of how much it influenced him in his own change of position. This was what he calls the argument *ex effectu,* the argument from the result. The result of the council's activities was division within its own ranks. The result of the work of the papacy was the reunion of the Roman and Greek churches. Since the formal decree of union had been signed in Florence on July 5, 1439, this particular argument was an especially persuasive one. Besides, it was not entirely new. The *Concordantia* had spoken of the requirement that councils end in tranquility, and Cusanus quotes Augustine's comment on the importance of considering the results of a council in

---

[36] For the distinction between the *cathedra* or *sedes* and the one occupying it, *sedens,* see Koch, *Briefwechsel,* letter no. 4, pp. 40-41. The development of the various interpretations of infallibility is well summarized in Aimé-Georges Martimort, *Le Gallicanisme de Bossuet* (Paris, 1953), chap. i. Particular attention is given to the *sedes-sedens* distinction (pp. 556ff) since it was important in Bossuet's thinking.

order to determine whether it was a true council.[37] The result was the ultimate proof that the members of the minority at the council had God on their side, since their actions had led to the reestablishment of unity with the Greek church.

While such an argument may sound strikingly like a type of political pragmatism—whatever succeeds is right—it is not. Given the theological assumption that the Holy Spirit was guiding and watching over the church, it seemed to follow that one could judge from events where divine inspiration was present. If the pope had not been right, God would never have permitted the reunion with the Greek church to take place.

The initial break between the pope and the conciliar majority had occurred when the pope confirmed the decree of the minority and sent them to Constantinople to arrange for the council of union. This had been followed by a papal decree formally transferring the council from Basel to Ferrara. The council had repeatedly refused to recognize a papal decree transferring it, and an earlier effort of the pope to do so had failed in the face of opposition from a united council. Cusanus then had to justify the validity of the second papal transfer in 1437 against the opposition of a majority of those present at the council.

To do so, he resorted to the papal power to act for the building up of the church *(ad aedificationem ecclesiae)*. The expression was derived from the Scriptures (II Cor. 10:8), but the idea was a variation on the Aristotelian concept of *epieikeia* or equity, which Cusanus and all political theorists of his time granted to the ruler, to act in cases of necessity or utility for the public good even if it meant

---

[37] Augustine is quoted both in *DCC* (Book II, chap. v, p. 107) and in Cusanus' letter to the representative of the emperor (Koch, *Briefwechsel*, letter no. 5, p. 48; see also p. 46).

departure from the established law. The most important use of this principle by the conciliarists had been the justification during the Great Schism of the convocation of a council without the consent of the pope.[38]

It was because he had this general power to act for the good of the church that the pope transferred the council to Ferrara, says Cusanus. He wished to avoid a schism (and even to the most extreme conciliar theorists, such as Marsilius of Padua, the pope held his office *propter vitare schisma*). He used the power which he had from Christ to preserve the unity of the church, and therefore transferred the council to Italy. From the context it appears that the schism to which Cusanus is referring is both the division at Basel and that between the Eastern and Western churches. His argument is that the interest in bringing about union is so great that the pope can use his special power to further the interests of the church in order to transfer the council. He neglects to note, of course, that the schism at Basel would never have arisen had it not been for the activities of the pope, and his act of transferring the council to Ferrara was hardly calculated to improve matters.[39]

Once again, Cusanus had taken a concept which he had developed in the *Concordantia* and had used it for a different purpose. The admitted papal power to dispense and interpret for the good of the church became a justification for positive papal action to subvert the Basel council. Like the modern conception of emergency powers of the executive, the grant of *epieikeia* to the papacy left open the pos-

38 St. Paul's statement is paraphrased in *DCC*, Book II, chap. xvii, p. 182, where the pope's power is said to be granted "ad aedificationem, non ad destructionem." A general power to dispense or interpret conciliar decrees is also granted the pope, in chap. xx, 206.

39 The argument from the papal power "ad aedificationem" is presented in Koch, *Briefwechsel*, letter no. 4, pp. 41 and 44, and letter no. 5, p. 48.

sibility that the pope, using the plea of necessity, would simply disregard the decisions of the council. In this case, he not only had disregarded them but had gone directly against the majority decision (although there was some question of the representative character of the majority).

In the modified theory developed by Cusanus immediately after his change of position, the conception of the pope ruling the church as *caput ecclesiae* had replaced that of a church under the direction of the bishops as *capita ecclesiae* under a papal administrator. The pope's position was a divinely intended one. Only he could call the council, and enough power inhered in the office that a minority of the council which was united with him could outweigh a conciliar majority. However, many elements in his theory were not changed from the *Concordantia*. There was still the same emphasis on consent and representation. A council which had the consent of the whole church was considered to be superior to the pope. Infallibility was not the exclusive prerogative of the pope, since the cardinals, as representatives of the provinces, were to give the consent of the church. Even the seemingly limitless grant of power to the pope *ad aedificationem* was derived from *De Concordantia Catholica*. Despite the fact that he was writing in defense of the pope, it was not until after the writing of *De Docta Ignorantia* that Nicholas of Cusa's basic conceptions of representation and consent were fundamentally altered, so as to permit the development of a new theory of papal supremacy.

CHAPTER X

·   ·   ·

LEARNED IGNORANCE

THE VISIT to Constantinople seems to have been of decisive importance in the philosophical development of Nicholas of Cusa. At least, this is his own interpretation of the origin of the reflections which gave rise to his most famous work, *De Docta Ignorantia*. In the letter to Cardinal Giuliano Cesarini which concludes the work, he describes it as a divine revelation.

> I was returning by sea from Greece, when, by what I believe was a supreme gift from the Father of Lights from whom is every perfect gift, I was led in the learning that is ignorance *(docta ignorantia)* to grasp the incomprehensible; and this I was able to achieve not by way of comprehension but by transcending those perennial truths which can be reached by reason.[1]

From this time forward, all of Nicholas' writings, speeches, and sermons are permeated by what he regarded as the great discovery which would make him famous in the history of philosophy. Even in his political writings, the technical terminology of his philosophical works is utilized. Now a philosophical conception which he regards as peculiarly his own gives to his thought a unity (if not

1 Nicolas Cusanus, *Of Learned Ignorance*, trans. Heron, p. 173 (163). The reference to "a perfect gift from the father of lights" is a paraphrase of James 1:17. In the quotations from *De Docta Ignorantia (DDI)*, I will use Father Heron's excellent but rather free translation, with occasional phrases from the Latin text of the Heidelberg edition, Nicolai de Cusa, *Opera Omnia*, vol. I, *De Docta Ignorantia*, ed. Ernst Hoffmann and Raymond Klibansky (Leipzig, 1932). The pagination in the Latin text is given in parentheses.

always a clarity) which it did not possess when he attempted in *De Concordantia Catholica* to synthesize the divergent traditions which had preceded him.

It is difficult, however, to accept on its face value Cusanus' statement that the principles of the *Docta Ignorantia* came to him in a flash of divine revelation. There are too many evidences of his early acquaintance with the elements of the Neo-Platonic tradition which contained most, if not all, of the essential doctrines of the "new" type of knowledge which he was espousing.

Briefly summarized, the argument of the *Docta Ignorantia* is as follows: The human mind learns by comparison of the unknown with the known. But this comparison can only give us approximate rather than absolute knowledge. Especially in dealing with God, in whom there is neither more nor less, our finite intellects cannot comprehend the infinite by any comparison with finite things, for God's infinitude far exceeds the limited capacities of the human reason. But although we cannot comprehend God's true nature, we do know that He is the one Absolute Maximum, characterized by the threefold qualities of unity, equality, and connection. We know that all rational conceptions of opposites or contradictions are resolved in this Infinite Transcendence. In Him, both the Maximum and Minimum coincide. Everything that is in the world develops from Him and He is in all things and contains everything in Himself. Christ forms the link between God, the Absolute Maximum, and the universe, which is the "maximum" of created things. He is both God and man, limited and absolute, created and creator.

The philosophical doctrines of the *Docta Ignorantia* which are important for Cusanus' later political theory can be summarized under four principal headings. First is the *docta ignorantia* itself, the belief that the wise man is learned only if he is aware of the limitations of finite human reason, particularly in comprehending the infinite transcendence of God. Secondly, the doctrine of the *coincidentia oppositorum* teaches that all things are united in God, even those which appear to us as opposed. God therefore contains everything in Himself, and the universe is the unfolding of His nature (*complicatio et explicatio*). Finally Cusanus holds that the universe reflects God's threefold nature (*trinitas universi*) so that every unity is also at the same time threefold.

The ideas of learned ignorance and the coincidence of opposites have a very ancient genealogy. St. Augustine uses the term *docta ignorantia* in one of his letters (Letter CXXX). It is possible that Cusanus knew this work, but a more likely source was the mystical writings of St. Bonaventure. In Bonaventure's *Breviloquium,* which is in the library at Kues, he would have read, "Our spirit in the manner of fire not only is directed upward but also, by a certain learned ignorance, it is swept up above itself into the darkness . . ."[2] The idea which the term expresses was almost a commonplace of the theological literature of the Middle Ages. The approach to God through the *via negativa* was described by the mystical writers as the progressive removal of all temporal and limited ideas about God so as to attain the "super-essential darkness" which is God in Himself and apart from all other relationships. An earlier chapter has reviewed the development of this tradition from the writings of Pseudo-Dionysius and his intermediary, Scotus Eriugena. Dionysius' *Divine Names* itself speaks of knowing

2 Bonaventure, *Breviloquium,* Part V, chap. vi, in *Tria Opuscula* (Florence, 1938), p. 188. ". . . ad modum ignis spiritus noster non solum efficitur agilis ad ascensum, verum etiam quadam ignorantia docta supra se ipsum rapitur in caliginem." A study by Francis Caminetti of the influence of Bonaventure on Cusanus is shortly to be published in the *Mitteilungen* of the Cusanus-Gesellschaft.

God through knowledge and ignorance (*ignorantia* in most medieval Latin translations).[3]

The same work also contains an anticipation of Cusanus' "coincidence of opposites." In the fourth chapter of the *Divine Names,* Dionysius states that God's Being even includes non-Being, and His Goodness can be conceived in a certain way to include Evil, since a full understanding of Goodness requires a knowledge of its opposition to Evil.[4] The same idea is developed by Eriugena, in a passage quoted in an earlier chapter which refers to God as "the opposition of oppositions, the contrary of contraries."

Yet Cusanus specifically denied the influence of Dionysius the Areopagite on the fundamental conception of the *Docta Ignorantia.* In his *Apologia Doctae Ignorantiae,* he wrote, "I confess, my friend, that I had not seen Dionysius nor any of the true theologians at the time that I received this conception from above, but I went swiftly to the writings of the doctors, and I found nothing but variations on my revelation."[5]

In view of the clear dependence of the structure of the *Concordantia* on the Dionysian hierarchies, this statement is difficult to explain. Cusanus refers specifically to Diony-

---

3 *De Divinis Nominibus,* chap. vii—in *Dionysiaca* (I, 404), which contains the Latin versions of Hilduin, Saracenus, and Grosseteste, which use the word *ignorantia,* and of Eriugena which does not.

4 *De Divinis Nominibus,* chap. iv (in *Dionysiaca,* I, 230-354). Ernst Hoffmann, "Die Vorgeschichte der Cusanischen *Coincidentia Oppositorum,*" introduction to *Über den Beryll,* trans. K. Fleischmann (Leipzig, 1938), pp. 1-35, traces the idea in earlier writers, most of them not read by Cusanus. More useful is the recent work of Rudolf Haubst, who shows that the "coincidence of opposites" came from Heimericus de Campo, who was in turn influenced by the commentaries of Albertus Magnus on Dionysius and by the theological works of Raymond Lull (cf. Haubst, *Das Bild,* pp. 64-69, 313-14, and "Zum Fortleben Alberts des Grossen," pp. 437-440).

5 Nicolai de Cusa, *Apologia Doctae Ignorantiae,* p. 12. "Fateor, amice, non me Dionysium aut quemquam theologorum verorum tunc vidisse, quando desuper conceptum recepi; sed avido cursu me ad doctorum scripta contuli et nihil nisi revelatum varie figuratum inveni."

sius' works twice in the *Concordantia*.[6] As early as 1431, he noted in a sermon that Dionysius was the originator of the *via eminentiae*, or method of attributing to God to a superlative degree the perfections which are found in His creatures. Beginning with his Christmas sermon, 1438, Nicholas' sermons are filled with references to Dionysius' *Divine Names* and *Celestial Hierarchy*.[7] As the *Docta Ignorantia* was completed in 1440, the question of the influence of Dionysius' writings on its composition is a significant one.

How are we to interpret Cusanus' denial of prior acquaintance with Dionysius, in view of these indications to the contrary? One possibility is to read the next sentence after the passage denying prior acquaintance with Dionysius. There Nicholas refers to Dionysius' letter to Gaius which mentions the *"scientia ignorationis,"* and it is possible that Nicholas meant that he had not seen this particular anticipation of his doctrine before his shipboard revelation. Vansteenberghe in his biography proposes a similar explanation when he interprets the statement as referring only to the *Mystical Theology*, a Greek text of which Nicholas brought back from Constantinople.[8] (Nicholas had only a rudimentary knowledge of Greek, but he could have received help from those on the ship.)

However, the statement seems to go further and to deny any direct acquaintance with Dionysius' works. In view of the vast influence that Dionysius exercised and the wide knowledge of his works, it is likely that, despite the doubts

6 *DCC*, Book I, chap. vi, p. 55 (a reference to the *Ecclesiastical Hierarchy*), and Book II, chap. xx, p. 232 (a mention of Dionysius in a quotation from a conciliar decree).

7 On the influence of Dionysius on Cusanus' sermons, see Josef Koch, *Predigten, Untersuchung über Datierung, Form, Sprache, und Quellen*, in *SBH* 1941-42, no. 1 (Heidelberg, 1942), p. 32; and Rudolf Haubst, *Die Christologie des Nikolaus von Kues* (Freiburg, 1956), p. 27.

8 Vansteenberghe, *Nicolas*, p. 414.

raised above, the statement is correct. Nicholas could have acquired a rather complete knowledge of the fundamentals of Dionysius' theories from Eriugena, Bonaventure, and Albertus Magnus, and the vocabulary used in the first book of the *Concordantia,* when Cusanus outlines his hierarchical system, seems to support this view.[9] In this interpretation, the early references to Dionysius are all derived from second-hand sources, and his first reading of the original (in Latin translation) would have taken place in 1438, after his "revelation" but before the occurrence of the specific quotations in his sermons.

Although the concepts of learned ignorance and the coincidence of opposites had only an indirect influence on Nicholas' political theory, the other two central ideas of the *Docta Ignorantia* were immediately applied in his political writings. The view of the universe as composed of triadic divisions (*trinitas universi*) had already been an essential part of the system outlined in the *Concordantia Catholica.* Nicholas probably derived this conception from Raymond Lull and Heimericus de Campo, when he wrote the *Concordantia,* but it is clear from passages in the seventh chapter of the second book of *Docta Ignorantia* that by the time of the composition of the latter work, there was a further dependence on the ideas of the twelfth century Platonism of the school of Chartres.[10]

The philosophical writings of the theologians of Chartres were also the source of the description of the relationship of God and the universe as one of *complicatio* and *ex-*

9 E.g., *DCC,* Book I, chap. ii, pp. 35-36, where references to the *Concordantia* as *theophanica,* and the description of lower ranks as "shades" of the higher, seem to be derived from Eriugena and Albertus. Cf. Ludwig Baur, *Nicolaus Cusanus und Ps. Dionysius im Lichte der Zitate und Randbemerkungen des Cusanus,* in *SBH* 1940-41, no. 4 (Heidelberg, 1941), pp. 10, 20, and 26.

10 See intro. to *DDI* (Heidelberg edition), p. xii. Nicolai de Cusa, *Apologia,* p. 24, also contains a specific reference to a Chartres commentary.

plicatio. Like the other concepts in the work, the *complicatio-explicatio* duality is, first of all, a theological conception. It is a way of stressing the dependence of all creation on its Creator. The idea is developed most fully in the third chapter of Book II of *De Docta Ignorantia,* which discusses, "How the Maximum (i.e., God) Envelops *(complicet)* and Develops *(explicet)* All Things." In demonstrating the relationship of God and the World, Cusanus draws a parallel with the relationship between a point and a line, rest and motion, and unity and plurality. In the same way that "the plurality of things is a development *(explicatio)* of the unity which is God, God in His unity embraces all things, while His unity is developed in plurality." God therefore contains everything in creation, and is present in all created things. To the fundamental concept of the coincidence of opposites—all things, even opposites, are in God—there is added an emphasis upon the radical dependence of every being in God and His simultaneous presence in everything which He has created.

As in the case of other "original" ideas of Nicholas of Cusa, the conception just outlined has a very long history. Boethius in the *Consolation of Philosophy* uses similar terms when he compares providence and fate. "Providence contains *(complectitur)* all things, however diverse and however infinite, while fate moves particular things in time, place, and form. Thus providence is the unfolding *(explicatio)* of the temporal order as united in the foresight of the divine mind, while fate is this same uniting, worked out and unfolded *(explicata)* in time."[11]

Recently published texts of twelfth century commentaries on Boethius' *De Trinitate* illustrate the development

---

11 Boethius, *The Consolation of Philosophy,* Book IV, prose 6 (Latin text with English trans. by H. F. Stewart and E. K. Rand, New York, 1918). Note that the verb *complector* is used instead of *complico.* The latter is used in a different sense in Book III, prose 12.

of this conception in the writings of the school of Chartres. In a manuscript, now identified as written by Thierry of Chartres, it is stated that "the whole (*universitas*) which Absolute Necessity has contained (*complicavit*) simply in Himself is unfolded (*explicata*) in the truths of forms and images which we call ideas."[12] A similar idea is also expressed in a Paris commentary on the same work: "God is unity containing (*complicans*) in Himself the universe of things in a certain simple fashion. The unfolding (*explicatio*) of this content (*complicationis*) is all things which were, which will be, and which are."[13] The similarity between some of Cusanus' ideas in *De Docta Ignorantia* and those of Thierry of Chartres in *De Sex Dierum Operibus* was noticed as early as 1909, when Duhem accused Cusanus of plagiarism and drily remarked that the confusion and obscurity of Cusanus' writings were much clarified by Thierry's work.[14]

Although the terms were drawn from the school of Chartres, the ideas which they expressed go back to Greek speculations on the relation of the One and the Many. As noted in an earlier chapter, the contrast between a God who is unity and contains all things, and a world of plurality dependent on Him, is a Christian and Neo-Platonic development of Greek logical theories which were applied

[12] "Haec igitur universitas, quam in quandam simplicitatem in se complicavit Absoluta Necessitas, explicatur in formarum atque imaginum veritates quas ideas dicimus." *Archives d'histoire*, 23:284 (1956). The text is preceded by a commentary: N. Haring, "A Commentary on Boethius *De Trinitate* by Thierry of Chartres," at pp. 259-265. See also Raymond Klibansky's introduction to the Heidelberg edition of the *Docta Ignorantia*, p. xii, and footnotes on pp. 17 and 81ff.

[13] "Deus est unitas complicans in se rerum universitatem simplicitate quadam. Cujus complicationis explicatio est omnia que fuerunt, que erunt, et que sunt." J. M. Parent, *La Doctrine de la création dans l'école de Chartres* (Paris, 1938), p. 183.

[14] L. Duhem, "Thierry de Chartres et Nicolas de Cues," *Revue des sciences philosophiques et theologiques*, 3:525-531 (1909).

to the One Creator who is the source of all creation.[15] This attempt to achieve an immediate intuition of all reality is a theme which recurs in Western (and Eastern) thought, both religious and secular, and Cusanus was by no means the last from his native country to concern himself with it.

Not a few of the representatives of the Neo-Platonic and mystical traditions in the Middle Ages, for example, Eriugena and Eckhart, were accused of the heresy of pantheism. Cusanus himself, who drew on these writers, was not exempt from this charge. Because of his view of the world as the *explicatio* of God, he was accused of heresy by a Heidelberg professor, Johannes Wenck. Wenck, a partisan of the council, published a work, *De Ignota Literatura,* which listed the errors which he had found in the *Docta Ignorantia.* He accused Nicholas of denying the principle of contradiction in his doctrine of the coincidence of opposites, thereby attacking the very foundation of knowledge. The analysis of the relation of God and the world as one of *complicatio* and *explicatio* Wenck saw as pantheistic and a denial of the Christian doctrine of the creation.[16]

Nicholas replied in his *Apologia Doctae Ignorantiae,* accusing Wenck of misinterpreting his doctrines. Against "the Aristotelian sect," Nicholas maintains that the coincidence of opposites is the beginning of the ascent into mystical theology. Truth is one, and the principle of con-

15 Klibansky, *Ein Proklos-Fund,* p. 28, attempts to prove from a phrase in the Strasbourg manuscript mentioned earlier that Nicholas actually derived the inspiration for the *Docta Ignorantia* from Proclus' *Commentary on the Parmenides.* However, a recent reexamination of the manuscript has indicated that the brief excerpt from Proclus was written by Cusanus after the composition of the *Docta Ignorantia.* Cf. Haubst, "Die Thomas- und Proklos-Exzerpte," pp. 22-23, 26-34, 50-51.

16 The text appears in E. Vansteenberghe, "Le 'De Ignota Litteratura' de Jean Wenck de Herrenberg," *Beiträge zur Geschichte der Philosophie des Mittelalters,* vol. VIII, no. 6 (Münster, 1910). See especially pp. 26, 29, and 35.

tradiction which is based on oppositions, while valid for use
by the dialectical reason, cannot deal with the higher realm
of intellectual knowledge. Cusanus adds that St. Thomas
recognized the dangers of a pantheistic interpretation of
some of Dionysius' statements but urged the importance of
reading them in their context. The same point, he says,
can be made about the *De Docta Ignorantia*. Nicholas then
cites a long list of authorities who used the same terminology without any pantheistic intent.[17]

Cusanus could have constructed a more effective refuta-
tion by quoting other passages from the *De Docta Ignorantia* which emphasize God's transcendence and at the same
time speak of the utter dependence of the world upon Him.
In the discussion of the *complicatio-explicatio* relationship,
Nicholas brings this out:

> It would seem as though God, who is unity, is multiplied
> in things . . . and yet we know that any multiplication of
> that unity, which is infinite and the maximum, is impossible.
> If we consider things without Him, they are as number with-
> out unity—nothing; if we consider Him without things He
> exists and they do not.[18]

To charge Nicholas with pantheism is to distort the subtle
analysis involved in the use of the terms derived from the
equally orthodox school of Chartres.

Contractio is another conception, related to that of
complicatio-explicatio, which appears in the *Docta Ignorantia* and is later used in Cusanus' political writings. It is
discussed in Book II, chapters iv-vii, in connection with the
relation of God and the universe. God is the absolute
Maximum. The universe is a maximum as well, since it
is unlimited, unified, and nothing beyond it can be imag-

17 *Apologia,* pp. 6, 17, 28, and 31.
18 *DDI,* Book III, chap. iii, p. 78 (71).

ined. The difference between the universe and God is that the universe is the maximum *contractum*—the particular expression of God in all created reality. It is like Him in that it is unlimited, simple, and unified. It is unlike Him in that it is relative and dependent on God. The universe is capable of further specification in individual things, and in each of these it is present by *contractio*. Nicholas gives the parallel of humanity as a whole and the individual man. In one man, humanity receives its finite (*contracta*) expression. The process from the unity of God and of the universe to the plurality of created things is one of *contractio* or particularization.

While he was writing the *De Docta Ignorantia,* Nicholas gave a Christmas sermon which contained many of the same ideas. After explaining to his listeners (one wonders how many understood him) that the way of negative theology is truer, because it leads us to a conception of God as "infinite unity, containing (*complicans*) all things," he said that we describe God in terms "such as spirit, intelligence, reason, justice, truth, and all those terms removed from the sensory world" because these attributes are *contractior* (more particular).[19] The use of this term even for abstract ideas illustrates Cusanus' theory of the various levels of contraction in the world. As he explains it, the universe is the first *contractio* (particularization), followed by the various genera and species, so that only on the fourth level of contraction do we arrive at the individual.[20] We apply to God the terms of truth, justice, and so forth, because they exist on a higher level of contraction (*contractior*) than the material world.

19 *"Dies Sanctificatus" vom Jahre 1439,* ed. Ernst Hoffmann and Raymond Klibansky, in *SBH* 1928-29, no. 3 (Heidelberg, 1929), p. 14.
20 *DDI,* Book II, chap. vi. The same chapter denies the Platonic doctrine of a separate world of Ideas. For Cusanus, universals exist only as "contracted" in individuals or, when known, as "contracted" in the intellect.

Yet, at the same time Nicholas' thought emphasizes the uniqueness of the individual thing. No two created beings are exactly alike, nor can they be simply subsumed into higher species and genera. There is a continuum of infinite degrees and grades between the created and the Creator. Moreover, each individual thing is a microcosm reflecting and "contracting" within itself the whole of the universe and its Creator. "Everything is in everything."[21]

The emphasis on the importance of the individual, and the contrast with the infinitude and ultimate unknowability of God, led Ernst Cassirer, thirty-five years ago, to single out *De Docta Ignorantia* as the first work to break with the hierarchical world order (*Stufenkosmos*) of Pseudo-Dionysius. Cusanus' work placed the infinite Creator at such a distance from men's limited rational faculties that, according to Cassirer, they were encouraged to turn their attention away from the attempt to comprehend the Deity through philosophy and theology to the less ambitious but more fruitful task of studying the finite and individual world around them. For Cassirer, as for other more recent students of the history of philosophy, Nicholas of Cusa was the first philosopher of modern times.[22]

A similar position was taken about the same time by the Heidelberg expert on Nicholas of Cusa, Ernst Hoffmann. For him the importance of the *Docta Ignorantia* lay also in setting the stage for the scientific discoveries of the Renaissance. For him, too, Cusanus broke with the *Stufenkosmos* of the Neo-platonists. He did this, however, not

21 *DDI,* Book II, chap. v. The ideas that each individual thing differs from every other thing and all things are in all things are derived from the Neo-Platonic tradition. See A. O. Lovejoy, *The Great Chain of Being,* Cambridge, 1936, chap. i, and discussion in Chapter III of this book.

22 Ernst Cassirer, *Individuum und Kosmos,* p. 10. An English translation will be published late in 1963 in the Harper Torchbook series. Cf. also G. de Santillana, ed., *The Age of Adventure* (New York, 1956), pp. 47-63. in the Mentor History of Philosophy series.

as the herald of a new age, but by reverting to the real doctrine of Plato, before the Neo-Platonic concepts of emanation and hierarchy were engrafted on the Platonic dualism of the world of the Idea and the world of appearances. According to Hoffmann, the astronomical revolution associated with Galileo would have been impossible if it had not been for the rejection of the Neo-Platonic *cosmos*, graded in a hierarchy of value. Only when it was believed that everything outside of God was of the same limited and finite value could the shift from quality to quantity, from evaluation to measurement, which characterizes modern science, take place.[23]

Both of these writers and others who have followed them exaggerate the extent of Cusanus' break with the medieval hierarchical universe. It is true that Nicholas describes the universe as infinite in at least two places in the *Docta Ignorantia,* and that he denies that the earth is the most inferior part of the universe and its center.[24] Moreover, the *Docta Ignorantia* contains a brilliant discussion of the relativity of knowledge to the standpoint of the observer, pointing out that a man on earth, on the sun, or on some other planet will always think of himself as at the center.[25] (These observations are known to have been of interest to Kepler and Copernicus in the next century.) However, the denial that the earth is the center of the universe is based on the distinction which Cusanus is attempting to make between the infinity of God and the finitude and change-

---

[23] Ernst Hoffmann, "Platonismus und Mittelalter," in *Vorträge der Bibliothek Warburg* (1923-24), ed. Fritz Saxl (Berlin, 1924), pp. 15-82; and by the same author, *Das Universum des Nikolaus von Cues,* in *SBH* 1929-30, no. 3 (Heidelberg, 1930).

[24] *DDI*, Book II, chap. i, p. 70 (64), chap. iv, p. 81 (73), chaps. xi-xii, pp. 107-118 (99-110).

[25] *DDI*, Book II, chap. xii, p. 111 (103). Cf. Raymond Klibansky, "Copernic et Nicolas de Cues," in *Léonard de Vinci et l'expérience scientifique* (Paris, 1953), pp. 225-235.

ability of the created world. Only God can be the center of the universe, says Cusanus, since only He is a fixed reference point in a world of change. The earth appears to be nearer the center, but its revolution around its "conjectural" pole is never perfect and "the various motions of the spheres" have no precise center except God. Neither is "the sphere of the fixed stars" the outermost point of the universe (*circumferentia*), since God is both center and circumference.[26] The earth is not the basest and lowest of the planets, because "in the world, there is neither a maximum nor a minimum in perfections, movements, and figures."[27]

From the mention of "the spheres" and "poles," it is evident that Nicholas has not broken with the Ptolemaic universe in his discussion, but only attempted to raise questions about the finite character of the universe in relation to the infinite perfection of God. The universe has no center because this would be a basis of value other than God. The world is infinite in the sense of being without limits, but it is an inferior type of infinity to that of the Divine.[28] Cusanus' conception of the physical universe is not completely clear in the *Docta Ignorantia*, but it seems to be without spatial limitation and, at the same time, composed of spheres rotating around poles which are themselves in motion. The poles are not at rest, and the universe has no center or circumference, because only in God is there absolute rest, an absolute center and circumference, and an absolute maximum and minimum.

Nevertheless, there remains a hierarchy of value in the created universe. It is still composed of degrees of being,

26 *DDI,* Book II, chap. xi, pp. 107-108 (100-101).
27 *DDI,* Book II, chap. xii, p. 112 (104).
28 The universe is *privative infinitum,* in chapter i of Book II. It is described as *infinitas contracta* in chapter iv, and in chapter xi, it is neither infinite nor finite but "without limits" (*careat terminis*).

hierarchically differentiated. If at the summit of this hierarchy Cusanus postulates a vast gulf yawning between finite man and an infinite God, he is not really saying anything very new. This conception was part of the "negative theology" of the Middle Ages, and the medieval Neo-Platonists saw no opposition between this and the belief in a hierarchical universe. Hoffmann is correct in linking this conception to Plato's *chōrismos,* or separation of the limited and changing world of appearances and the unlimited and real world of Ideal Forms (and above all, the Idea of the Good in Book VII of the *Republic*), but this conception never disappeared from the Neo-Platonic tradition in the Middle Ages. All the while that medieval scholasticism was trying to define and even confine God in rational formulations, the Neo-Platonic and mystical traditions were asserting his infinity and incomprehensibility.

A universe of hierarchical degrees of being and value is essential to the argument of Cusanus' *Docta Ignorantia.* As he says in the opening chapter of Book II, "for any given finite being, there is a greater or lesser necessarily to be found," but for the Infinite, there is no greater or lesser.[29] Chapter six of the same book describes how the descent is made from the One to the Many, from God to individual things (*gradualiter descendentes ad particulare*). Below God is the universe, which is subdivided into various genera of being. These in turn are divided into species, each of which is constituted of individuals.[30] God contains (*complicat*) all of them, but some are on a higher level of being (*contractior*) than others. The highest species of one genus coincides with the lowest species of the next, and every link between species is by grades (*omnis connexio gradu-*

29 *DDI,* Book II, chap. i, p. 70 (63).
30 *DDI,* Book II, chap. vi, pp. 86-87 (79).

ativa est).[31] While it is true that, according to Nicholas, one can never by the study of these genera and species (the *via eminentiae* or positive way) arrive at an adequate understanding of the Godhead, this was also admitted in the Neo-Platonic theology. At the end of the dialectical ascent to union with God, there is still an infinite distance which can only be traversed by mystical intuition.

The Neo-Platonic conception of creation as a process of emanation or flowing out of creative power from God through successive hierarchical levels of creation was outlined by Nicholas, seven years earlier, in the opening chapters of *De Concordantia Catholica,* and he still uses language in the *Docta Ignorantia* which assumes a hierarchial order in the world. He still describes the process of creation as a flowing out *(fluere),* although the verb *explicare* seems to replace it more and more in his later writings.[32]

The ideas of a hierarchical universe and of all creation as the *explicatio* of God are not necessarily incompatible. One can speak of God as present everywhere in the world of His creation, and still believe that certain things are more like Him and higher in their value than others. What the *Docta Ignorantia* seems to imply is a greater emphasis than in the earlier Neo-Platonic writers upon the concentration of all power and potentiality in God, the head of hierarchy. This development also took place when the ideas of *complicatio* and *explicatio* were applied to church and empire. The old hierarchies remained, but their heads were considered to possess all ruling power *complicative* in their persons.

31 *DDI,* Book III, chap. i, p. 129 (120).
32 See, for instance, the use of *fluit* in the Letter to Rodrigo Sanchez de Arevalo, written in 1442, and reproduced as appendix 3 to *DAP,* at page 106. For the history of the use of *fluere* in the Neo-Platonic tradition, see Heinz-Mohr, *Unitas Christiana,* p. 298, n. 3.

The idea of an ascending hierarchy of being is not as foreign to Plato himself as Hoffmann would have it. The theory of knowledge of Book VII of the *Republic* assumes that there are degrees of knowledge which can only be attained by careful study and spiritual preparation, and this hierarchy of knowledge corresponds to a hierarchy of being, the object of this knowledge. Similarly in the *Timaeus,* creation is described in terms of a descending hierarchy in the universe. Among the Platonic writings not known to the Middle Ages, the *Symposium* with its hierarchy of the objects of *eros* and the Seventh Letter with its degrees of knowledge could also be cited.

Despite the dualism of Plato's epistemology, hierarchical elements are also present in his thought although they are not as clearly delineated as in the writings of the Neo-Platonists. Similarly, Cusanus' *Docta Ignorantia* may have emphasized the incommensurability of God, and spoken less about the degrees of being in the universe, but both elements were still present in his writing. Cusanus' cosmology, like his political theory, retained traditional elements, and he never gave up the idea of a hierarchy of levels of reality from matter through living life, through animals, man, and up to pure spirits and ultimately to God.

CHAPTER XI

·　　·　　·

EXPLICATIO PETRI

THE DISCUSSION of Nicholas' new philosophical theories provides the background for the use of certain of these philosophical terms in his political discussions in the years which followed the publication of the *Docta Ignorantia.* The belief in a natural hierarchy in the political, social, and ecclesiastical order remained a part of his thought, but his newly developed philosophical vocabulary, especially the concepts of *contractio* and *complicatio-explicatio,* achieved a prominent position in the formulation of Cusanus' political theory after 1440.

Our sources for his political philosophy in this period are more meager than previously. He did not write any major political work after the change from the council to the pope, and after 1439 even his letters with one exception were not concerned with political topics. A record of his thinking on the controversy between the pope and the Council of Basel after 1440 is contained in the reports of the meetings of the *Reichstag,* where he appeared as one of the representatives of the pope and argued in favor of the abandonment of the German position of neutrality between pope and council.[1] A manuscript in the Trier

1 Cusanus' speeches in 1441 are reported in *RTA,* vol. XV, pt. 2, ed. Hermann Herre (Gotha, 1914), on pp. 639-646 (second-hand reports on his speeches at the Mainz Princes' Congress), 761-765 (John of Segovia's description of Nicholas' answer to his speech at the same meeting), 765-772 (Nicholas' reply to a list of questions submitted to him by the emperor's representative), and 874-876 (his report to Cardinal Cesarini on his speeches at the meeting). A summary of a propapal speech attributed by the editor to Cusanus (pp. 646-47) has been demonstrated, on grounds both of manu-

library, containing a dialogue against the "Amedists" (the partisans of Amadeus of Savoy, elected antipope by the Council of Basel in November 1439), has also recently been identified as of Nicholas' authorship. Its arguments are substantially identical with those of the speeches before the *Reichstag*, and it appears to date from the same period.[2] Probably the best summary statement of the changes of Nicholas' political and ecclesiastical theories as a result of the writing of *De Docta Ignorantia* is contained in his letter to Rodrigo Sanchez de Arevalo, written from the *Reichstag* session in Frankfurt on May 20, 1442. Since Arevalo was also a philosopher and churchman on the side of papacy (since 1439) and Cusanus did not have any polemical purpose in writing to him, the letter is particularly valuable as a statement of Nicholas' later position. It was utilized by Robert Bellarmine in his defence of the papal position after the Reformation, when the Protestant publicists quoted conciliar writings such as the *Concordantia*.[3]

script evidence and of doctrinal content (it asserts, in a way that Cusanus would not, that the pope "is over all laws, both human and divine"), to be that of a Heidelberg professor, Johannes Risen. Cf. Rudolf Haubst, "Nikolaus von Kues und Johannes Wenck, Neue Erörterungen und Nachträge," *Römische Quartalschrift*, 53:81-88 (1958). The speeches in 1442 are reported in *RTA*, vol. XVI, pt. 2, prepared by Hermann Herre and ed. Ludwig Quidde (Stuttgart-Gotha, 1928), on pp. 407-432 (Cusanus' memorandum on his speeches at the Frankfurt Reichstag in June 1442) and pp. 539-543 (his reply to the conciliar representatives at the same meeting).

2 *Dialogus Concludens Amedistarum Errorem ex Gestis et Doctrina Concilii Basiliensis* (henceforth referred to as *Dialogus*), contained in Trier Municipal Library Manuscript 1927/1426. A typescript copy has been made by Josef Koch, who discusses the question of Nicholas of Cusa's authorship in "Über eine aus der nächsten Umgebung des Nikolaus von Kues stammende Handschrift der Trierer Stadtbibliothek," in the collection of essays dedicated to Gerhard Kallen, *Aus Mittelalter und Neuzeit* (Bonn, 1957), pp. 117-135.

3 *Epistola Nicolai de Cusa ad Rodericum de Trevino, Archidiaconum, Oratorem Regis Castellae*, printed as appendix 3 in Kallen, ed., *DAP*, pp. 106-112. For further information on Rodrigo Sanchez, see Richard H. Trame, *Rodrigo Sanchez de Arevalo, 1404-1470* (Washington, 1958). Arevalo was present at Basel from 1433 to 1439. He voted with the conciliar

EXPLICATIO PETRI

Although these sources are different in character and purpose, they were all written in the same period, the two years following the publication of *De Docta Ignorantia,* and they are markedly similar in their general position, both indicating a general continuity with Cusanus' earlier thought and reflecting the changes which his philosophic writing and his polemical activity on behalf of the papacy had introduced into his theories. In the effort to reconstruct Cusanus' political philosophy at this time, they can be considered together.

As in everything which he had written previously on the subject of political theory, his writings and speeches in 1441 and 1442 continue to emphasize the themes of representation and consent. He repeats the argument for the pope which he had made in his letters in 1439, that the council is drawn *from* the church and cannot be considered to be a universal council unless its decrees are accepted by the consent of the whole church. In the case of Basel, the pope, the patriarchs, and the representatives of the leading kingdoms of Europe have been opposed to its decisions, particularly to the deposition of Pope Eugene and the election of an antipope. The same requirements which were listed in *De Concordantia* and utilized in the letters in 1439 are also repeated. To be a true council, it must be properly convened, be truly representative, carry on its discussions freely, and conclude in agreement. At least in the last two respects, Cusanus' charges, the Council of Basel is deficient.[4]

The canon law discussions of the relations of head and members of the ecclesiastical corporation are again cited.

---

majority on the site of the union council in 1437. Like the other delegates from Castile, he withdrew from the council in 1439 in protest over the deposition of the pope.

4 *RTA,* XV, 762, 874; XVI, 414, 417. *Dialogus,* p. 8 (in typescript).

Now, instead of outlining a theory whereby the pope with a minority of the council should prevail, he notes that canon law provides that, where there is a disagreement among the members of a provincial council, the ultimate decision should go to the head of the *universitas*—the metropolitan or archbishop.[5] He argues that a similar procedure should be used for the *universitas* of the whole church. Where the council is divided, the decision should be referred to the pope.

The attacks on the voting system at Basel become increasingly strong. Again and again Cusanus denounces the council for taking its decisions by a vote of all present, without considerations of hierarchical status. Mere *numerositas*, he says, does not suffice. The great weakness of the council was that it admitted any simple priest to vote on an equal basis with the great ecclesiastical dignitaries. Cusanus criticizes the council's reliance on "arithmetic" and "mathematical abstractions," and its majorities which were composed of the very lowest grades (*infimis*) of the ecclesiastical hierarchy, even in one case utilizing the personal servant of one of the bishops in order to break a tie vote.[6]

The use of this argument indicates how far the earlier ideas of the infallibility of the majority, as expressed in parts of the *Concordantia*, have receded into the background, and how much more importance is now being given to hierarchical considerations, for, Nicholas asks, "Does not one pope or prince have greater authority in his vote than one manservant?"

Cusanus now develops a new conception of the power of the pope over the council. The pope must call the coun-

5 *RTA*, XV, 639, 874, and XVI, 418. The complex discussions by the medieval canonists on this subject are summarized by Tierney, *Foundations*, pp. 108-117.

6 *RTA*, XV, pp. 646, 763, 874; XVI, 410, 429, 543; and *Dialogus*, pp. 8 and 29.

cil, and if he does not, none can be held. Once it is convened, his presence or that of his representative is necessary in order for any business to be transacted. Where previously his participation had been required only for decisions on dogma, now it is necessary that he approve all decrees of the council for them to go into effect. "The apostolic see has this privilege in the councils, that where it does not consent, it [the conciliar decree] is not carried, and where it consents, it is carried."[7] Without his consent there is no council, because the council must act with the consent of both head and members.

When Nicholas discusses the reasons for the important position of the pope as head of the church, we get some indication of his new theories concerning the relations of pope and church. "The unity of the Church is from the confession of Peter, and through Peter it is communicated to the world . . . Whatever we have in the church was in Peter and from Peter, and all its faith, and there is no power of binding and loosing except in the chair of Peter."[8]

Here there is a completely new theory being enunciated as to the source of power (*jurisdictio*) in the church. For all Cusanus' talk about the importance of consent, he has admitted that all power comes from the pope, and the pope's consent is really all that matters in the council. While his speeches may still have echoes of the older theories of consent as justification for rule, the dominant theory now becomes one which concentrates power in the papacy.

[7] *RTA*, XV, 763. "Sedes vero apostolica haberet hoc privilegium in conciliis, quod, ubi non ipsa consentit, non valet, ubi consentit, valet." See also *RTA*, XV, 663, 771; XVI, 417-419; and *Dialogus*, p. 20.

[8] *RTA*, XV, 640, 644. "Quod unitas ecclesie esset a confessione Petri et per Petrum orbi communicata . . . ita quod, quidquid in ecclesia habemus, fuit in Petro et ex Petro, omnem quoque fidem; nullamque esse ligandi et solvendi potestatem nisi in cathedra Petri . . ."

In a statement to the Frankfurt *Reichstag* in 1442, he used the terminology of the *Docta Ignorantia* to express his ideas: "There is nothing in the church which is not first in Peter or his successor, and through the medium of the pope in all others . . . all power flows from the head of the church where there is a plenitude of power, and is particularized (*contracta*) in the church . . . all power which is unfolded (*explicata*) in the church is contained (*complicatorie*) in the pope as in a causal principle."[9]

On May 20, 1442, Nicholas wrote a letter to Rodrigo Sanchez de Arevalo, who was being sent by the King of Castile to the *Reichstag* then in progress at Frankfurt.[10] In the letter Nicholas uses the same argumentation, announcing at the outset that he is going to discuss the relation of the pope and the council "according to the rules of learned ignorance (*doctae ignorantiae*)." Just as the variety of beings in the world is an unfolding of one God, so the church is a mystical unfolding of the grace of Christ. This mystical church is represented in the sensory *(sensibilis)* world by a visible organization with a visible head, the pope. This church had its beginning with Peter's confession of faith "in the rock which is Christ," and can be called the *explicatio Petri* since the variety of believers receives its unity from the confession which he made.[11]

From the conception of unity in Peter's confession, Cusanus moves to that of unity in Peter's successor, and

9 *RTA*, XVI, 421 and 423. ". . . nichil est in ecclesia, quod non sit prioriter in Petro et ejus successore et per ejus medium in aliis . . . Fluit igitur a capite ecclesie, ubi est plenitudo potestatis omnis potestas contracta que est in ecclesia . . . omnis potestas que est explicata in ecclesia est in papa ut in principio causali complicatorie . . ."

10 Trame, *Rodrigo*, pp. 53-57.

11 The use of the verb *explicare* to discuss the relationship of the pope and the church (although without Cusanus' metaphysical overtones) has also been noted in the conciliar writings of Gerson and Zabarella. Cf. Heinz-Mohr, *Unitas Christiana*, p. 336, n. 262 and 265.

always in terms of *explicatio* and *complicatio*. The church as the unfolding of Peter reveals itself through its hierarchical ranks—patriarchs metropolitans, archbishops, bishops, and presbyters—all of whom can be viewed as particular (*contractas*) expressions of the general power of the church. This power is found in its fullness in the pope, the head and prince of the church, and includes within it all other powers in the church. Since all power is derived from the pope, he cannot be subordinated to any or all of the local officers of the church, since "it is irrational to say that a prince in his kingdom is both above and below [the people]: Reason does not allow this coincidence of contradictories, and certain most learned men have understood this when they have said that the prince is exempt from the laws and cannot be judged by his subjects."[12]

From the concepts of *explicatio* and *contractio* which were already outlined in his *Docta Ignorantia*, Cusanus seems to have derived a most extreme theory of papal supremacy. All power comes from the pope as the head of the hierarchy, and all other church offices depend completely upon him. In *De Concordantia Catholica*, Nicholas had specifically denied that all power in the church came from a divine grant to Peter or to the pope. Even after the change from the council to the pope, when the pope's position as *caput* had been greatly enhanced, Cusanus had maintained that it was to both the pope and the bishops that Christ had given the power to govern the church.[13] Now it appears that he has developed a new theory of papal

---

[12] Letter to Rodrigo, p. 109. "Unde irrationabiliter dicitur principem in eo regno, ubi est princeps, praeesse pariter et subesse. Ratio enim contradictoriorum coincidentiam non admittit. Quod sapientissimi quidam intellexerunt, qui principem solutum legibus et non posse a subditis judicari dixerunt." The reference to the *princeps* as *legibus solutus* is drawn from Roman law, and the *sapientissimi* were probably the civil lawyers.

[13] *DCC,* Book II, chap. 13, p. 154; Koch, *Briefwechsel,* p. 40.

absolutism in which all power is given to the papacy and distributed to the church through the pope.

Nicholas' former conceptions of consent and representation have also been completely altered. While there is mention of consent in the speeches to the *Reichstag*, it is almost always the consent of the pope which is discussed, not that of the church. There is no reference to the earlier theory of consent as the basis for all political and ecclesiastical authority. In the letter to Rodrigo, it is not a question of the delegation of authority from below to ecclesiastical superiors, nor of participation in lawmaking by those subject to them (the *quod omnes tangit* principle). Now all authority comes from above. It is concentrated (*complicata*) in the head and flows out from him to the lesser grades in the hierarchy of authority.

It is similar in the case of representation. As already noted, two theories of representation were present in *De Concordantia*. The first book of *De Concordantia*, when it discussed the pope or the bishop as representing his church, used terms (for example, the bishop as *figura ecclesiae*) which assumed a theory of representation in which the representative embodies or personifies the thing represented (personification theory). In other discussions, particularly when he outlined the role of the cardinals in the church constitution, Nicholas seemed to be thinking in terms of elected representatives (delegation theory) chosen by consent and acting in accordance with a legally prescribed set of rights and duties.

However, in the *Concordantia*, even when he used the first theory of representation, Cusanus also combined it with a theory of propinquity of representation (*presidentiae particulares*) which justified the superiority of the council to the pope on the grounds that the local authorities who participated in the council were more representative of those subject to them because they were closer to them. The pope represented ("impersonated") the church less well because he was farther removed from the *congregatio fidelium,* and therefore he was subordinated to a council made up of bishops and other local representatives. (The same theory was used with regard to the pope's authority in other councils; in councils of the diocese of Rome, for instance, his authority as *caput* or *presidens* was greater than in the universal council in which he was farther removed from those represented.)

In the letter to Rodrigo this theory has been dropped, and we find the personification theory of representation, combined with Neo-Platonic notions of hierarchy. Just as the ascent of the hierarchy of being brings one closer to the One, so in the ascent of the ecclesiastical hierarchy the church is better represented by the higher ranks (in the higher "contractions" of church power), and above all, by the pope at its summit. There is still discussion of the local (*particulares*) church rulers, but their power and authority are derived not from consent or from propinquity to those below, but by a "flowing down" or "unfolding" of the power of Peter which is contained in the papacy, *complicative.* The pope's position in the ecclesiastical hierarchy seems not unlike that of God in relation to the various gradations of the created universe.

The same development towards papal absolutism can be traced in another conception which was originally used with a quite different purpose in the *Concordantia. Epieikeia,* the Aristotelian legal theory of equity, which had been used there to justify the calling of a council without the pope's consent, is now used to justify the papal transfer of the council from Basel to Ferrara. In the *Concordantia,* Nicholas dealt with the papal right to transfer the council, since the pope had tried early in the history of the council to transfer it to Italy. He stated there that if there had been sufficient cause to transfer the council, the pope, using *epieikeia,* would have been justified in doing so, but in that case he would have had the consent of the council, since it too would have been aware of the good reasons for the transfer. In the *Reichstag* speeches, he uses the same argument. The first transfer, he says, was done without good reason, while the 1437 transfer was justified by the fact that it was done to avoid schism and bring about unity with the Greeks. The fact that the council objected the second time as well is not mentioned. (John of Segovia defending the council at the Mainz *Reichstag* of 1441 replied to Cusanus by quoting the *Concordantia* on the necessity of consent by the council to any change in its site.[14])

In Cusanus' writings and speeches after 1440, a new element is added to this argument. For the first time the words *plenitudo potestatis* are used to describe the authority of the pope in transferring the council. The whole concept of a full or unlimited power in the church would have been repugnant to Nicholas at an earlier period. Now, however, he talks on two different occasions of a papal transfer of the council "out of the fullness of his power," and at another point, in the *Dialogus,* he uses the same term to describe the power of the pope over the councils.[15] Cusanus seems to have developed a new attitude to the papal office. The *plenitudo potestatis,* which he earlier would grant only to the whole church, now inheres in the pope as the source and the fulfillment of all power in the church hierarchy.

14 *DCC,* Book II, chap. 25, pp. 226-227. *RTA,* XV, 763; *Dialogus,* p. 24; *Monumenta Conciliorum Generalium Saeculi XV,* III (Vienna, 1886), 566.
15 *RTA,* XV, 645; XVI, 431; *Dialogus,* p. 10. See also *RTA,* XVII (ed. Walter Kämmerer, reprinted Göttingen, 1956), 211.

If Nicholas had said nothing else, it would appear that he had rejected all his previous conciliarist opinions in favor of thoroughgoing papalism. However, this believer in the "coincidence of opposites" still retained elements of his former position in his new synthesis, and he continued to utilize conceptions, derived from the canonistic tradition, providing for corporate action to limit the ruler. Although he set limits around these procedures which made them largely ineffective in practice, it is significant that, in keeping with his belief in the virtue of a median position, Cusanus always qualified the grant of unlimited power which he seemed to have made to the pope.

In the letter to Rodrigo, the most thoroughgoing statement of a theory of papal supremacy, Nicholas says that "there is no absolute power to rule except that of God on high."[16] The papal power exists for the building up of the church, and every member of the church is subject to the pope only in so far as the pope promotes the good of the church. "Where that ruler commands something which does not tend to the building up of the church entrusted to him, that command does not proceed from his ruling power, so that there is no obligation to obey him." Thus one rather broad theoretical limit has been set upon the absolute power of the pope—the good of the church. This limitation is immediately applied to the question of church offices. The pope may not interfere with lower church offices, since the order and status of the universal church were established by Peter for the building up of the church. Only in cases of utility or necessity may the pope make temporary exceptions in the rules or order of the ranks of the church, using his power of *epieikeia* or dispensation.[17]

---

16 Letter to Rodrigo in *DAP*, p. 109. ". . . non est potestas principis absoluta nisi Dei summi."

17 Letter to Rodrigo, p. 110. "Ubi vero ipse princeps ea fieri mandaret,

A parallel may perhaps be drawn between this view of papal power and the concept of the universe in the *Docta Ignorantia* as the *maximum contractum,* reproduced *(explicatum)* in lower "contractions" but itself not absolute, as is God. Limits are set upon papal power. The church may be an *explicatio* of his power, but he may only act for its benefit and he must respect the existing distribution of church offices.

There was another limit on papal power, which was accepted by both the papalists and conciliarists—the possibility of papal heresy. On the basis of Distinction 40, chapter 6, of Gratian's *Decretum* it was believed that the pope could be judged if he was guilty of heresy. Nicholas of Cusa, even after the development of the philosophy of "learned ignorance," was still a good canon lawyer and accepted this on its face.

He also accepted, even in his conciliar period, the belief that the *sedes Romana* was protected from error in matters of faith by divine grant in the New Testament. How could the doctrine of infallibility of the *sedes Romana* be reconciled with the acceptance of the possibility of papal heresy?

The analysis of the *Concordantia Catholica* and of the letters written in 1439 has shown how Nicholas had harmonized the two beliefs previously. In the *Concordantia,* the *sedes* meant the pope in his patriarchal council, while, in 1439, infallibility was granted to the pope with his cardinals, not to the pope alone. The pope could err and had done so. It was only when he acted together with his council or cardinals that he was protected from error.

---

quae ad finem aedificationis ecclesiae illi creditae non tenderent, non procederet iussio a principatu; quare ei tunc obedire non esset necesse." See also *RTA*, XVI, 418 and 431, where the papal power to transfer the council must be exercised *in aedificationem ecclesiae* and *causis racionabilibus existentibus.*

Now Cusanus goes one step further. While admitting the possibility of personal heresy by the pope, he seems to believe that he is infallible when he makes formal decisions on matters of faith. "No pope when speaking from the papal see (*in sede*) or in judgment has ever decreed that anything must be held other than what is Catholic doctrine, although at times he has also erred."[18] Nicholas is stating what is now Catholic doctrine, as defined by the Vatican Council of 1870, which limits papal infallibility to cases when he is teaching *ex cathedra* on questions of faith and morals. This marks an important change in the direction of papal absolutism in Cusanus' theory, since it eliminates all possibility of corporate expression of the consent of the church, and extends the divine promise of protection from error to the pope alone, rather than in association with any other body in the church.

Moreover, although he admits the possibility of heresy by the pope as an individual, Nicholas speaks of the pope as departing less (*minus recedit*) from the truths of faith. Although he can err just as anyone else can, he is less likely to do so (*minus deviabilem*) and, as a matter of historical record, he has actually fallen into heresy less often than the councils.[19]

Yet, in theory at least, an additional limit has been set upon the absolute supremacy of the papacy besides the requirements that he act for the good of the church and

---

[18] *RTA*, XV, 768. ". . . ut nullus pontificum in sede seu in judicio decreverit hucusque aliud quam id, quod catholicum est, tenendum, licet ipse eciam aberravit aliquando." See also H. Paetzoldt, *Die Lehre des Nikolaus Cusanus von der Kirche auf Grund seiner Predigten* (Breslau, 1938), p. 47, n. 50, for a quotation from a 1454 sermon which explicitly distinguishes between papal statements *in cathedra* and those which are made *private*. For earlier examples in canonist writings, see Tierney, *Foundations*, p. 39, n. 2.

[19] *RTA*, XVI, 425. ". . . sed sicut papa est deviabilis, ita quisque aliorum; immo presumi debet papam minus deviabilem." See also *Dialogus*, p. 30.

maintain the existing distribution of church offices—he must observe the doctrinal decrees of the church councils and popes who have gone before him. He can dispense with church law for reasons of utility or necessity, but the dispensing power cannot apply to church doctrine, since exceptions to dogma would constitute heresy.

Papal power, vast as it was under Cusanus' new theory, was thus not completely unlimited. By maintaining heretical opinions, the pope could forfeit his office, and by acting against the good of the church or altering the apostolic constitution of offices, he could exceed his powers. Yet these theoretical limits would be largely meaningless if the pope himself were the sole judge of the good of the church or of heretical doctrine. It was important to know who was to decide when these vague theoretical limits on the papacy were transgressed, and what institutional restraints could enforce them. Even in his propapal utterances, Nicholas of Cusa seemed to feel the need for some kind of limitation on papal excess. For this purpose, the *via concilii* seemed very attractive as a means of controlling the pope. The Council of Constance had succeeded in bringing about the end of the Great Schism, and Constance had declared and Basel had reaffirmed the doctrine that the pope was subject to the council in matters of faith, reform, and the ending of the schism.

Yet at Basel the doctrine of conciliar supremacy had itself led to schism, the worst of all possible evils in the view of one who all his life labored for church unity. Moreover, the remnants of the Council of Basel were insisting on their right to depose the pope as they had done in 1439. How could a method be found to limit papal abuse of power and at the same time to deny the claim of the Council of Basel to superiority over the pope? What resort was there in the later theory of Nicholas in the event of papal heresy or persistent action against the good of the church?

In accepting the validity of the Council of Constance, but not that of Basel, Nicholas made use of that perennial resource of the conciliar theorists, the doctrine of necessity. When the church was divided and there was no certain pope, it was necessary to depart from the normal procedure and recognize the temporary right of the council to depose the disputed claimants and to elect a single undisputed pope. However, it was only against three disputed popes that a general superiority of the council could be acknowledged, although, of course, the pope was bound by the provisions of the Council of Constance which had been approved by the single undisputed pope after he had been elected.[20]

For a council to act against the pope in cases either of heresy or continued abuse of power, it had first to be convoked. But here, Nicholas' theory had abandoned his earlier belief that the emperor could call the council if necessary. Now, there is a single-minded concentration on the requirement of papal convocation, consent, and participation, even in a council which is being convoked to depose him on grounds of heresy. If it seems unlikely that the pope would consent to such proceedings, Nicholas once more raises the specter of schism. "Rather a bad pope should be tolerated than that occasion be given . . . of dividing the church."[21] If no council can be held because of papal obstinacy and the church is in real difficulty, the bishops can meet together (but not as a universal council) and provide for the

20 *RTA*, XVI, 432; and especially *Dialogus,* pp. 5 and 21.
21 *RTA*, XV, 772. ". . . quod pocius malus pontifex toleretur quam quod occasio detur . . . ecclesiam dividendi."

necessities of the church. However, if the necessity happens to be that of getting rid of the pope in the face of his repeated refusal to call a council, there does not seem to be much that can be done. The pope cannot be deposed, since the bishops by themselves are not qualified to do it. In addition, no decisions on faith can be taken, since for them to be valid the consent of the papacy is required.

Once the council has been properly convoked, as in the case of the Council of Basel, and a disagreement develops between the pope and council, which is to be followed? This was one of a number of specific questions put to Nicholas of Cusa by the emperor's representative at the 1441 *Reichstag,* and the same question was treated in Cusanus' speech to the *Reichstag* meeting the following year.

The case of papal heresy was fairly clear. If, once the council is in session, it becomes apparent that the pope is persisting in heresy, he can be deposed by a universal council. This action has a merely declaratory force, since by embracing heresy he has already deposed himself. Here Cusanus is following accepted canonistic doctrine (and he is opening the door to trumped-up charges of papal heresy, such as those actually used in the deposition of Eugene). His real difficulty arises when he comes to the case of a nondoctrinal difference between the pope and the council, such as the one which had actually taken place at Basel. He had said that the pope must work for the good of the church. What if the council and the pope differed on the interpretation of the church's good?

On this point, Nicholas is of two minds. On the one hand, he quotes with apparent approval canon law texts to demonstrate that, aside from the case of papal heresy, no one can judge or sentence the pope except God. The best that the members of the council can do is discuss the problem with due reverence, but they may not take any action.[22] On the other hand, Cusanus admits that there are a number of learned men *(gravissimorum virorum)* who believe that a pope can be judged by a council. However, even granting their argument, he says, the judgment can only be carried out by a unanimous council. If it is divided, the part of the council which is on the side of the pope, so long as he is not a heretic *(quamdiu fuerit catholicus)*, is the church, and the others are schismatics.

Here we get a repetition in a different form of the "equal weight" theory outlined in Cusanus' letters in 1439. The fact that the pope is head of the church means that unless all the rest of the church is ranged against him, union with him means union with the church. Only if there is unanimous opposition by the entire church can he be deposed on grounds of abuse of power.

Cusanus does not seem to have been very happy with this view, although it had been his firm belief a few years before. However, it had the advantage of disproving the Basel council's claim to superiority over the pope (since a part of the Basel council had been in favor of the pope) and, at the same time, of providing for a way to check the pope without introducing a division or schism in the church (since, if the entire church was against him, there was not likely to be a schism). Moreover, as Nicholas admitted, the likelihood that such a situation would arise seemed very slight.

The approach of unanimous resistance to papal abuse is also the one which Cusanus favors in his letter to Rodrigo. Without ever mentioning the councils, he says that the church can disobey the pope if he persists in acting against its interests, and can "withdraw" from him if he violates

---

22   *RTA*, XVI, 423, and *Dialogus*, p. 10.

fundamental church law (*statuta sanctorum patrum*), thus exceeding the limits of his authority (*exiens vires potentiae suae*).[23] However, he adds that this can only take place when there is no danger of schism (that is, only by unanimous withdrawal). Whether this withdrawal is permanent or temporary—whether he is recommending disobedience or deposition—is not clear. However, in the *Reichstag* of 1442, he recommends disobedience rather than deposition and he once again shows his fear of schism. If the pope commands actions which are clearly against the interests of the church (and in case of doubt, the presumption is in his favor), he should be disobeyed. While disobedience may be less efficient in dealing with a recalcitrant pope, Cusanus says, it avoids the great danger which all theories of deposition and conciliar supremacy involve—schism and disunity within the church.[24]

The canonistic tradition had provided an intricate analysis of the relations of the head and members of the ecclesiastical corporation, and Nicholas, arguing as a canon lawyer for the supremacy of the pope, still was required to discuss the problem of controlling the pope. His general belief in finding a middle or concordant position impelled him to try to harmonize the antithetical viewpoints of the papalists and the conciliarists.

When he was a conciliarist, in *De Concordantia Catholica,* his theory inclined toward the papacy much more than

---

[23] Letter to Rodrigo, pp. 110-111. Nicholas admits that the pope can dispense from church law "for reasons of utility or necessity" (*ex causa utilitatis aut necessitatis*) and restricts the possibility of withdrawal to cases of papal illegal action "for a personal and unworthy reason" (*ex aliqua particulari non digna causa*).

[24] *RTA*, XVI, 424. "Unde cum juris remedium sit, non obedire prelato in hiis, que contra deum et universalem statum ecclesie Christi existunt, ut est concors omnium sentencia, tunc prelato ecclesie eciam pessimo per nonobedienciam resistitur, ubi ecclesiam destruere vellet, et hoc est remedium sine scismatis periculo et est optimum et equissimum."

those of most of the conciliarists at Basel. The pope normally was to call the council, and his representatives were to preside over it if they were in attendance. He was to be consulted on any decree on matters of church dogma. He had substantial powers of dispensation from church law, and he represented the church in his person, although not as well as did the universal council. The *sedes Romana* in the sense of the pope in his patriarchal council was infallible, although the universal council was superior to the pope alone.

The later statements of Nicholas in favor of the pope, which seemed to derive all church authority from him, still retained elements of the conciliarist position. Although only the pope can call the council and preside over it, and although he must consent to all its decrees for them to be valid, the bishops can still provide for the necessities of the church in the face of papal inaction. Once the council has been called, they can depose the pope on grounds of heresy, and, at least in the view of some, a unanimous council can also act against him if he is working against the interests of the church. In any event, if the pope abuses his powers, the church can disobey him, and if he persists, it can "withdraw" from him.

Even where there are substantial differences between the theories of 1433 and those of 1442, they utilize the same basic theoretical categories. The necessity of universal consent, which in 1433 was used to justify conciliar superiority, is the basis of Cusanus' argument after 1437 that the Basel council is no longer a universal council. The papal power of dispensation or *epieikeia*, discussed at length in 1433, is used to justify his transfer of the council to Ferrara. In 1433, 1439, and 1442, it is maintained that the *sedes Romana* is infallible. However, in each case, the *sedes* is defined differently. Even Cusanus' theories of representation, however different they may appear in practice, are not basically dissimilar in 1433 and 1442. In both cases the ruler personifies or typifies the political or ecclesiastical community, and the transition from the statements in Book I of the *Concordantia,* where the bishop is the *figura* of his church, to the letter to Rodrigo, where the church is viewed as the *explicatio Petri,* is not a difficult one.

Yet, for all the similarities, there is a very fundamental shift in Nicholas' thinking between the two dates. In the early period the dominant note is that of the medieval legal tradition, the belief in the right of the organized community to participate in lawmaking and to set and enforce limitations on the ruler. In 1442 the dominant note is that set by the theories of medieval Platonism and the *Docta Ignorantia.* All power flows from the head of the hierarchy and is concentrated in it. If qualifications are introduced in this theory, so that one could not describe it as a medieval anticipation of Bodinian theories of sovereignty, nor even as a statement of extreme papalism such as those of James of Viterbo and Aegidius Romanus, it is because of the survival of elements of canonistic legalism in Cusanus' thought, and because of his philosophical preference for a conciliatory position, a *coincidentia oppositorum.*[25] Yet, forced to choose between council and pope, now he chooses the pope where earlier he would have chosen the council. Even with all the qualifications which he adds, Nicholas of Cusa has become the exponent of papal monarchy in the church.

[25] Carl Schmitt, *The Necessity of Politics* (London, 1931), argues that "the Catholic theory of politics" is based on the *complexio oppositorum.*

CHAPTER XII

. . .

THE GERMAN CARDINAL

DESPITE Nicholas' efforts as *Hercules Eugeniorum* at various meetings of the *Reichstag*, the emperor was indecisive, and the German princes remained neutral or favorable to the council. Relations between Germany and the papacy worsened as a result of a papal attempt to depose the prince-archbishops of Cologne and Trier, and it was not until 1447 that the electors of the empire submitted to the pope. Nicholas carried out his work of persuasion and diplomacy at Nuremberg in 1444, at Frankfurt in 1446, and at Aschaffenburg in 1447. Complete reconciliation with Germany was achieved with the conclusion of the Concordat of Vienna in 1448, which specified which benefices would be filled by Rome and which were elective. A clause in the concordat, which was later to be important for Nicholas, provided that bishops were to be elected by their chapters, except in cases in which (1) Rome had not been duly notified of the result, or (2) the election was uncanonical in form, or (3) an urgent reason persuaded the pope with the advice of the cardinals to name a worthier person.[1] With the signing of the concordat and the resignation of the antipope in 1449, the conciliar period was terminated.

Cusanus' active service on behalf of the papacy was rewarded by Eugene IV, who, just before his death in 1447,

---

[1] Nicholas was called *Hercules Eugeniorum* by Aeneas Sylvius in his history of the Council of Basel. For the terms of the Concordat of Vienna, see Feine, *Rechtsgeschichte*, p. 401. The relevant section says, ". . . nisi ex causa rationabili et evidenti, et de fratrum consilio, de digniori et utiliori persona duxerit providendum."

named him a cardinal. Eugene's successor, Nicholas V, confirmed the appointment, which had been secret,[2] and Cusanus was formally invested with the cardinal's red hat in January 1450. Shortly thereafter he was named Bishop of Brixen (now Bressanone), an independent bishopric just south of the Brenner Pass in the Tyrol. Apparently the pope feared that the Archduke of the Tyrol was in the process of swallowing up the bishopric, and he wished to put a person of great juristic and diplomatic talents and experience into the office in order to resist the archduke.

Much of the rest of Nicholas of Cusa's life was devoted to intermittent conflict with Archduke Sigismund of the Tyrol. At the very beginning, Nicholas ran into difficulty because the pope had named him instead of Leonard Wiesmayer, the archduke's chancellor, who had been elected by the diocesan chapter. As a basis for his nomination the pope was able to cite the clause of the Vienna Concordat concerning uncanonical elections (he claimed that the chapter had been surrounded by the archduke's armed men during the voting), as well as the clause providing for the nomination of a more worthy person for an urgent reason. While the initial conflict was settled in 1451 by a direct appeal to the emperor (the temporal overlord of the Prince-Bishop of Brixen), the difficulties with the archduke continued until Cusanus' death.

In 1450-51 the pope sent Nicholas to Germany and the Low Countries to preach the Jubilee (Holy Year) indulgence, and armed with full powers to end abuses such as simony and concubinage and to enforce the monastic rules. This last reform effort before the Reformation was only moderately successful, and in some cases it ran into very

2 See the excerpts from Cusanus' official biography, *Historia Reverendi Domini Nicolai de Cusa,* quoted in Vansteenberghe, *Nicolas,* p. 86, n. 4.

formidable opposition.[3] (Many of the manuscripts in the collection at Kues were purchased during this trip.[4])

It was in this period that Nicholas started to build the library and the hospice for the aged which still exist at Kues. According to Nicholas' intention, the latter was to house six members of the nobility, six clergymen, and twenty-one indigent unmarried or widowed men at least fifty years of age—a total of thirty-three, one for each year of Christ's life. The hospice, which still functions today, the oldest private foundation in Europe, was endowed with a fund of 10,000 florins and now receives the income from local vineyards. The building was begun in 1452 and in 1458 a charter gave the foundation legal standing; Cusanus never saw the completed buildings, for his last visit to Kues took place during his reforming mission in 1451. During these years he was also in regular correspondence with the Teutonic Knights, whose interests he, as the German cardinal, was expected to protect, both against the independence efforts of the Hanseatic League and the rival claims of Poles and Czechs to territories in dispute then as now.[5]

In 1452 Nicholas came into the diocese of Brixen, and the controversy with the archduke flared up over the question of jurisdiction over a local convent. In different forms

3 For one example, see the account by E. Vansteenberghe, "Le Cardinal-legat Nicolas de Cues et le clergé de Liége" in *Leodium*, 15:103-114 (1922), describing the resistance of the clergy of Liége.

4 Sabbadini, *Scoperte*, I, 16-27.

5 For the itinerary of the reform trip, see Koch, *Nikolaus von Cues und seine Umwelt*, pp. 116-148. The correspondence with the Teutonic Knights has been published by Erich Maschke, *Nikolaus von Kues und der Deutsche Orden*, in *SBH* 1955, no. 1 (Heidelberg, 1956). The charter for the foundation at Kues is analyzed in Klaus Mörsdorff, *Die Scabini-Frage in der Stiftungsurkunde des St. Nikolaus-Hospitals in Bernkastel-Kues*, in *Sitzungsberichte der Bayerischen Akademie der Wissenschaften*, Phil.-hist. Klasse, no. 4 (Munich, 1958).

it continued to agitate the cardinal and his diocese from 1452 until the final departure of Nicholas for Rome in 1460. The pope excommunicated Sigismund after he had laid siege to Nicholas in one of the castles of the Prince-Bishop of Brixen and had forced him to sign a humiliating surrender. The dispute was finally settled only in 1464, a few weeks after Nicholas' death.[6]

In the midst of controversies and feverish diplomatic activity, Nicholas found time to write spiritual works, including four dialogues in 1450 collectively known as *Idiota,* because one of the persons in the dialogue is called "the simpleton."[7] Although Nicholas was active in European political and ecclesiastical life, he wrote little that is of direct political relevance, and the development of his ideas must be deduced from his actions, from occasional passages in his theological treatises, and from a single work on the reform of the church, written very near the end of his life.

Various attempts have been made to draw connections between Cusanus' philosophical position and his political theory, sometimes leading to directly opposing conclusions. One writer on medieval theory asserts that Cusanus' Platonism led to "his hierocratic philosophy after 1440."[8] Another sees in the theories of the *Docta Ignorantia* the basis for a type of religious and political pluralism.[9] Both

[6] The principal account of the feud is A. Jäger, *Der Streit des Cardinals Nicolaus von Cusa mit dem Herzog Sigmund von Österreich,* 2 vols. (Innsbruck, 1861). It is summarized in Vansteenberghe, *Nicolas,* pp. 140-211. Insight into Cusanus' methods of historical research is provided in the documents surrounding one stage of the dispute in the South Tyrol in 1456, published and analyzed in Hermann Hallauer, "Eine Denkschrift des Nikolaus von Kues zum Kauf der Ämter Taufers und Uttenheim in Südtirol," *Mitteilungen,* 1:76-94.

[7] Available in English as *The Idiot,* reprint of 1650 translation with introduction by W. R. Dennes (San Francisco, 1940).

[8] Alois Dempf, *Sacrum Imperium* (Berlin-Munich, 1929), p. 560.

[9] Bauer, "Sacrum Imperium," pp. 238-239.

authors fail to discuss Cusanus' actual political activities and writings in his later life, preferring to project political conclusions from philosophical premises which themselves are not always clear.

It is true that Nicholas used the terminology of the *Docta Ignorantia* in explaining his position on church government. Yet this did not lead him either to papal theocracy or to a system of representative government in the church. The analysis of the letter to Rodrigo Sanchez de Arevalo has revealed that at the same time that he spoke of the church as the *explicatio Petri* he also left open the possibility for resistance of the church to papal decrees. The pope is limited by the end of the good (*aedificatio*) of the church. If he commands anything "which does not tend to its good," he may be disobeyed. Moreover, if the papal decrees violate the fundamental law of the church and are issued for personal or unworthy reasons rather than out of necessity, the church can withdraw from him.[10] However, this can only be done if there is absolute unanimity in opposition to the pope. In practice, these qualifications were not likely to limit papal power seriously since, in any doubtful situation, the doubt was to be resolved in favor of the pope. The same requirement of unanimity undermined Cusanus' reluctant concession in his speech to the *Reichstag* that perhaps a council might in extreme cases take action against the pope. Here again action could only be taken by unanimous decision.

The requirement of unanimous opposition probably did not seem as unrealistic to Nicholas as it may today. It must be remembered that he continued to believe that the church was acting under the inspiration of the Holy Spirit, and in cases of prolonged abuse by the pope he was con-

10 Letter to Rodrigo, pp. 110-111.

fident that the required unanimity would be brought about by divine influence.

Cusanus' position should be compared with that of Rodrigo Sanchez de Arevalo, the recipient of his letter, to demonstrate that Nicholas never went as far in his conception of papal authority as did the most convinced defenders of the pope. The Vatican library contains a dialogue which is based on Rodrigo's debates with a defender of the council before the emperor in Vienna in 1440. In the dialogue Arevalo asserts that the council has no jurisdiction over the pope. If the pope falls into heresy, he is *ipso facto* cut off from the faith, but he is deposed by God, not by the council. Arevalo takes issue directly with the decrees of the Council of Constance, which Nicholas never attacked. The Spanish ecclesiastic declares that the decree *Sacrosancta,* asserting conciliar supremacy, was not accepted by the whole council nor approved by the popes, an essential prerequisite for its canonical validity. Moreover, it directly contradicted the canons and decrees of former councils which had declared the pope to be head of the church.[11]

The second article of the dialogue goes still further. Arevalo uses Boniface VIII's bull *Unam Sanctam* to argue the absolute necessity, for salvation, of submission to the papacy. He illustrates this by the comparisons popular with theorists of the direct power of the papacy in temporals, such as the subordination of the members of the body to the head and of the river to its source. A later work, the *Defensorium Ecclesiae,* written in 1466, carries these arguments still further.[12] Arevalo argues that the temporal power must be subordinated to the spiritual

11 Trame, *Rodrigo,* pp. 36-44, summarizing *Codex Vaticanus Latinus* 4002.
12 Martin Grabmann, *Studien über den Einfluss der Aristotelischen Philosophie* (Munich, 1934), pp. 114-127, summarizing *Codex Vaticanus Latinus* 4106.

because the soul is superior to the body, because the lower end must serve the higher end, and because monarchy is the natural order of the universe. His conclusion is that the pope possesses "despotic and absolute power" and that "the rulership possessed by the church and the Roman pontiff, its head, is a rulership over the whole world both as to spiritual and temporal matters, while the rulership possessed by emperors and kings is ministerial and instrumental, being subservient to him, and subject to change and revocation at the command of the ruling authority of the church and the Roman pontiff."[13]

The hierocratic or theocratic theory of the fifteenth century papalists, if Arevalo is typical, went much further than Nicholas was willing to go. It asserted the exemption of the papacy from any control by the council or the church as a whole, and subscribed to the doctrine of the direct power of the pope over all temporal rulers. It is true that those defenders of the papacy who were influenced by the Thomistic tradition tended to take a more moderate position on the question of the relations of the spiritual and temporal powers. A theory of the indirect power of the papacy was developed at this time by John of Turrecremata, one of the staunchest opponents of the claims of the conciliarists, but he was the exception to the majority of fifteenth century theologians and jurists in the post-conciliar period.[14] Most of them shared the opinion of the fourteenth century apologist for the papacy, James of Viterbo, that

[13] Grabmann, *Einfluss*, p. 127. "Principatus ecclesie et romani pontificis eius capitis est principatus totius orbis quoad spiritualia et temporalia et principatus imperialis et regalis est ministerialis et instrumentalis et eidem subministrans et deserviens mobiliter et revocabiliter ad jussum principatus ecclesie et romani pontificis."

[14] Grabmann, *Einfluss*, p. 132, quotes Turrecremata's *Summa de Ecclesia* which concludes that the pope may intervene in temporals only "quantum necesse est pro bono spirituali conservando."

the pope is "the chief of the kings of the earth."[15] Like Arevalo, they reasoned from the hierarchy of ends and the necessary subordination of the lower to the higher, an argument which Boniface VIII had consciously derived from Dionysius.[16]

In the *Concordantia Catholica*, Nicholas of Cusa had taken a different position. He had argued for parallel hierarchies in church and empire and assumed that the guidance of the Holy Spirit would prevent conflict. Did he later abandon this duality of hierarchies in favor of theocratic monism, as he had abandoned the structure of representative councils on which the hierarchies were based?

His sermons after his change to the side of the papacy emphasize the absolute necessity of union with Rome and use terms drawn from his philosophical vocabulary as well as from the later canon lawyers to demonstrate the absolute supremacy of the pope. "Peter is the rock of the edifice of the church in which the whole building is contained (*complicatur*)," he preached in 1454. "In every multitude of the same kind, there is one, in whom is full power (*plenitudo*) with respect to all."[17]

If one wanted to demonstrate theocratic tendencies in Cusanus' later years, reference could also be made to his frequent threats to invoke the "secular arm." On his reform trip through Germany and the Low Countries, Nicholas was always ready to utilize the force at the disposal of the civil authority to effect reform of the recalcitrant

15 James of Viterbo, *De Regimine Christiano*, Part II, chap. 3, quoted in McIlwain, *Growth*, p. 262.
16 See above, Chapter III, n. 48.
17 Herbert Paetzold, *Die Lehre des Nikolaus Cusanus*, p. 39, n. 8, "Petrus est lapis aedificii ecclesiae in quo totum complicatur aedificium," and p. 49, n. 54, "In omni multitudine unius generis reperitur unum, in quo est plenitudo respectu omnium."

clergy.[18] However, the papal bull creating his legation had authorized him to make use of the secular arm, and this was for the Middle Ages a normal instance of the cooperation of the two powers. It did not necessarily imply any subordination of the temporal to the spiritual power. The *Concordantia Catholica* reflects a similar attitude when it discusses the relations of the parallel hierarchies of church and empire. Each would help the other, and, as the example of the Crusades demonstrates, there was nothing unusual about the use of force in aid of the church in the Middle Ages.

Nor was it unusual for the church to possess temporal power, but here *De Concordantia* had expressed itself for reform. At least it had said temporal administrators should be appointed for church lands and the pope should be supported by a collection throughout the church. In practice in later years Cusanus showed himself most tenacious with regard to the temporal privileges of the church. In his interminable feud with the Archduke of the Tyrol over his diocese of Brixen, he showed no inclination to surrender any of his temporal possessions to the jurisdiction of the secular ruler. A similar concern to defend the legal rights of the church was also manifested in his intervention against the Hanseatic League in favor of the religio-military order of the Teutonic Knights. As a canonist, he attempted to uphold what he felt to be the established rights of the church, and if he seems in his later years to have been working for the extension of the temporal power of the church, it was not so much because of his philosophical or theological beliefs as because of his training and background

18 How recalcitrant they could be is indicated by one attempt to poison the papal legate, and another case, mentioned earlier, of violent resistance from the clergy of Liége. For examples of the appeal to the secular arm, see Koch, *Nikolaus von Cues und seine Umwelt*, pp. 52 and 61, and Maschke, *Nikolaus von Kues und der Deutsche Orden*, pp. 57 and 63.

as a canon lawyer and his position as a leading churchman. In the letter to Rodrigo, Nicholas had described the pope as containing *complicative* all power in the church. Since the emperor and other temporal rulers were in the church, this might be interpreted as the assertion by Nicholas of the complete theocratic subordination of the temporal to the spiritual. However, a single passage in a late philosophical work, *De Beryllo*, completed in 1458, seems to indicate that Nicholas continued to believe in parallel structures in the spiritual and temporal hierarchies. In *De Beryllo* he develops the same general philosophical ideas which had been set forth in the *Docta Ignorantia*. At one point he quotes an apocryphal letter of Plato on the "universal King" who is the first principle of all things. Then he applies this to secular government:

> Every state is ordered by its ruler and receives from him its direction and its existence. The various things which are found individually in the state are first united in the king as his being and his life, as Proclus says. Dukes, counts, soldiers, judges, laws, weights, and measures, and the like, all have their being in the king, as the personification of the state, in whom all things which can exist in the state have their reality. The law of the state which is written on parchment is in the king living law; and thus it is for everything of which he is the originator. Whatever has its being and name in the state has it from him. . . You see, then, that exactly as the law written on dead parchment is in the prince living law, so, in the First Principle, all is life, time is eternity, and all created things, the Creator.[19]

[19] Nicolai de Cusa, *Opera Omnia*, vol. XI/1, *De Beryllo*, ed. Ludwig Baur (Leipzig, 1940), chap. xv, pp. 14-15. "Omnis enim republica per regem et ad ipsum ordinata, et per ipsum regitur et existit. Quae igitur in republica reperiuntur distincta, prioriter et conjuncte in ipso sunt ipse, et vita, ut addit Proclus: duces, comites, milites, judices, leges, mensurae, pondera, et quaequae talia, omnia sunt in rege, ut in publica persona in qua omnia quae possunt esse in republica, actu existunt ipse. Lex ejus in pellibus scripta est, in ipso lex viva, et ita de omnibus quorum ipse auctor

The above excerpt provides an interesting parallel with the letter to Rodrigo. In the same way as the letter portrays the pope as containing within himself everything that is in the church, the paragraph quoted conceives the king as containing in potentiality everything that is in the kingdom. The same theory of representation as personification is put forward, and there is the same omission of the element of corporate consent which had been so important in the earlier theories of the conciliar period. The king *is* the kingdom. He is the source of law, and the community has no independent legislative powers. While the passage does not exclude the possibility of papal overlordship, its whole tone is such as to emphasize the ruler's temporal supremacy and to reassert the parallelism of function present in Cusanus' earlier thought.

Naturally, the few sentences quoted above should not be taken as representing a fully developed political theory. They are suggested by a supposed letter of Plato cited in Proclus' commentary on the *Republic,* and the whole discussion is devoted to proving a theological and metaphysical rather than a political point. However, it shows that Cusanus' increasing tendency towards a unitary conception of rulership in church and state was accompanied by continued parallelism rather than theocracy in his church-state theory. Just as the *Concordantia* had seen empire and church as two parallel hierarchies of rulers and councils, so the excerpt from *De Beryllo* and the letter to Rodrigo see pope and king each as incorporating and personifying all the powers of those over whom they rule.

The discussion in *De Beryllo* centers around the king or the prince, while the *Concordantia* had discussed the posi-

---

est, et ab ipso omnia habent, quae habent . . . Ecce sicut lex scripta in pellibus mortuis, est lex viva in principe, sic in primo, omnia sunt vita, tempus in primo est aeternitas, creatura creator."

tion of the emperor and had been addressed to Emperor Sigismund. When *De Beryllo* was written, twenty-five years after the *Concordantia*, there was much less hope for reform of the empire, and the emperor himself was not the strong leader that Sigismund had been. Yet Nicholas never completely abandoned his hope for a reform of the empire, nor his ideal conception of the union of all temporal kings under the leadership of a strong emperor. In one of his last philosophical works, *De Ludo Globi*, written in 1462, there is a passage which shows that he still thought of other kingdoms as in some sense subordinate to the empire, and reverting to it when they became vacant.

The subject under discussion is the relationship of the soul to the body. When the soul infuses the body, Cusanus says, it is like a king in a little kingdom which is a part of the great kingdom of the universe. But when the soul departs, the body reverts to the "universal kingdom" of the rest of the physical world. In the same way, the kingdom of Bohemia belonged to the empire before it had its own king, and, in the same way, it will revert to the empire if it ceases to have its own king. Just as the citizen of Bohemia is subject to his own king directly, and to the emperor indirectly, so man is under the rulership of his own soul immediately, and mediately he is subject to the "kingdom of the world."[20]

The yearning for a universal empire and universal church, and the hopes for universal agreement among men which characterized *De Concordantia Catholica*, remained with Nicholas until his death. If we see in his letters a certain rigidity and inflexibility, and a readiness to appeal to authority, there is in his philosophy a desire for harmony and spontaneous agreement which is the very opposite of a

---

[20] Nicolai de Cusa, *Opera* (Basel, 1565), *De Ludo Globi*, Book I, p. 218.

rigorist view. The best expression of this, in his later years, is the religious dialogue, *De Pace Fidei*.[21]

The work was written shortly after the fall of Constantinople in 1453. Cusanus was deeply affected by this event, having been to Constantinople in connection with the preparations for the Council of Ferrara-Florence. The problem of relations with the Islamic world had concerned him since the time of the Council of Basel, when he acquired a twelfth century collection of writings on Mohammedanism which may have inspired *De Pace Fidei*.[22] The conflict with Islam suggested to him the larger problem of relations between men of the many diverse religious faiths throughout the world. Could a unity be found in this diversity? Was a concordance or agreement of faiths possible? In the face of the intensity with which men defended the religious beliefs which they held as absolutely true, and which they attempted to enforce on others, could the evil of religious disagreements, and even wars, be ended by some common agreement on faith?

Nicholas poses this question in the opening chapter of *De Pace Fidei*, and he imagines a heavenly gathering of representatives of many nations and religions to discuss it. Successively a Greek, Italian, Arab, Indian, Chaldean, Jew, Scythian, Frenchman, Persian, Syrian, Turk, German, Tartar, Armenian, and Bohemian engage in discussion with Christ, St. Peter, and St. Paul. The discussion demonstrates to them that there are certain elements common to or implicit in all religions. These elements, however, are not

21 Nicolai de Cusa, *Opera Omnia*, vol. VII, *De Pace Fidei*. The late Bruno Decker has published two articles analyzing *De Pace Fidei*: "Nikolaus von Cues und der Friede unter den Religionen," in *Humanismus, Mystik, und Kunst in der Welt des Mittelalters*, ed. Josef Koch (Leiden-Cologne, 1953), pp. 94-121, and "Die Toleranzidee bei Nikolaus von Kues und in der Neuzeit," in *Nicolò Cusano, Relazioni presentate al Convegno Interuniversitario di Bressanone* (Florence, 1962), pp. 5-24.

22 Introduction to *De Pace Fidei*, p. xxxix.

those of the later Deism or natural religion, although Cusanus was claimed by Enlightenment thinkers as a spiritual ancestor.[23] The common doctrines on which all could agree included the necessity of Divine Revelation, the Trinity, the Incarnation, and the Redemption, even the doctrine of Transubstantiation in the Eucharist. The dialogue thus appears ultimately to be an apologetic for the Catholic religion, attempting to find in other religions elements which resemble or imply these Catholic doctrines.

In it Nicholas attempted to demonstrate the philosophical necessity of the Trinity on the basis of the Neo-Platonic and Augustinian concepts of unity, equality, and connection. He pleaded for toleration of a wide diversity of rites within a common consensus which he felt men of good will could find. Religious truth is one, but God has revealed it to different nations in different ways. Nicholas saw a merit in this diversity since it would induce competition among the various rites.

One of the reasons that he was claimed by the later reformers as a spiritual ancestor was his statement in this work that faith and not works provides the way to salvation.[24] It is also interesting that in the dialogue there is no mention of the veneration of the Virgin Mary, nor of the church hierarchy, nor even of the position of the pope in the church.[25] If the articles which Nicholas proposed

23 A German translation in 1787 with additions by Johann Semler transformed Cusanus into an eighteenth century rationalist. See the introduction to a more recent German version by L. Mohler, *Über den Frieden im Glauben* (Leipzig, 1943), pp. 85-87.

24 O. Menzel, *Johannes Kymeus, Des Babsts Hercules wider die Deudschen, SBH* 1940-41, no. 6 (Heidelberg, 1941), pp. 66-69. A forthcoming article in the *Mitteilungen* of the Cusanus-Gesellschaft will discuss his indirect influence on Martin Luther. Bodin's argument for religious toleration in his *Colloquium Heptaplomeres* (French translation by Roger Chauviré, *Le Colloque de Jean Bodin*, Paris, 1914, especially pp. 67 and 108) shows that he was familiar with *De Pace Fidei*.

25 Decker, "Die Toleranzidee," p. 8, interprets Cusanus' statement that

as rationally demonstrable and acceptable to all religions seem to involve more than most of them would be likely to accept, it is because he maintained, even late in his life, his faith in the possibilities of agreement among men as a result of free discussion and the assistance and inspiration of the Holy Spirit. Perhaps he was too optimistic, and certainly the work glosses over very fundamental differences in a most imprecise fashion, but it demonstrates that the appeal to authority, which he was quite ready to make in actual practice during his reforming missions and in his struggles as Bishop of Brixen, was foreign to his fundamental philosophical outlook, which sought agreement and compromise among different points of view rather than the imposition of an authoritarian command. In religion, as in politics and philosophy, he was seeking a universal concord, a coincidence of opposites.

This concern for harmonization of disagreements seems to have been reflected in the fact that Cusanus spent much of his life in mediating political controversies. In his conciliar period he was involved in the negotiations with the Hussites, and was sent to settle a dispute in Bavaria. In 1452 he was even selected to mediate the Hundred Years War between England and France, but the opposition of the English prevented his going. The only dispute which he does not seem to have had much success in settling was that involving his own diocese in Brixen and the Archduke of the Tyrol.

In the last part of his life after he had left Brixen, we

---

there could be a wide variety in church offices—*officia ecclesiastica* (*De Pace Fidei*, p. 62)—as implying a willingness to tolerate alternative structures of authority in the church. However, Nicholas specifies that this must be done without impairing the faith (*salva fide*). It is not altogether clear whether papal supremacy and episcopal authority were considered an essential part of the faith by Cusanus. The next sentence indicates only that diversity among the nations will be allowed (and even encouraged) in "their devotions and ceremonies."

once more have a record of Cusanus' political principles. In 1458 his friend, Aeneas Sylvius Piccolomini, ascended the papal throne as Pius II, after an intrigue-ridden election which he has described in his *Commentaries*.[26] Nicholas was not present for the election but shortly thereafter went to Rome. In January 1459 he was appointed vicar-general of the Papal States. As an adviser and confidant of the pope, he was actively involved in the politics of the great families of northern Italy, but he continued his efforts to settle the Brixen affair and to carry out the reform of the church in Italy.[27]

Despite the Vienna Concordat, conciliar agitation was still widespread in the German empire. In Cusanus' own disagreement with Sigismund of the Tyrol, the appeal to the council was used both by Sigismund and by his secretary, Gregory of Heimburg, a contemporary of Cusanus at Padua and Basel, and a lifelong antagonist of the papacy. Aeneas himself had remained at Basel several years after the departure of Cusanus, and after his election to the papacy he found it necessary to issue the bull *Execrabilis*, on January 19, 1460, which prohibited the appeal from papal decrees to the council. The movement for a revival of the council in Germany reached its height in early 1461, when the *Reichstag* of Nuremberg demanded a general council to hear the appeal of the archbishop-elect of Mainz who had been excommunicated by the pope.

Nicholas was not unsympathetic to the archbishop, but his attitude to the council was now very different from his position at Basel.[28] He still saw the council as an instrument of reform, and he had been urging and planning a

26 Leona C. Gabel, ed., *Memoirs of a Renaissance Pope* (New York, 1959), pp. 79-87.

27 Erich Meuthen, *Die letzten Jahre des Nikolaus von Kues* (Cologne-Opladen, 1958), *passim*.

28 Gabel, *Memoirs*, p. 372.

council to be assembled at Mantua for the twofold purpose of the reform of the church and the organization of a crusade against the Turks. Its participants were to include princes, prelates, and ambassadors, but "not every copyist and schoolmaster as at Basel."[29] Nicholas had also used diocesan and provincial councils during his reform mission in Germany and in his own diocese of Brixen, but it was always clear that this was at the behest and under the authority of the pope. In Germany, Brixen, and Mantua the councils were to be assembled to give effect to papal directives, not to give consent to church law, as *De Concordantia Catholica* had proposed earlier.

Yet the idea of the expression of the consent of the church had not disappeared from the ecclesiology of Cardinal Cusanus. However, instead of being located in the universal council which now appeared to be the source of divisions and disagreements in the church, it was to be embodied in the college of cardinals. The occasion for the last expression of Cusanus' theory of the church constitution was a draft project for church reform which he drew up at the request of Pius II, who had invited suggestions for a papal program of reform.[30]

In Cusanus' reform proposal some of the familiar themes of his youth recur. Once more there is the comparison of the church to the human body, with a functional cooperation of the different parts under one head, Christ, and united by the Holy Spirit. This cooperation has as its objective the *aedificatio* of the church, a phrase which continu-

29 ". . . el concilio a Mantua . . . per reformatione de la gesia, in lo quale non voria potesse intrare ogni copista et pedagogo, come fu a Basilea, ma solum signori et prelati et ambassatori." Letter from Bartolomeo Bonatto to Barbara Gonzaga, 9 October 1461, reproduced in Meuthen, *Letzten Jahre,* p. 253.

30 The complete text of the reform proposals along with a comparison with Pius II's legislation appears in Ehses, "Der Reformentwurf," pp. 274-297.

ally recurs throughout the work. Christ, not the pope, is described as head of the church, but subsequently Nicholas states that papal power is not limited by any human law *(humana constitutione restringibilis)*, although the pope is obliged to observe the decrees of previous ecumenical councils *(statuta sanctorum patrum)*.

In the reform proposal, the college of cardinals replaces the council as the institution to represent the consent of the faithful to papal rule. Speaking in the draft as the pope would do, he says:

> In that college is a certain type of consent of the whole church spread throughout the world; and therefore they elect the pastor of the church, and the one to whom they consent is the one to whom the church, which they represent, consents. Therefore they comprise the daily full council of the church acting as representatives of the nations, and they are the parts and members of our mystical body, that is, of the holy, Roman, catholic, and apostolic church, and they are in us, as the church in its pope, and we in them, as the bishop in his church.[31]

[31] Ehses, "Reformentwurf," p. 292. "In ipso enim collegio est quidam totius dispersae per orbem ecclesiae consensus; ideo et eligunt pastorem ecclesiae, et in quem ipsi consentiunt, ecclesia, quae in ipsis est repraesentative, etiam consentit. Faciunt igitur nobiscum quotidianum compendiosum ecclesiae concilium quasi legati nationum, et sunt partes et membra corporis nostri mystici, sc. sanctae Romanae apostolicae et catholicae ecclesiae, et ipsi sunt in nobis, ut ecclesia in suo Pontifice, et nos in ipsis, ut episcopus in ecclesia."

Evidence of the importance of the cardinals and the church council in the ecclesiology of Cusanus in his later years is contained in a diagram of the structure of the church council now in the library at Kues—see Marx, *Verzeichnis*, no. 106 f.187v). Drawn up probably by his secretary, Peter Erckelentz, it illustrates the council as nine concentric circles around a center which is Christ, and within a triangle which is the Trinity. Characteristically classified in three groups of three, they are labelled deacons, priests, bishops, followed by archdeacons, archpriests, and archbishops, and finally cardinal deacons, cardinal priests, and the pope. In the hierarchies described in Book I of the *Concordantia*, there was no mention of the cardinals.

Here, at the end of his life, Cusanus again returns, in a qualified fashion, to the theories of the *Concordantia*. Once again he bases the pope's power upon the elective consent of the whole church, as represented by the cardinals. Again he sees the cardinals as a corporate body or council in attendance on the pope, representing as ambassadors *(legati)* the various parts of the church.

Yet it is not clear whether the college of cardinals is to act as a real limit on the papacy. The language which is used in describing the relationship of the pope and the cardinals is that of the integralist theory of representation, present in the *Concordantia* but more important after the change in Cusanus' allegiance. The cardinals are members of the pope's body and "in" him, as the church is in him and the bishop is in his church. Each is contained in the other, and there does not seem to be the possibility of the church or the college of cardinals acting to limit the powers of the pope. Nor is there any mention of the requirement in the *Concordantia* that the cardinals consent to dispensations and interim legislation. Aside from electing the pope, the representative role of the cardinals seems, at first glance, to be restricted to giving advice and assisting in papal administration. The theory of the reform proposal, despite traces of earlier conceptions of consent and representation, seems to assume, in practice, a system of papal absolutism.

Yet, from the pen of Pius II himself there is evidence that Nicholas went much further in his theory of the role of the college of cardinals in the church. At the end of 1461 Pius decided to create a number of new cardinals, including the elevation of the Bishop of Arras, who had the strong support of the King of France and the Duke of Burgundy. Before taking the step he consulted individually with his leading cardinals and recorded the discussions in his *Com-*

mentaries. When he asked Cusanus for his opinion, Pius records that he received strong criticism because of his failure to get the previous consent of the college of cardinals.

> "You are preparing to create new cardinals without any pressing reason merely at your own whim and you have no regard for the oath you swore to the sacred college in the conclave both before and after your elevation, namely, that you would on no account create cardinals unless with the consent of a majority of the college and according to the decrees of the Council of Constance. Now you ignore the ordinance of the synod and do not ask the consent of the college."[32]

Although this outburst may have been prompted only by personal pique at not being consulted, or, more likely, by opposition to the creation of a French cardinal, it also seems to indicate that although Nicholas may have rejected the doctrine of conciliar superiority he believed that the pope was obliged to consult the college of cardinals and get their consent on the creation of new cardinals, and that he based this on the Council of Constance, which the defenders of the papacy usually acknowledged only with considerable reservations.

Nicholas continued his dialogue with Pius with a denunciation of the corruption of the papal curia:

> "If you can bear the truth, I like nothing which goes on in this Curia. Everything is corrupt. No one does his duty. Neither you nor the cardinals have any care for the church. What observance of canons is there? What reverence for the laws? What assiduity in divine worship? All are bent on ambition and avarice. If I ever speak in a consistory about reform, I am laughed at. I do no good here. Allow me to withdraw. I cannot endure these ways. I am an old man and need rest."

32 Gabel, *Memoirs,* p. 228.

Pius relates that he replied to him that the primary responsibility for the preservation of the church rested on the pope, not on a cardinal. "You will have to give account of your advice, we of our rule. . . Know that you are a cardinal, not pope."[33]

For all of Nicholas' zeal for reform, he himself was guilty of some of the faults which he criticized in others. His reform proposal, as well as *De Concordantia Catholica,* had criticized the multiplication of absentee benefices, but all his life he collected church offices. At the time that he left the Council of Basel he held five church positions, and in the course of his life he proceeded to acquire approximately fifteen others. However, the income from many of them went to the building of the home for the aged in Kues. At the end of his life, because of the difficulties in the diocese in Brixen, he required a special subsidy from the college of cardinals in order to live on the magnificent scale expected of a cardinal resident in Rome. Upon his death relatives succeeded to a number of the church posts which he had held.[34]

The reform proposal had also described the cardinals as the representatives of the nations *(legati nationum)* in the church (a significant change in terminology from the *legati provinciarum* of the *Concordantia),* but Nicholas had warned the cardinals that they should not regard themselves as protectors of any nation or prince, but should make up their minds free of outside pressures. Yet, from

---

33 Gabel, *Memoirs,* p. 230. For evidence of the friendship of Aeneas and Cusanus, see Meuthen, *Letzten Jahre,* p. 107.

34 Meuthen, *Letzten Jahre,* pp. 89-103, 218-221; Koch, *Nikolaus von Kues und seine Umwelt,* pp. 79-100. The prohibitions on plural benefices appear in *DCC,* Book II, chap. 28, p. 288, and in Ehses, "Reformentwurf," pp. 288-289. Meuthen, "Die Pfründen," pp. 59-63, emphasizes the historical circumstances surrounding Cusanus' acquisition of benefices, notably the fact that this was the normal method of support for the higher ranks of the clergy in papal service.

the time of the composition of *De Concordantia Catholica* he himself had been conscious of his nationality.[35] As the German cardinal, he endeavored to represent the interests of his nation at the Holy See. This meant preventing the Poles from securing a bishop in Silesia and protecting Breslau against the pressures of the Bohemians. As the stormy discussion with Pius II indicates, he also labored to limit French influence at the papal curia. His excessive concern with the German national interest was noted by Pius II, who described him as "a German too devoted to his nation."[36]

The narrowness of Cusanus' nationalism stands in apparent contradiction to the universality of his theories, but this combination of contradictory elements is characteristic of his thought. There is a consistency, almost to the point of repetitiveness, about his works, and at the same time they contain within themselves elements which are difficult to reconcile. Yet Nicholas tries to reconcile them, and this is the one stream that runs through all his writings—the attempt to unite opposite tendencies in a harmonious *concordantia*. *Concordantia* was proposed first as a legal conception, with overtones of theology. Then it became a metaphysical dualism of *complicatio* and *explicatio*. But ultimately it was a mystical ideal, a yearning of a busy church diplomat and lawyer, whose whole life was devoted to reform and controversy, for the peace and tranquillity of the life of unity with the divine. He was never able to use the cell which he had reserved for himself at the Benedictine abbey of Tegernsee to which he had hoped to retire in old age. Nor was his library at Kues, with

35 *DCC*, preface, p. 2, on his German origin; Book II, chap. 29, p. 267, on Hugh of St. Victor as "our German"; Book III, chap. 32, p. 438, on the consequences to *Germania* if reform is not instituted.
36 Gabel, *Memoirs*, p. 372.

its window opening upon the sanctuary of the adjoining chapel, ever used by its builder. All his life he sought *concordantia,* but found only controversy.

Nicholas of Cusa was a transitional figure in an age of transition. Half his life was spent in Germany, where medieval forms of life and thought still were dominant. The other half was in Italy, bursting with the creative activity of the Renaissance. In this period of turmoil he attempted to reform a decaying social and ecclesiastical order, to harmonize the clash of interests in church and empire, and to bring peace to an age of conflict. His efforts at reform ended in failure, and half a century later the church was reformed in a different manner from that which he had proposed. Everywhere that he attempted to enforce monastic rules or consolidate church institutions, he met with opposition or apathy. He died within a few days of the death of Pius II, in August 1464, while on his way from Rome to Ancona to help the miserable remnants of the army raised in what was the last effort of a united Christendom to liberate the Holy Land. His monument is located in his titular church, San Pietro in Vincoli in Rome, on the opposite side of the nave from the Michelangelo *Moses.* By his own instruction, his heart is buried in front of the altar in the chapel of St. Nicholas in Kues.

CONCLUSION

THE CONCILIAR movement is usually examined from the point of view of what "might have been." In the history of political theory it is seen as an abortive effort to constitutionalize the church and a last attempt, at the dawn of the age of absolutism to assert a theory of the role of representative institutions in government. In the history of religion, it is viewed as the final possibility of reforming the medieval church and removing the abuses which led to the Reformation.[1]

Yet, as the examination of the most sophisticated and complex of the theories of the conciliar movement has shown, both of these views are oversimplifications. It is true that the Council of Constance, by ending the Great Schism, had given enormous prestige to the *via concilii* as a method of reform in the church. However, when unity was restored to the papacy, it was difficult to maintain the conciliar thesis which had sounded so attractive in a time of schism. The whole weight of tradition and of canon law, while providing some arguments for conciliarism, provided many more for papal supremacy. On the one side there were discussions in canon law of the right of the church to correct the pope, and there was the example of the early church councils and the tradition of the equality of all bishops. Yet, on the other side, there was the belief that Christ had established Peter and his successors in a special position of primacy, that there was a deposit of faith which had to be infallibly interpreted by the church, and that the

---

1 See, for example, Figgis, *Gerson to Grotius*, p. 63: "The child they nurtured was constitutionalism"; and Will Durant, *The Reformation* (New York, 1957), p. 257: "Had there been more Nicholases, there might have been no Luther."

church hierarchy under the pope had a special role in mediating God's revelation.

The popes had originally been able to carry out their program of centralization because from Gregory VII forward they had proclaimed a program of ecclesiastical reform and legal centralization. If local abuses scandalized the faithful, they could be reformed by a mission from Rome, such as that on which Nicholas of Cusa embarked in 1451 and 1452. If someone felt he did not get justice from the local ecclesiastical courts, he could always appeal to Rome. When the papacy was divided, the church looked elsewhere for the initiative of reform—to the universities, to the emperor, and to the general council. However, when unity was restored, the initiative was again with the pope, since the council was only to meet every ten years, and canon law required that the pope himself convoke it and give his consent to its decrees. He took advantage of this initiative, and when it came to a contest between pope and council the pope won.

What would have happened, what might have been, if the council had won? It is difficult to say. However, there were evidences at Constance and at Basel of rising nationalistic feelings and divisions, and it seems not unlikely that if the principle of conciliar supremacy in the determination of religious questions had ultimately triumphed, the council would have divided as it always had tended to do once an immediate outside threat was removed, and ultimately the Christian church would have separated into national churches. To some extent this is what happened in the Reformation, on both the Catholic and Protestant side, but a strong papacy remained as the means of union of the Catholic Church, where with the triumph of conciliarism there might have been only a titular or symbolic head.

It must be remembered that the primary role of the

church was to protect the deposit of faith, God's revelation, by means of its infallible teaching *magisterium*. The divisions in the Council of Basel which alienated Nicholas of Cusa were an anticipation of what would happen to a church based on the principle of majority rule. If the church was to be a single body to interpret infallibly the revealed deposit of faith, and if those infallible interpreters were to be selected by succession to the Apostles, it was difficult to combine this conception with a legal theory which had been developed to describe the members of a business venture or private association. Nor, despite his quotations from Cyprian, could Nicholas put his faith for long in the infallibility of the majority. He did not have any Rousseauean belief in the wisdom of the ordinary layman or even of the ordinary priest. Moreover, it was not a question of wisdom, but of divine guidance in the interpretation of revelation, and church history provided numerous examples of councils which issued contradictory decrees. If infallibility and consistency were desired, only the pope could provide them.

When Nicholas made the distinction between the power of orders which was transmitted by succession, and that of jurisdiction which was derived from consent, he attempted to answer the objection that church power was derived from above, not from below. But when he gave the power to make church law to the council, he demanded too much of that body. He wanted the council to be unanimous on questions of faith. When, instead, it became divided, he turned to an institution which could better assure the unity which he saw as a mark of divine inspiration. The council could restore unity to a divided papacy, but once restored, the pope was better situated to maintain it.

Tradition and canon law, as well as the nature of the church as the infallible guardian of a single revealed truth, made the triumph of the papacy a likelihood, but many other ingredients of the propapal theory were also already contained in Nicholas of Cusa's conciliarism. In the *Concordantia,* he admitted that the pope was normally the one to call the council, and after he changed positions he only had to add the qualification that no one but the pope could do so. He admitted that the pope must be consulted in all decisions on faith, and he only had to extend this to a requirement of consent to all conciliar decisions to undercut conciliar supremacy. He admitted that the pope had an emergency power to act for the good of the church, and the pope only had to assert this emergency power to transfer the council to Italy where he could control it. He believed in the infallibility of the church and even of the papal *cathedra* on church dogma, and only had to interpret this *cathedra* as consisting of the pope alone, rather than the pope in council or with his cardinals, to get to a theory of papal supremacy.

Moreover, his fundamental political categories, while including corporative elements, also utilized conceptions of representation and consent which were as applicable to the pope as to the council. Representation was virtual, that is, the ruler was said to "figure" or personify all those below him, and although earlier Nicholas seemed to believe that lower rulers better represented their subjects than did those on the upper levels of the hierarchy, his later philosophical speculations led him to see the one at the summit of the hierarchy as the source of all power and the most representative of all. In addition, the radical demand for participation in law and government which the *quod omnes tangit* maxim seemed to imply was weakened in practice by Cusanus' admission in the *Concordantia* that tacit consent and customary obedience to rulership and law were sufficient.

While the provisions of canon law and the necessity for an infallible authority were not arguments applicable to the secular ruler, theories of representation and consent could be applied to the empire as well as to the church. There was a transfer from the speculations about the nature of the government of the church to that of the secular order, and this is why the conciliarists are studied in the history of political theory, rather than only in the history of religion. While it is something of an exaggeration to say that "the road from Constance to 1688 is a direct one; Nicholas of Cusa, Gerson, and Zabarella are the ancestors through pamphlets like the *Vindiciae contra Tyrannos* of Sidney and Locke,"[2] it is true that Gerson argued for conciliarism on the grounds that the mixed constitution was the best form of government (and if Nicholas did not repeat this argument, he proposed a church constitution which was in fact constructed on this model), while Turrecremata defended papal monarchy with arguments that monarchy was the political ideal. When Nicholas defended a conciliar structure in the church, the parallelism of his thinking on church and state also required that the empire be governed in the same way. After the change to the side of the pope, Cusanus continued this parallelism and described both the pope and the secular ruler as containing *(complicatio)* all those subject to them. Thus, even if special reasons led to the defeat of the system of representative councils in the church, the victory of the papacy was, by the principle of parallelism, a victory for absolutism in political thought as well.

Conversely, the philosophical and legal justification for rule of the church by councils is important to the history of political theory since it represents an attempt by the

2 Harold Laski, "Political Theory in the Later Middle Ages," *Cambridge Medieval History*, VIII (Cambridge, 1936), 638.

CONCLUSION

Middle Ages to deal with the problem of institutionalization of the very considerable theoretical restraints which
it imposed on the ruler. In the process of the legalization
of what had previously been traditional or religious relationships in church and state, the lawyers could not allow
for the feudal remedy of self-help, *diffidatio,* and tyran-
nicide. Some institutional means had to be found to limit
the ruler, and some of the arguments which Cusanus
developed for the superiority of the representative council
were applicable with equal or greater force to the secular
order. Consent might not be the basis of legitimacy in an
ecclesiastical order based on the transmission by succession
of an infallible objective revelation, but it could do quite
well as a theory of legitimacy of the secular ruler. The
feudal belief in the community as the source of law
harmonized with the natural law argument that the original
equality of men demanded that they consent to the law
to which they were subject.

In Cusanus' theory, the origin of these theories of consent and representation was an ecclesiastical one. He was
a churchman, accustomed to argue from canon law or
theology to politics. It is true that there were feudal
precedents for his theories in the Imperial *Reichstag* and
other councils, but the primary inspiration for Nicholas'
conciliarism came from canon law and theology. From the
canon lawyers came the conception of the church as a
corporation consisting of a head and members, and the
requirement that on some matters all the members should
be consulted. From other passages in canon law came
precedents for collective action of the members of the
ecclesiastical community against the head. From mystical
theology and neo-Platonism came the view of the universe
as an order of hierarchy and correspondence, as well as
his later theory of absorptive representation.

The church council was justified as the representative institution which could consent to law and limit the ruler, and Nicholas proposed a parallel system for the empire, although he was never very precise about the details of his proposal. If conciliarism is seen as a last attempt to justify the role of medieval representative institutions, Nicholas of Cusa's thought might have been the basis for the development of some type of parliamentarianism in Germany.

In some passages Nicholas even seems to anticipate the later doctrine of the separation of powers. In one place he states that he does not believe that the pope, who is the supreme judge of all Christendom, should make the laws which he is to enforce. In another, he sees the pope as a judge and administrator, to carry out laws made by the council. These councils would, of course, be quite different from modern parliaments. Votes would undoubtedly have been weighted in accordance with hierarchical status. The ruler or pope would also have participated and exercised considerable influence (although he could conceivably be overruled by the council). Moreover, in Cusanus' theory, the church councils would be restricted to clergymen appointed from above, with the consent of the faithful, and in the councils of the empire the laws would made by the wise and would receive tacit consent by being observed. It is not quite accurate, therefore, to describe Nicholas as "among the leading champions of popular sovereignty,"[3] but we can say that his theories restated and systematized the medieval principles of consent and ultimate derivation of political authority from the whole people at a time when those principles were about to be overshadowed by the claims of the centralizing monarchies.

Just as in the church the initiative returned to the pope

---

[3] Otto von Gierke, *The Development of Political Theory,* trans. Bernard Freyd (New York, 1939), p. 149.

once unity had been restored to the church, so in the secular order the monarchs were able to assert effective control of the representative institutions which emerged from the Middle Ages. The principle of hereditary succession and royal legislation supplanted claims that the community as represented in council or parliament had the right to make law or elect the ruler. In the case of Germany, the princes succeeded in undermining the vestiges of imperial control and carried out a similar absolutist policy. Neither Cusanus' pleas for a strong central government in the empire, nor for legislation and election by councils or assemblies, were heard with any sympathy. This was understandable, since he was a churchman and his writings were directed to churchmen in language which they could best appreciate. *De Concordantia Catholica* was also directed to the emperor, but after the death of Sigismund his immediate successors were less and less concerned with reform and centered their attention upon their own kingdoms, so that there was no hope for initiative from them.

In addition, Nicholas of Cusa's theories contained other elements derived from ecclesiastical sources which tended away from the encouragement of representative assemblies. The older mystical and hierarchical view of society became the basis of an organic theory of the state and the church in which the head could not be separated from the members since both were members of the single unified body politic. As Nicholas had said after his change to the papal side, a body without a head cannot act because it is "acephalous." While this view did provide that the members should carry out their functions in the social hierarchy without interference from above (as in Nicholas' provision in the letter to Rodrigo that no pope, no matter how powerful, could interfere with the distribution of church offices), it could never become the basis of any action by the community against its head, since no increase in numbers or quantity could balance the higher status or quality of the ruler (except in the single case of the unanimous action of the whole church).

It was not only the hierarchical tradition which predisposed Nicholas to favor absolutism. In the secular order, he desired a strong ruler and disliked feudal decentralization and fragmentation. He saw the emperor as the most promising secular instrument of reform, where the councils had been the means of reform for the church. Thus his theories regarding the empire were already predisposed to absolutism for the same reason that he ultimately transferred his allegiance to the pope—efficiency, the argument *ex effectu.*

This had its basis in Nicholas of Cusa's philosophy and theology. He was looking for harmony, *concordantia,* a unity in diversity—but, first of all, for unity. When he saw it in the emperor, he urged that the emperor's powers be strengthened. When he did not find it in the council, he turned to the pope. The old faith in the action of the Holy Spirit to harmonize and unify a divergent council through free consent was abandoned in the face of the facts of conciliar disunity and conflict, and he looked to an outside agency to impose the unity which he sought.

Although the influence of Cusanus' philosophical ideas on the thinkers of the Italian Renaissance in the fifteenth century has been exaggerated by some German writers, his cosmological conceptions are known to have influenced later writers such as Giordano Bruno, Kepler, and Leibniz.[4] Descartes also mentions him to prove that the belief

4 Paul O. Kristeller, *The Philosophy of Marsilio of Ficino* (New York, 1943), p. 15, and Ernst Cassirer, "Ficino's Place in Intellectual History," *Journal of the History of Ideas,* 6:492, n. 27 (1945). Ficino mentions Cusanus once in a letter.

in an infinite universe does not contradict religious ortho-doxy.[5] The influence of Cusanus' political and ecclesiastical theories is more difficult to trace. His name was invoked successively by the religious reformers, both Protestant and Catholic, by the thinkers of the Enlightenment (particu-larly for his religious proposals), by the Romantic move-ment, by German nationalism, and even, more recently, as an anticipation of Nazism.[6] In Germany an enormous amount of scholarly work has been done on everything from the shape of his head to the etymology of his name, and even a number of sensational novels have been written about him. A whole generation of students of philosophy and history in Berlin, Heidelberg, and elsewhere has been fascinated by this complex and controversial thinker.[7] For Nicholas of Cusa, churchman, lawyer, mystic, mathemati-cian, astronomer, reformer, and philosopher, is a many-sided and interesting historical personality. He stands be-tween two historical ages. In his critical attitude to history, in his interest in Greek and in mathematics, in his concern with the philosophical investigation of the cosmos, he anticipates many Renaissance characteristics. Yet his polit-ical thought is thoroughly medieval in its assumptions and

5 Alexandre Koyré, *From the Closed World to the Infinite Universe* (New York, 1958), p. 6.
6 On Cusanus and the romantic movement, see W. Lenartz, *Nicolaus Cusanus-Joseph Görres* (Kolmar, 1944). Gerhard Kallen, *Nikolaus von Cues als politischer Erzieher* (Leipzig, 1937), makes Cusanus a prototype of Nazism, pp. 17 and 20, while Georg Pick, "Nikolaus von Kues und Gregor Heimburg," *Nationalsozialistische Monatshefte*, 14:260-273 (1943), sees in him a conflict between "the Aryan soul" and "the oriental ideas" of the Catholic church (p. 260).
7 Fictional biographies of Cusanus include B. von Selchow, *Der unend-liche Kreis* (Leipzig, 1935), and H. Künkel, *Schicksal und Liebe des Niklas von Cues* (Leipzig, 1936). The former makes Cusanus' birth illegitimate, and the latter adds spice to his biography by inventing a love affair with a nun involved in the feud at Brixen. A long quotation from Cusanus also appears in the opening chapter of the Nobel-prize-winning novel of Her-mann Hesse, *Das Glasperlenspiel* (translated into English as *Magister Ludi*, New York, 1949).

in its content. He looks for a single unifying principle in philosophy and in politics. God, not man, is the beginning and end of all activity, and the Catholic religion and a supernatural outlook are basic assumptions of all his works. His political thought is a last restatement before the breakdown of the medieval "ideal of an organically harmonious Christendom, multiple in function, one in spirit . . . [towering] over the ambitions and antagonisms which it is powerless to reconcile."[8] The ancient order, based on the double authority of Peter and Caesar, was passing away, but before it departed it was given one final magnificent summation in the writings of the last of the medieval political theorists, Nicholas of Cusa.

8 E. F. Jacob, "Nicholas of Cusa," p. 49.

SELECTED
BIBLIOGRAPHY
INDEX

SELECTED BIBLIOGRAPHY

I. PRIMARY SOURCES

A. Works of Nicholas of Cusa

1. LATIN EDITIONS

Nicolai Cusae, *Accurata recognitio trium voluminum operum*, 3 vol., Paris, 1514 (reprinted, Frankfort, 1961).

Nicolai de Cusa, *Opera*, Basel, 1565.

Nicolai de Cusa, *Opera Omnia*, pub. by Heidelberger Akademie der Wissenschaften, Leipzig-Hamburg, 1932-1959. Vol. I. *De Docta Ignorantia (DDI)*, ed. Ernst Hoffmann and Raymond Klibansky, Leipzig, 1932. Vol. II. *Apologia Doctae Ignorantiae*, ed. Raymond Klibansky, Leipzig, 1932. Vol. VII. *De Pace Fidei*, ed. Raymond Klibansky and Hildebrand Bascour, O.P., Hamburg, 1959. Vol. XI/1. *De Beryllo*, ed. Ludwig Baur, Leipzig, 1940. Vol. XIV. *De Concordantia Catholica (DDC)*, ed. Gerhard Kallen, Book I, Leipzig, 1939.—Book II, Leipzig, 1941.—Book III, Hamburg, 1959.

Nicolaus von Cues, *Texte seiner philosophischen Schriften*, ed. Alfred Petzelt, vol. I, Stuttgart, 1949.

Cusanus-Texte, issued in the *Sitzungsberichte der Heidelberger Akademie der Wissenschaften*, Philosophisch-historische Klasse *(SBH)*:

Briefwechsel des Nikolaus von Kues, part 1, ed. Josef Koch, in *SBH* 1942-43, no. 2, Heidelberg, 1944.

Briefwechsel des Nikolaus von Kues, part 4, *Nikolaus von Kues und der Deutsche Orden*, ed. Erich Maschke, in *SBH* 1956, no. 1, Heidelberg, 1956.

De Auctoritate Presidendi in Concilio Generali (DAP), ed. Gerhard Kallen, in *SBH* 1935-36, no. 3, Heidelberg, 1935.

"Dies Sanctificatus" vom Jahre 1439, ed. Ernst Hoffmann and Raymond Klibansky, in *SBH* 1928-29, no. 3, Heidelberg, 1929.

Vier Predigten im Geiste Eckharts, ed. Josef Koch, in *SBH* 1936-37, no. 2, Heidelberg, 1937.

SELECTED BIBLIOGRAPHY

De Concordantia Catholica Libri Tres, facsimile of vol. III of the 1514 Paris edition, ed. Gerhard Kallen, Bonn, 1928.

Dialogus Concludens Amedistarum Errorem ex Gestis et Doctrina Concilii Basiliensis, typescript of Trier manuscript 1927/1426, in possession of Professor Josef Koch, Cologne.

Reformatio Generalis, in Stephan Ehses, "Der Reformentwurf des Kardinals Nikolaus Cusanus," *HJ,* 32:281-297 (1911).

2. ENGLISH TRANSLATIONS

The Idiot, 1650 London trans. with introduction by W. R. Dennes, San Francisco, 1940.

Of Learned Ignorance, trans. Germain Heron, O.P., with introduction by D. J. B. Hawkins, London, 1954.

Unity and Reform; Selected Writings of Nicholas de Cusa, trans. and ed. John Patrick Dolan, Notre Dame, Indiana, 1962.

The Vision of God, trans. E. Gurney Salter, New York, 1928.

3. FRENCH TRANSLATIONS

De la docte ignorance, trans. L. Moulinier, with introduction by Abel Rey, Paris, 1930.

Oeuvres choisies de Nicolas de Cues, ed. and trans. with introduction by Maurice de Gandillac, Paris, 1942.

4. GERMAN TRANSLATIONS

Über den Beryll, trans. Karl Fleischmann, with introduction by Ernst Hoffmann, Leipzig, 1938.

Über den Frieden im Glauben, trans. Ludwig Mohler, with introduction, Leipzig, 1943.

Vom Globusspiel, trans. Gerda von Bredow, with introduction, Hamburg, 1952.

B. Works by Other Authors before 1500

Augustine, *The City of God,* trans. John Healey, London, 1931.

Aristotle, *Nicomachean Ethics,* Loeb Classical Library (Greek text), London, 1947.

———— *Politics,* trans. Ernest Barker, Oxford, 1946.

———— *Politics,* Loeb Classical Library (Greek text), London, 1950.

PRIMARY SOURCES

Boethius, *The Consolation of Philosophy,* Loeb Classical Library (Latin text), New York, 1948.

Conrad of Gelnhausen, *Epistola Concordiae,* in E. Martène and U. Durand, *Thesaurus Novus Anecdotorum,* vol. II, Paris, 1707, cols. 1200-1225.

Corpus Juris Canonici, ed. Emil Friedberg, 2 vols., Leipzig, 1879-1881.

Corpus Juris Civilis, ed. Paul Krueger and Theodor Mommsen, 3 vols., Berlin, 1882-1895.

D'Ailly, Pierre, *De Ecclesiae, Concilii Generalis, Romani Pontificis, et Cardinalium Autoritate,* in Louis Ellies du Pin, *Joannis Gersonii Opera Omnia,* vol. II, Antwerp, 1706, cols. 925-960.

Dietrich of Niem, *De Modis Uniendi et Reformandi Ecclesiam in Concilio Universali,* ed. H. Heimpel, Leipzig, 1933.

Dionysius the Areopagite, *Dionysiaca,* 2 vols., Bruges, 1937.

Durandus, Gulielmus, *Tractatus de Modo Generalis Concilii Celebrandi,* Paris, 1531.

Gerson, Jean, *De Auferibilitate Papae,* in *Joannis Gersonii Opera Omnia,* ed. Louis Ellies du Pin, vol. II, Antwerp, 1706, cols. 209-224.

———— *De Potestate Ecclesiastica,* in Louis Ellies du Pin, *Joannis Gersonii Opera Omnia,* vol. II, Antwerp, 1706, cols. 225-256.

Gratian, *Decretum cum glossis Johannis Teutonici et annotationibus Bartholomei Brixiensis,* Venice, 1514.

Henry of Langenstein, *Epistola Concilii Pacis,* in Louis Ellies du Pin, *Joannis Gersonii Opera Omnia,* vol. II, Antwerp, 1706, cols. 809-840.

John of Paris, *De Potestate Regia et Papali,* in Simon Schard, *De Jurisdictione, Autoritate, et Praeeminentia Imperiali, ac Potestate Ecclesiastica,* Basel, 1566, pp. 142-224.

Lupold of Bebenburg, *Tractatus de Juribus Regis et Imperii Romani,* in S. Schard, *De Jurisdictione,* pp. 328-409.

Marsilius of Padua, *Defensor Pacis,* ed. C. W. Previté-Orton, Cambridge, 1928.

———— *Defensor Pacis,* ed. Richard Scholz, 2 vols., Hanover, 1932-1933.

Plato, *Parmenides,* trans. F. W. Cornford, New York, 1951.

SELECTED BIBLIOGRAPHY

———— *Republic,* trans. F. W. Cornford, New York, 1945.

———— *Timaeus,* trans. Thomas Taylor, Washington, 1944.

Plotinus, *Enneads,* trans. Thomas Taylor, London, 1895.

Proclus, *The Elements of Theology,* trans. E. R. Dodds, Oxford, 1933.

———— *Parmenides nec non Procli Commentarium in Parmenidem,* ed. R. Klibansky and C. Labowsky, London, 1953.

Thomas Aquinas, *Summa Contra Gentiles,* trans. English Dominicans, 5 vols., London, 1923-1929.

———— *Summa Theologica,* trans. English Dominicans, 22 vols., London, 1911-1925.

William of Occam, *Breviloquium,* ed. L. Baudry, Paris, 1937.

———— *Dialogus,* in M. Goldast, *Monarchiae Sancti Romani Imperii,* Frankfurt, 1668, II, 396-957.

———— *Octo Quaestiones,* in *Opera Politica,* vol. I, ed. J. G. Sikes, Manchester, 1950, pp. 1-223.

Zabarella, Franciscus, *Tractatus de Schismate,* in S. Schard, *De Jurisdictione,* pp. 688-711.

C. Documentary Sources

Deutsche Reichstagsakten (RTA)

Vol. XIII, ed. Gustav Beckmann, Stuttgart-Gotha, 1916-1925.

Vol. XIV, ed. Helmut Weigel, Stuttgart, 1933-1936.

Vol. XV, ed. Hermann Herre, Gotha, 1912-1914.

Vol. XVI, ed. Hermann Herre and Ludwig Quidde, Stuttgart-Gotha, 1928.

Vol. XVII, ed. Walter Kämmerer, Göttingen, 1956 (reprint).

Haller, Johannes, et al., *Concilium Basiliense,* 8 vols., Basel, 1896-1936.

Mansi, J. D., ed., *Sacrorum Conciliorum Nova et Amplissima Collectio,* vol. XXIX, Venice, 1788 (reprinted Paris, 1904); vol. XXXI, Supplement, Paris, 1901.

Monumenta Conciliorum Generalium Saeculi XV, vols. II, III, Vienna, 1857, 1886.

Poggii Epistulae, ed. T. de Tonellis, 3 vols., Florence, 1832-1861.

Ambrosii Traversari Epistolae, ed. Petrus Cannetus, Florence, 1759.

II. SECONDARY SOURCES

A. Books

Ancelet-Hustache, Jeanne, *Master Eckhart and the Rhineland Mystics*, New York, 1957.

Avondo, Edoardo Ruffini, *Il Principio maggioritario nella storia del diritto canonico*, Modena, 1925.

Barraclough, Geoffrey, *Papal Provisions*, Oxford, 1935.

Baur, Ludwig, *Nicolaus Cusanus und Ps. Dionysius im Lichte der Zitate und Randbemerkungen des Cusanus*, in *SBH* 1940-41, no. 4, Heidelberg, 1941.

Berges, Wilhelm, *Die Fürstenspiegel des hohen und späten Mittelalters*, Leipzig, 1938.

Bett, Henry, *Nicholas of Cusa*, London, 1932.

Bohnenstädt, Elisabeth, *Kirche und Reich im Schriftum des Nikolaus von Cues*, in *SBH* 1938-39, no. 1, Heidelberg, 1939.

Brehier, Emile, *The Philosophy of Plotinus*, Chicago, 1958.

Brockhaus, Clemens, *Nikolai Cusani de Concilii Universalis Potestate Sententia*, Leipzig, 1867.

Butler, Dom Cuthbert, *Western Mysticism*, London, 1922.

Carlyle, R. W. and A. J., *A History of Medieval Political Theory in the West*, 6 vols., Edinburgh-London, 1903-1936, 2nd impression, 1950.

Cassirer, Ernst, *Individuum und Kosmos in der Philosophie der Renaissance*, Leipzig, 1927.

Clarke, Maude V., *Medieval Representation and Consent*, London, 1936.

Colomer, Eusebio, *Nikolaus von Kues und Raimund Llull*, Berlin, 1961.

Combes, André, *Jean Gerson, Commentateur Dionysien*, Paris, 1940.

Conger, George P., *Theories of Macrocosms and Microcosms in the History of Philosophy*, New York, 1922.

Copleston, F. W., *A History of Philosophy*, vols. II, III, London, 1950, 1953.

Dempf, Alois, *Sacrum Imperium*, Berlin-Munich, 1929.

Dickinson, John, *The Statesman's Book of John of Salisbury*, Cambridge, Mass., 1927.

SELECTED BIBLIOGRAPHY

Durantel, J., *Saint Thomas et le Pseudo-Denis*, Paris, 1919.

Düx, Johann Martin, *Der deutsche cardinal Nicolaus von Cusa*, 2 vols., Regensburg, 1847.

Elliott, W. Y., and N. McDonald, *Western Political Heritage*, New York, 1949.

d'Entreves, A. P., *Aquinas, Selected Political Writings*, Oxford, 1939.

―――― *The Medieval Contribution to Political Thought*, Oxford, 1939.

―――― *Natural Law*, London, 1951.

Feibleman, James K., *Religious Platonism*, London, 1959.

Feine, H. E., *Kirchliche Rechtsgeschichte*, vol. 1, Weimar, 1950.

Figgis, John Neville, *Studies of Political Thought from Gerson to Grotius*, New York, 1960 (reprint of Cambridge, 1916 edition).

Friedrich, Carl J., *Constitutional Reason of State*, Providence, 1957.

Fromherz, Uta, *Johannes von Segovia*, Basel-Stuttgart, 1960.

Gabel, Leona C., ed., *Memoirs of a Renaissance Pope*, New York, 1959.

Gandillac, Maurice de, *La Philosophie de Nicolas de Cues*, Paris, 1941.

Garin, Eugenio, *Studi sul Platonismo medievale*, Florence, 1958.

Gewirth, Alan, *Marsilius of Padua*, 2 vols., New York, 1951-1956.

Gierke, Otto von, *Das deutsche Genossenschaftsrecht*, vol. III, Berlin, 1881.

―――― *The Development of Political Theory*, trans. Bernard Freyd, New York, 1939.

―――― *The Political Theories of the Middle Age*, trans. F. W. Maitland, Cambridge, 1900.

Gill, Joseph, *The Council of Florence*, Cambridge, Mass., 1959.

Gillet, P., *La Personnalité juridique en droit ecclesiastique*, Malines, 1927.

Grabmann, Martin, *Studien über den Einfluss der Aristotelischen Philosophie*, in *Sitzungsberichte der Bayerischen Akademie der Wissenschaften* (Phil.-hist. Klasse) 1934, no. 2, Munich, 1934.

SECONDARY SOURCES

Haller, Johannes, *Papstum und Kirchenreform*, Berlin, 1903.

Hamman, Adelbert, *La Doctrine de l'église et de l'état chez Occam*, Paris, 1942.

Haubst, Rudolf, *Das Bild des einen und dreieinen Gottes in der Welt nach Nikolaus von Kues*, Trier, 1952.

———· *Die Christologie des Nikolaus von Kues*, Freiburg, 1956.

Hefele, C. J., *Conziliengeschichte*, trans. and rev. H. Leclercq, *Histoire des Conciles*, vols. VI, VII, Paris, 1914-1916.

Heimpel, Hermann, *Dietrich von Niem*, Münster, 1932.

Heinz, Mohr, Gerd, *Unitas Christiana*, Trier, 1958.

Henle, R. J., *St. Thomas and Plato*, The Hague, 1956.

Hirsch, Karl, *Die Ausbildung der konziliaren Theorie im XIV. Jahrhundert*, Vienna, 1903.

Hoffmann, Ernst, *Nikolaus von Kues, Zwei Vorträge*, Heidelberg, 1947.

——— *Das Universum des Nikolaus von Cues*, in *SBH* 1929-30, no 3, Heidelberg, 1930.

Honecker, Martin, *Nikolaus von Cues und die griechische Sprache*, in *SBH* 1937-38, no. 2, Heidelberg, 1938.

Hopper, Vincent F., *Medieval Number Symbolism*, New York, 1938.

Hughes, Philip, *A History of the Church*, vol. III, New York, 1947.

Huizinga, J., *The Waning of the Middle Ages*, London, 1924.

Hyma, A., *The Christian Renaissance*, Grand Rapids, 1924.

Inge, W. R., *Christian Mysticism*, London, 1899, reprinted New York, 1956.

Iung, Nicolas, *Alvaro Pelayo*, Paris, 1931.

Jacob, E. F., *Essays in the Conciliar Epoch*, 2nd ed., Manchester, 1953.

——— ed., *Italian Renaissance Studies*, London, 1960.

Jedin, Hubert, *A History of the Council of Trent*, trans. Ernest Graf, vol. I, London, 1957.

Kallen, Gerhard, *Die handschriftliche Überlieferung der Concordantia catholica des Nikolaus von Kues*, in *SBH* 1963, No. 2, Heidelberg, 1963.

——— *Nikolaus von Cues als politischer Erzieher*, Leipzig, 1937.

Kern, Fritz, *Kingship and Law in the Middle Ages*, Oxford, 1948.

SELECTED BIBLIOGRAPHY

Klibansky, Raymond, *The Continuity of the Platonic Tradition during the Middle Ages*, London, 1939.

—— *Ein Proklos-Fund und seine Bedeutung*, in *SBH* 1928-29, no. 5, Heidelberg, 1929.

Koch, Josef, ed., *Humanismus, Mystik und Kunst in der Welt des Mittelalters*, Leiden-Cologne, 1953.

—— *Nikolaus von Cues und seine Umwalt*, in *SBH* 1944-48, no. 2, Heidelberg, 1948.

—— *Predigten, Untersuchung über Datierung, Form, Sprache, und Quellen*, in *SBH* 1941-42, no. 1, Heidelberg, 1942.

Koyré, Alexandre, *From the Closed World to the Infinite Universe*, New York, 1958.

Kristeller, Paul O., *The Classics and Renaissance Thought*, Cambridge, Mass., 1955.

—— *The Philosophy of Marsilio Ficino*, New York, 1943.

de Lagarde, Georges, *La Naissance de l'esprit laique*, 6 vols., Paris, 1942-1948.

Lewis, Ewart, *Medieval Political Ideas*, 2 vols., New York, 1954.

Lovejoy, Arthur O., *The Great Chain of Being*, Cambridge, Mass., 1936.

de Lubac, Henri, *Corpus Mysticum*, Paris, 1949.

Marrou, Henry, *Saint Augustin et l'Augustinisme*, Paris, 1955.

Marx, J., *Verzeichnis der Handschriften-Sammlung des Hospitals zu Cues*, Trier, 1905.

McIlwain, C. H., *The Growth of Political Thought in the West*, New York, 1932.

Mennicken, Peter, *Nikolaus von Kues*, Trier, 1950.

Menzel, Ottokar, *Johannes Kymeus, Des Babsts Hercules wider die Deudschen*, in *SBH* 1940-41, no. 6, Heidelberg, 1941.

Meuthen, Erich, *Die letzten Jahre des Nikolaus von Kues*, Cologne-Opladen, 1958.

Morrall, John B., *Gerson and the Great Schism*, Manchester, 1960.

Mundy, John H., and Kennerly M. Woody, eds., *The Council of Constance*, New York, 1961.

Nicolay, Wilhelm, *Essays über Nicolaus von Cues*, Frankfurt, 1954.

Paetzoldt, Herbert, *Die Lehre des Nikolaus Cusanus von der Kirche auf Grund seiner Predigten*, Breslau, 1938.

SECONDARY SOURCES

Parent, J. M., *La Doctrine de la création dans l'école de Chartres*, Paris, 1938.

Pastor, Ludwig, *The History of the Popes*, vols. I, II, London, 1891.

Patch, Howard R., *The Tradition of Boethius*, New York, 1935.

Pérouse, Gabriel, *Le cardinal Louis Aleman*, Paris, 1904.

Plöchl, W. M., *Geschichte des Kirchenrechts*, vol. II, Vienna, 1955.

Posch, Andreas, *Die "Concordantia catholica" des Nikolaus von Cues*, Paderborn, 1930.

Pralle, Ludwig, *Die Wiederentdeckung des Tacitus*, Fulda, 1953.

Rashdall, Hastings, *The Universities of Europe in the Middle Ages*, 3 vols., 2nd ed., rev. F. M. Powicke and A. B. Emden, Oxford, 1936.

Roques, R., *L'Univers Dionysien*, Paris, 1954.

Rotta, Paolo, *Il cardinale Nicolò da Cusa*, Milan, 1928.

———— *Nicolò Cusano*, Milan, 1942.

Sabbadini, Remigio, *Le Scoperte dei codici latin e greci ne' secoli XIV e XV*, 2 vols., Florence, 1905-1914.

Sabine, George H., *A History of Political Theory*, 3rd ed., New York, 1961.

Saitta, Giuseppe, *Nicolò Cusano e L'umanesimo italiano*, Bologna, 1957.

Scholz, Richard, *Die Publizistik zur Zeit Philipps des Schönen*, Stuttgart, 1903, reprinted 1962.

Schultz, Rudolph, *Die Staatsphilosophie des Nikolaus von Kues*, Meisenheim am Glan, 1948.

Schürmeyer, Walter, *Das Kardinalskollegium unter Pius II*, Marburg, 1914.

Sciacca, M. F., *Saint Augustin et le Néoplatonisme*, Louvain, 1956.

Shorey, Paul, *Platonism, Ancient and Modern*, Berkeley, 1938.

Stumpf, Theodor, *Die politischen Ideen des Nicolaus von Cues*, Cologne, 1865.

Thorndike, Lyon, *Science and Thought in the Fifteenth Century*, New York, 1929.

Tierney, Brian, *Foundations of Conciliar Theory*, Cambridge, 1055.

SELECTED BIBLIOGRAPHY

Trame, Richard H., *Rodrigo Sanchez de Arevalo*, 1404-1470, Washington, 1958.

Ullmann, Walter, *The Growth of Papal Government in the Middle Ages*, London, 1955.

—— *Medieval Papalism*, London, 1949.

—— *The Origins of the Great Schism*, London, 1948.

—— *Principles of Government and Politics in the Middle Ages*, London, 1961.

Valois, Noel, *Le Pape et le Concile*, 1418-1450, 2 vols., Paris, 1909.

Vansteenberghe, Edmond, *Le cardinal Nicolas de Cues*, Lille, 1920.

Vilmain, Jean Joseph, *Les Principes de droit public du cardinal Nicolas de Cues*, Strasbourg, 1922.

Volkmann-Schluck, K. H., *Nicolaus Cusanus*, Frankfurt, 1957.

Whittaker, Thomas, *The Neo-Platonists*, 2nd ed., Cambridge, 1928.

Zellinger, Eduard, *Cusanus-Konkordanz*, Munich, 1960.

Zibermayr, Ignaz, *Die Legation des Kardinals Nicolaus Cusanus und die Ordensreform*, Münster, 1914.

B. Articles

Archibald, Katherine, "The Concept of Social Hierarchy in the Thought of St. Thomas Aquinas," *The Historian*, 12:28-54 (1949).

Bauer, Roger, "Sacrum imperium et imperium germanicum chez Nicolas de Cues," *Archives d'histoire*, 21:207-240 (1954).

Congar, Yves M. J., "Quod Omnes Tangit ab Omnibus Tractari et Approbari Debet," *Revue historique de droit français et étranger*, 36:210-259 (1958).

Cranz, F. Edward, "St. Augustine and Nicholas of Cusa in the Tradition of Western Christian Thought," *Speculum*, 28:297-315 (April 1953).

Decker, Bruno, "Nikolaus von Cues und der Friede unter den Religionen," in *Humanismus, Mystik, und Kunst in der Welt des Mittelalters*, ed. Josef Koch, Leiden-Cologne, 1953, pp. 94-121.

—— "Die Toleranzidee bei Nikolaus von Kues und in der Neuzeit," in *Nicolò Cusano, Relazioni presentate al Con-*

vegno Interuniversitario di Bressanone, Florence, 1962, pp. 5-24.

Duhem, L., "Thierry de Chartres et Nicolas de Cues," *Revue des sciences philosophiques et theologiques*, 3:525-531 (1909).

Ehses, Stephan, "Der Reformentwurf des Kardinals Nikolaus Cusanus," *HJ*, 32:281-297 (1911).

Hallauer, Hermann, "Eine Denkschrift des Nikolaus von Kues zum Kauf der Ämter Taufers und Uttenheim in Südtirol," *Mitteilungen*, 1:76-94 (1961).

Haring, N., "A Commentary on Boethius *De Trinitate* by Thierry of Chartres," *Archives d'histoire*, 23:259-265 (1956).

Haubst, Rudolf, "Nikolaus von Kues und Johannes Wenck. Neue Erörterungen und Nachträge," *Römische Quartalschrift für Christliche Altertumskunde und Kirchengeschichte*, 53:81-88 (1958).

——— "Die Thomas- und Proklos-Exzerpte des 'Nicolaus Treverensis' in Codicillus Strassburg 84," *Mitteilungen*, 1:17-51 (1961).

——— "Zum Fortleben Alberts des Grossen bei Heymerich von Kamp und Nikolaus von Kues," *Studia Albertina*, Supp. IV of *Beiträge zur Geschichte der Philosophie und Theologie des Mittelalters*, Münster, 1952, pp. 420-447.

Hoffmann, Ernst, "Platonismus und Mittelalter," *Vorträge der Bibliothek Warburg (1923-24)*, ed. Fritz Saxl, Berlin, 1924, pp. 17-82.

Honecker, Martin, "Ramon Lulls Wahlvorschlag Grundlage des Kaiserwahlplanes bei Nikolaus von Kues?" *HJ*, 57: 563-574 (1937).

Jacob, E. F., "Nicholas of Cusa," in *Social and Political Ideas of Some Great Thinkers of the Renaissance and Reformation*, ed. F. J. C. Hearnshaw, London, 1925, pp. 32-60.

Kallen, Gerhard, "Die politische Theorie im philosophischen System des Nikolaus von Cues," *HZ*, 165:246-277 (1942).

——— "Der Reichsgedanke in der Reformschrift 'De Concordantia Catholica' des Nikolaus von Cues," *Neue Heidelberger Jahrbücher*, Heidelberg, 1940, pp. 59-76.

Kleinen, Hans, and Robert Danzer, "Cusanus Bibliographie (1920-1961)," *Mitteilungen*, 1:95-126 (1961).

Klibansky, Raymond, "Copernic et Nicolas de Cues," in *Léo-*

SELECTED BIBLIOGRAPHY

nard de Vinci et l'expérience scientifique au seizième siècle, pub. by Centre National de la Récherche Scientifique, Paris, 1953.

────── "Plato's Parmenides in the Middle Ages and the Renaissance," *Medieval and Renaissance Studies*, 1:281-335 (1943).

Koch, Josef, "Nikolaus von Cues als Mensch," in *Humanismus, Mystik, und Kunst in der Welt des Mittelalters*, ed. J. Koch, Leiden-Cologne, 1953, pp. 56-75.

────── "Nikolaus von Kues," in *Die grossen Deutschen*, ed. H. Heimpel, T. Heuss, and B. Reifenberg, Berlin, 1956, pp. 275-287.

────── "Platonismus im Mittelalter," *Kölner Universitätsreden*, no. 4, Krefeld, 1948.

────── "Über die Universalität des Nikolaus von Kues," *Zur Feier der Einweihung des Nikolaus-von-Kues-Gymnasiums*, Bernkastel-Kues, 1962, pp. 7-12.

────── "Über eine aus der nächsten Umgebung des Nikolaus von Kues stammende Handschrift der Trierer Stadtbibliothek," in *Aus Mittelalter und Neuzeit*, ed. Josef Engel and Hans Martin Klinkenberg, Bonn, 1957, pp. 117-135.

Krchňák, Alois, "Die kanonistischen Aufzeichnungen des Nikolaus von Kues in Cod. Cus. 220 als Mitschrift einer Vorlesung seines Paduaner Lehrers Prosdocimus de Comitibus," *Mitteilungen*, 2:67-84 (1962).

Lagarde, Georges de, "L'Idée de représentation dans les oeuvres de Guillaume d'Ockham," *Bulletin of the International Committee of Historical Sciences*, 9:425-451 (1937).

Laski, Harold J., "Political Theory in the Later Middle Ages," *Cambridge Medieval History*, vol. VIII, ed. C. W. Previte-Orton and Z. N. Brooke, Cambridge, 1936, pp. 620-645.

Leicht, P. Sylvio, "Un Principio politico medievale," *Rendiconti della Reale Accademia dei Lincei* (Scienze Morali), 5th series, XXIX (1920), 232-245.

Lewis, Ewart, "Organic Tendencies in Medieval Political Thought," *American Political Science Review*, 32:849-876 (1938).

Mantese, Giovanni, "Ein notarielles Inventar von Büchern und Wertgegenständen aus dem Nachlass des Nikolaus von Kues," *Mitteilungen*, 2:85-116 (1962).

Martin, Victor, "Comment s'est formée la doctrine de la

superiorité du concile sur le pape," *Revue des sciences religieuses*, 17:212-243, 261-289, 404-427 (1937).

McNeill, John T., "The Emergence of Conciliarism," in *Medieval and Historiographical Essays*, ed. James L. Cate and Eugene N. Anderson, Chicago, 1938, pp. 269-301.

Meister, Alois, "Die humanistischen Anfänge des Nikolaus von Cues," *Annalen des historischen Vereins für den Neiderrhein*, XLIII (1896), 1-21.

Meuthen, Erich, "Die Pfründen des Cusanus," *Mitteilungen* 2:15-66 (1962).

—— "Die universalpolitischen Ideen des Nikolaus von Kues in seiner Erfahrung der politischen Wirklichkeit," *Quellen*, 37:192-221 (1937).

—— "Nikolaus von Kues und der Laie in der Kirche," *HJ*, 81:101-122 (1962).

—— "Obedienz- und Absolutionslisten aus dem Trierer Bistumsstreit (1430-1435)," *Quellen*, 40:43-64 (1960).

Moulin, L., "Sanior et Maior Pars," *Revue historique de droit français et étranger*, 36:368-397, 491-529 (1958).

Post, Gaines, "A Roman-canonical Precept, 'Quod Omnes Tangit' in Bracton," *Traditio*, 4:197-251 (1946).

Randall, J. H., Jr., "The Development of the Scientific Method in the School of Padua," in *Roots of Scientific Thought*, ed. Philip Wiener and Aaron Noland, New York, 1957, pp. 139-146.

Rice, Eugene, "Nicholas of Cusa's Idea of Wisdom," *Traditio*, 12:345-368 (1957).

Sabbadini, Remigio, "Niccolò da Cusa e i conciliari di Basilea alla scoperta dei codici," *Rendiconti della Reale Accademia dei Lincei* (Scienze Morali), 5th series, XX (1911), 3-41.

Schmidt, Alois, "Nikolaus von Kues Sekretär des Kardinals Giordano Orsini?" in *Aus Mittelalter und Neuzeit*, ed. Josef Engel and Hans Martin Klinkenberg, Bonn, 1957, pp. 137-143.

Shepard, Max A., "William of Occam and the Higher Law," *American Political Science Review*, 26:1005-1023 (1932), and 27:24-38 (1933).

Sigmund, Paul E., "Cusanus' *Concordantia*: a Re-interpretation," *Political Studies*, 10:180-197 (1962).

—— "The Influence of Marsilius of Padua on XVth Century

SELECTED BIBLIOGRAPHY

Conciliarism," *Journal of the History of Ideas*, 23:392-402 (1962).

Tierney, Brian, "Pope and Council: Some New Decretist Texts," *Medieval Studies*, 19:197-218 (1957).

Ullmann, B. L., "Manuscripts of Nicolas of Cues," *Speculum*, 13:194-197 (1938).

Van de Vyver, E., "Annotations de Nicolas de Cues dans plusieurs manuscrits de la bibliothèque royale de Bruxelles," *Nicolò Cusano, Relazioni presentate al Convegno Interuniversitario di Bressanone*, Florence, 1962, pp. 47-62.

Vansteenberghe, E., "Le Cardinal-legat Nicolas de Cues et le clergé de Liége," *Leodium*, 15:103-114 (1922).

——— "Le 'De Ignota Litteratura' de Jean Wenck de Herrenberg," *Beiträge zur Geschichte der Philosophie des Mittelalters*, vol. VIII, no. 6 (Münster, 1910).

——— "Quelques lectures de jeunesse de Nicolas de Cues," *Archives d'histoire*, 3:275-284 (1928).

Wackerzapp, Herbert, "Der Einfluss Meister Eckharts auf die ersten philosophischen Schriften des Nikolaus von Kues, 1440-1450," *Beiträge zur Geschichte der Philosophie und Theologie des Mittelalters*, vol. XXXIX, no. 3 (Münster, 1962).

C. Unpublished Manuscript

Liese, Hermann, "Nikolaus von Cues auf dem Reichstag von Frankfurt, 1442," MS, Cologne (in possession of Professor Josef Koch).

INDEX

INDEX

INDEX

in, 130; council theories in, 131; imperial authority in, 131, 188-217; civil hierarchy in, 132-134; relation of church and state in, 134-136; organic analogies in, 134-136; and church constitution, 158-187; and civil constitution, 188-217; and representation, 267-270; and infallibility, 272, 278

De Conjecturis, 124

De Docta Ignorantia, 2, 6, 24, 62, 124, 235, 243, 244-263, 266-267, 272, 280, 284-285; sources of, 244-249; criticism of, 252-253

De Ludo Globi, 292

De Mente, 24

De Pace Fidei, 6, 124, 293-294

Decretals, 76, 78, 89, 91

Decretalists, 11, 69

Decretists, 11

Decretum, 67-89, 107-109, 124, 129, 139-140, 159-160, 169, 196, 201. *See also* Gratian

Descartes, 312

Devotio moderna, 21

Dialogus, 270

Dietrich of Niem, 108-110

Dionysius the Aeropagite, 45-51, 57-65, 88, 113, 115, 127-130, 246-249, 255. *See also* Neo-Platonism

Dishypatus, John, 223

Docta ignorantia, 245-246, 249, 266

Donation of Constantine, 196-197, 205

Durandus, Gulielmus, 13, 85-89, 99, 106, 130

Eckhart, Meister, 56, 61-62, 66, 252

Empire, constitution of, 188-217; and secular authority, 84-85, 132-134; and consent, 191-192, 200, 204-206; and elective rulers, 192-194; and church constitution, 194-195; and papal power, 195-202, 208; and Donation of Constantine, 196-197; and enforcing Christian laws, 202-203, 206; and church councils, 206-208; reform of, 208-216; hierarchical rule in, 210-211; centralized army in, 211; secret ballot in, 211-212; judi-

cial improvements in, 212-213; imperial councils, 213-215

Enlightenment, 2

Epieikeia, 96, 101, 118, 181-182, 241-243, 269-271

Episcopalism, 77, 161-162

Eriugena, Scotus, 46, 51-52, 56, 61, 246-247, 249, 252

Eugene, Pope, 19, 31-35, 221-222, 231, 234, 263, 281-282

Eusebius of Caesarea, 42

da Feltre, Vittorino, 22

Ferrara-Florence, Council of, 232, 234

Figgis, John N., 3

Frequens, 17-18

de Gandillac, Maurice, 5

George of Trapezunt, 44

Gerson, Jean, 14, 56, 62-63, 113-117

von Gierke, Otto, 3

God, 126-127, 244-250, 254-258, 260

"Golden Bull," 12

Gratian, 67-68, 80-81

Greek Church, 222-225

Gregory VII, 12, 305

Gregory IX, 69

Gregory XII, 16

Gregory of Heimburg, 225-226, 296

de Groote, Gerard, 21

Grosseteste, Robert, 46

Heidelberg, University of, 22

Heidelberg Academy of Sciences, 5, 6

Heimericus de Campo, 25-26, 57, 60, 123, 249

Heinz-Mohr, Gerd 5

Henry of Langenstein, 13, 94, 101-103, 116

Hierarchy, ecclesiastical, 49-51, 82, 88, 91-92

Hierarchy of being, 40-51, 55-57, 62-65, 122-123, 256-260. *See also* Neo-Platonism

Hilduin, 51

Hobbes, Thomas, 190

Hoffmann, Ernst, 2, 6, 255-256, 258, 260

Holy Spirit, 115

INDEX

INDEX

HARVARD POLITICAL STUDIES